AF560799

INDIA IN 1857

BEFORE AND AFTER

By the Same Author

- Encyclopaedic History of the Sikhs and Sikhism (6 Volumes)
- European Women in India—Their Life and Adventures
- History of the Conquest of China
- International Law and Practice in Ancient India
- Legal & Political System in China
- Martial Law—Theory and Practice
- Military Dictionary and Encyclopaedia
- Military History of British India
- Origin & Development of Legal & Political System in India (3 Volumes)
- Political, Legal and Military History of India (10 Volumes)
- Portrait of a Political Murder—Trial and Execution of Z.A. Bhutto
- Rare Documents on Sikhs and Their Rule in the Punjab
- Studies in Islamic Law, Religion and Society
- Unity and Discipline through Law

INDIA IN 1857

BEFORE AND AFTER

Edited by

H.S. BHATIA
Chief Editor
Civil & Military Law Journal, New Delhi

DEEP & DEEP PUBLICATIONS PVT. LTD.
F-159, Rajouri Garden, New Delhi - 110 027

INDIA IN 1857
Before and After

ISBN 978-81-8450-083-7

Typeset by RAHUL COMPOSERS
358, Pocket-B, Phase-II, Sector 16-B, Dwarka, New Delhi - 110 075

Printed in India at MAYUR ENTERPRISES,
WZ Plot No. 3, Gujjar Market, Tihar Village, New Delhi - 110 018

Published by DEEP & DEEP PUBLICATIONS PVT. LTD.,
F-159, Rajouri Garden, New Delhi - 110 027 • Phone : 25435369, 25440916
E-mail : ddpubs@gmail.com • ddpbooks@yahoo.co.in
Showroom :
2/13, Ansari Road, Daryaganj, New Delhi - 110 002 • Telefax : 23245122

Contents

Preface

The Portuguese, the Dutch, the French and the English came ostensibly for trade but resolved to make India their colony. Sir George Dunbar in his "Political Games of the European Rivals" narrate episodes of open hostility, diplomatic moves and confrontation both at sea and land of European nations, unsettled political conditions in India and fluctuating situation resulting in British ascendancy at the end. India in the second half of the 18th century had broken up into a number of warring states. Many adventurers, European and some American soldiers, trained in European warfare and military discipline entered India and joined the fray to make fortune. Some amassed fantastic wealth. Clive, for instance, returned from India with gold and jewels which made him the richest commoner armies, conquered kingdoms, overturned princes and ruled provinces wielding much personal power. Other European soldiers of lesser fortune created conditions that paved the way for the establishment of English supremacy in India.

How the Great Uprising of 1857 originated? During the Company's times there had been several "Mutinies in the Indian Army" both European and Native including a few princely states and Bhai Maharaj Singh in the Punjab. What were the causes of these mutinies and how these were curtailed have been elaborately given in this book. Whether the Great uprising was a "Mutiny or War of Independence" has for long the subject of controversy both within and outside India. According to Dr. Ganda Singh there was nothing national about 1857 mutiny. It was at best a religious, not of the Muslim and Hindu soldiers of UP, who wanted to restore to the Mughal Emperor Bahadur Shah

Zafar, his throne, power and sovereignty. But Abul Kalam Azad maintains that "patriotism had to be reinforced by an appeal to religious passion", and the Uprising created a remarkable sense of unity among the Hindus and Muslims of India in this period. Dr. Nandalal Chatterji discloses that "during the Mutiny days hundreds and thousands of erstwhile dacoits suddenly abandoned their usual criminal pursuits and turned into patriotic rebels so as to fight the British Government". Proceedings of the military trial of the Mughal Emperor Bahadur Shah Zafar, a sequence to the unsuccessful Great Uprising of Indian soldiers is given in this book. After the findings of guilty by the Military Tribunal, the King was awarded a term of life imprisonment in exile, and transported to Rangoon where he died in early November, 1862 at the age of 87. The shock felt in England due to the events of the Great Uprising gave the East India Company its death blow and the Government of India was transferred from the Company to the Crown.

This book includes the events before and after the Mutiny of 1857. *Chapter One* gives : *British Rule in India—How and Why?*: Three-fold Policy of Conquest; Three-fold Principles of Rule; India Regarded as Fair Game for Plunder; Conquest by Trade; England's Unbounded Prosperity; British Connection, Good and Evil; Conquest By Deliberate Subjection; Subjection by Terror; Lal Pultan-Mutineers Blown Away; First Encounter between European and Native Troops; Bloody Bath at Vellore; Aggressive Policy against Native Rulers; British Seamen Surrender to Mughal; Conflict between Old and New Company.

Chapter Two includes : *Establishment of the Company in India* : Charter Granted to London Merchants; British Missions Sent to Jehangeer Court; Factory at Surat; Sir Thomas Roe on a Royal Mission; Portuguese Opposition; President of Company at Surat Appointed; Foundation of Madras Laid; Trade Opened in Bengal; Company takes over Bombay; Pomp and Show by the Bombay President; Revolt by Bombay Population; Key to Important Terms.

Chapter Three gives : *British Politico-Military Power in India:* Evolution of the British Indian Armed Forces; The Beginnings; The Army; The Navy; The Formative Period; During the Company's Times; Presidency Armies : Bengal, Madras, Bombay; Presidency Chief as C-in-C Origin of Presidency Armies; Different Patterns; Different Pays of Sepoys; Army of Bengal Presidency; *Lal*

Pultan-mutineers Blown Away; First Encounter between European and Native Troops; Trust Well Rewarded; Composition of Bengal Army; New Reorganisation; Camp Equipage and its Conveyance; New-modelling the Army; Great Promotions and New Raisings; Army of Madras Presidency; Cavalry Raised by Carnatic Nabob; Subadar's Pride Hurt; Firm Allegiance; Constitution of Company's Army; Remedying the Evil; Army of Bombay Presidency; Bombay Army Composed of all Classes; British Model; Exemplary Fidelity; British Political Power through Indian Troops; Government Essentially Military.

Chapter Four inludes : *British Flattery and Deceipt*: The Entertainment; The Attack Plan; A Fake Commercial Treaty.

Chapter Five gives : *Anglo-Sikh Wars of Freedom from British Rule* : First Sikh War with Exceedingly Stubborn Fighters; *Mudki* and Ferozeshah—British Guns Silenced; Aliwal and Sobraon—British Forces Skillfully Managed; Traitor Sikh Sardar—British Capture Punjab; The Punjab, a British Protectorate; The Revolt at Multan—British Sikh Governor Murdered; Ramnagar, *Chillianwala* and Gujarat—Sikh Terms for Peace Rejected by British; Power of Khalsa Broken; Supremacy but not Security; *Mudki*.

Chapter Six gives : *Maharaja Duleep Singh under British Protection in Mussoorie* : Looses Identity, Faith and Empire; Lord Dalhousie's Desire to Defeat Sikh Government and Abolish the Sikh Dynasty.

Chapter Seven describes *Dalip Singh : A Life in Struggle.*

Chapter Eight gives : *Bhai Maharaj Singh (Trailblazer)* : Saint-Patriot Bhai Maharaj Singh and His Martyrdom for National Freedom; His Patriotic Mission; Great Influence on the Sikh Soldiers; General Revolt Planned; His Arrest and *Persecution*; Six Years in the Solitary Cell; Bhai Maharaj Singh; Outstanding Example of a Martyr.

Chapter Nine gives : *Mutinies in the Indian Army* : European Mutinies; Native Mutinies; Proceedings of the Court Martial and Punishment; Opinion of the Adawlat; 1857, and Earlier Uprisings; Pre-mutiny Revolts in Princely States of Orissa.

Chapter Ten includes : *Bloody Incidents in Vellore.*

Chapter Eleven gives : *Fugleman of the Great Uprising.*

Chapter Twelve describes : *The Cartridge Fable* : Role of Christianity; School Education.

Chapter Thirteen gives : *The Great Uprising of 1857* : Indian Mutiny, 1857-58; A Spark to the Tinder; An Outworn Army; The Heroic Handful; The Holding of the Ridge; The Decision to Assault; "Nikkalseyn is Dead !"; The Capture of Delhi; The Tragedy of Cawnpore; The Infamy of the Nana; The March on Cawnpore; Sir Henry Lawrence; The Defence of the Residency; The First Relief of Lucknow; The Second Siege of the Residency; The Second Relief of Lucknow; The Advance of Tantia Tope; The Situation, Restored; The Final Occupation of Lucknow; The Rani of Jhansi; Sir Hugh Rose; A Double Victory; The Counterstroke of Tantia and the Rani; The Last Battles and the Final Reckoning; The End of "John Company"; Origin of the 1857 Great Uprising; And its First Martyr; When Delhi was Lost and Won by the English; The Sack of Delhi 1857-58 as Witnessed; Greatness of Ghalib; How could Ghalib stay in Delhi after the British Victory?; Sources of Study; Feelings Among the Natives Towards the Company's Government; Daily Increasing Poverty; Discontentment Leads to Insurrection; Down with the English; Ruin of the Upper Classes; Company's Indian empire like an island of sand.

Chapter Fourteen includes : *Bahadur Shah and the Administration Court of the Mutineers.*

Chapter Fifteen describes : *Military Trial of Delhi Emperor.*

Chapter Sixteen gives : *From Company to the Crown* : Crown and Company Courts Amalgamated; District Officer Evolved; Famine and Flood; Cooperative Societies Started; British Administration Entirely Western; Curzon's Reforms; Partition of Punjab and Bengal Provinces; Resentment throughout India; Dual Military Control; Indians Excluded from High Positions in Civil and Military Services; Lapses in British Behaviour; Nationalist Movement; English Radical Ideas; Poineers in Education; Indian National Congress Founded; Demand for Home Rule; All-India Muslim League; The Terrorist Movement; First Step in Constitutional Progress.

Chapter Seventeen gives : *Muslim Politics in the Punjab, Pro-1857* : Muslim Millet-adherents, Hindu United Congress, Education, Sikh, Gurudwaras, Nation; Origins of Muslims Political Activities; Three Types of Political Activities; Hindu Rise—A Threat to Muslims; The Second Era—Urdu *vs.* Hindi; Lahore Indian Association—A United and Divided House;

Hindu-Muslim Unity Societies Formed; Urban Punjabis and Communal Politics on (1884-87) Kine Slaughter; Municipal Elections aroused Hindu-Muslim Tension; Association and Congress almost Hindu Bodies; Communal Hate Circulars given to Attickson Commision; Muslims Oppose Congress (1885-90); Opposition to Congress Spreads; The Congress Meet the Challenge in Bombay; Energetic Congress Campaign.

Chapter Eighteen gives : *Sikhs : Gurudwaras/Nation*: Akali Dal Agitation; The Martial Sikhs and Non-Violence; Babar Akali Movement; Participation of Masses.

Chapter Nineteen includes : *Anglo-Sikh Wars : Some Prominent Features*; A. Proclamation of War; Sikh Soldiers Bring Humanity to Battle Field; British Officer Mistakenly in Sikh Army Escorted Back; Sikh Soldier Carries on his back War Wounded British Officer Miles away to Camp Hospital; Sikh Empire Lost by Treachery; Jammoo Rajah Betrays Sikh Cause; Residue Sikh Power Weakened; Treachery Rewarded; Another Treachery; Lord Dalhousie, Governor General of India wanted Sikh Government Defeated and their Dynasty Abolished.

I am grateful to all who have cooperated in finalising this book. I acknowledge with thanks the help of various librarians and authors of various books which have been referred to in this book.

H.S. BHATIA

British Rule in India—How and Why?

William Digby

*"According to Lord Macaulay, the man who first visualised that it was possible to found an European empire on the ruins of Mughal monarchy was Dupleix, who clearly saw that the greatest force which the princes of India could bring into the field would be no match for a small body of men trained in the discipline and guided by the tactics of the West. It is one of history great ironies **that the French paved way for British sway in India in one of the decisive battles**." (Ed.)*

THREE-FOLD POLICY OF CONQUEST

What were the principles on which our rule in India began. There were at first, no principles whatsoever. We were too much occupied in establishing a footing to trouble ourselves concerning the people and their interests present and future. From 1740 to nearly the end of the eighteenth century our controlling action was a scramble for wealth. The manner in which that wealth was obtained was a secondary matter, or, indeed, of no matter. We were in India to make money, and all shadow of pretence at even making money honestly, was cast aside.

Three-fold Principles of Rule

The present can only be understood as the facts and circumstances of the past are clearly apprehended. Whatever of deficiency exists in our mode of administration of India today so far as the Indian people are concerned, and whatever of unusual poverty is to be found on the Indian Continent, are as they are because of the system of rule which, with every good intention but mistakenly, was then begun and was finally adopted. Those principles of rule were three-fold:

1. *Conquest by Trade*—Exploitation of India undisguisedly—'naked and not ashamed'—1700-83.
2. *Conquest by Deliberate Subjection*—India for England first and last—1783-1833.
3. *Conquest by 'Pousta'*—A show of Fair Dealing accompanied with the maintenance, rigidly and uncompromisingly, of Indian National Inferiority—1833.
4. Jail and gun blast for mutiny and disobedience.

To understand the India of today each of the above mentioned aspects must be examined, and evidence adduced in support of the conclusions they compel. This evidence shall be as brief as may be, but the facts represented must be stated even if the reader has to suffer what, otherwise, might be deemed an over-weighting of official statement.

England did not enter into relations with India with empire in view. For a long time after the opportunity of seizing power was ours, we were not anxious to lay hold of it. In agonising tones, repeated again and again, the Committee of Merchants in London commanded their servants not to acquire additional territory. One of the greatest of the Governors General listened,—Hazael-like, with protest, and denial and that we could do such things—to the prophecy of an Ambassador from

Nepaul, who early in the nineteenth century declared British supremacy in India would not stay in its course until it reached the Indus.

Until 1774, when Warren Hastings was made the first Governor-General, little of blame, maybe, attached to the British in India, judged from the point of view of a State responsible for the good government of subordinate peoples. Till then, disguised as the position may have been by the presence of the French in Southern India and the frequent conflicts which took place with the Country Powers, as the phrase quaintly puts it, the British were adventurers, with so much to be said in their favour as may rightly be said of adventurers, and no more. If they possessed power it was mainly by deputy. The position then occupied was like unto that of the British people towards India before the Crown—that is, the nation—became directly responsible for Indian rule.

India Regarded as Fair Game for Plunder

As adventurers nearly two centuries ago the early Britons in Bengal and the sister Presidencies regarded the land and the people as fair game for plunder. Under King Edward VII, Emperor of India, and under the later Britons, as administrators, disguised with all the speciousness which Western civilisation abundantly supplies for such purposes, and glossed over with words of forceful sound but scant meaning, such as Secretaries of State delude themselves and the House of Commons with once at least in every year—the day on which the Indian idol is brought out for British worship—India is still fair game for plunder, and is plundered. Hard as the saying may sound in the ears of the ordinary Englishman, the plunder is proceeding far more outrageously today than at any preceding period. The thin whips of the early days of our rule have become bundles of wire thongs; the exactions of Clive and Hastings fall into insignificance by the side of the drain which, in ever-augmenting volume, is over-enriching one country at the cost of the life-blood of another. Behind the fairest product which any administration in the world's history has ever put in the window-front to challenge admiration, there lurks a degree of daily-increasing misery—not intended truly, and therefore, its very existence denied even when it is exposed to view—which few Britons dream of, and which far fewer realise. We did not *mean* to cause misery, we do not *desire* there should be misery, and, therefore, what is exhibited as such cannot be human misery. To believe it to be so is *maya,* illusion. There *is* illusion, but it is more correctly spelt delusion.

CONQUEST BY TRADE

'We are', say the Court of Directors, in their General Letter to Bengal, April 26, 1765, 'extremely anxious for the arrival of Lord Clive, and the gentlemen who accompanied him; as they have been so lately in England, they are the best judges of the opinion the Government and the nation entertain of the conduct of the English in Bengal for these last four years; which we are sorry to say is, in general, that they have been guilty of violating treaties, of great oppression, and a combination to enrich themselves.

'We do not here mean to enter into a discussion respecting the political conduct of our late Governor and Council; but must say that an unbounded thirst after riches seems to have possessed the whole body of our servants to a degree that they have lost all sight of justice to the Country Government and of their duty to the Committee.'

Burke tells the story with more of detail. He says :

> 'This new system of trade, carried on through the medium of power and public revenue, very soon produced its natural effects. The loudest complaints arose among the natives, and among all the foreigners who traded, in Bengal. It must have unquestionably thrown the whole mercantile system of the country into the greatest confusion. With regard to the natives, no expedient was proposed for their relief. The case was serious with respect to European powers. The Presidency plainly represented to the Directors that some agreement should be made with foreign nations for providing their investment to a certain amount, or that the deficiencies then subsisting must terminate in an open rupture with France.'[1]

The people not being so generally engaged in trade, and not having on their conquest of Bengal divested the ancient Gentu proprietors of their lands of inheritance, bad for their chief, if not their sole, support the share of a moderate conqueror in all offices civil and military. But your Committee find that this arrangement was of short duration. Without the least regard to the subsistence of this innocent people, or to the faith of the agreement on which they were brought under the British Government, this sum was reduced by a new treaty to £320,000, and soon after (upon a pretence of the present Nabob's minority, and a temporary sequestration for the discharge of his debts) to £160,000; but when he arrived at his majority and when the debts were paid (if ever they were paid) the sequestration continued; and so far as the late ad vices may be understood, the allowance to the Nabob appears still to stand at the reduced sum of £160,000.

The other resource of the Mahomedans, and of the Gentus of certain of the higher castes, was the army. In this army nine-tenths of which consists of native, no native, of whatever description, holds any rank higher than that of a Subahdar Commandant, that is, of an officer below the rank of an English subaltern, who is appointed to each company of the native soldiery.

'Your Committee would here be understood to state the ordinary establishment; for the war may have made some alteration. All the honourable, all the lucrative, situations of the army, all the supplies and the contracts of whatever species that belong to it, are solely in the hands of the English; so that whatever is beyond the mere subsistence of a common soldier and some officers of a lower rank, together with the immediate expenses of the English officers at their table, is sooner or later, in one shape or another, sent out of the country.'[2]

Governor Verelst, with great particularity, himself an observer of the events he describes, confirms all that Burke states.

Much of modern European national prosperity is based upon the plunder of nations representing ancient civilisations. Spain robbed South America; England—from Drake under Elizabeth to Blake under Cromwell-seized as many of the Lusitanian treasure ships on their way to Spain as she could, and appropriated what they carried. Later, in the development of the land and its dependencies even these additional riches were not enough; more money was needed by the country, and none was locally forthcoming. England was vigorously asserting herself on the Continent of Europe and elsewhere. For a time an issue of bank-notes helped the situation. But coin was needed, a metallic foundation for the paper issued, and at last coin was obtained from India. How it was obtained Macaulay has told in his Essays on Clive and Hastings. The historian's works are in the hands of, or are available to, every reader; I may, therefore, be pardoned if I simply call upon the memory of my reader and forbear quotation, especially as I have much, not within reach even of the ordinary student, with which I must deal.

England's industrial supremacy owes its origin to the vast hoards of Bengal and the Karnatik being made available for her use. Had this happened honourably and in the ordinary course of trade it would have been matter for satisfaction. Before Plassey was fought and won, and before the stream of treasure began to flow to England, the industries of our country were at a very low ebb. Lancashire spinning and weaving were on a par with the corresponding industry in India so far as machinery was concerned, but the skill which made Indian cottons a marvel of manufacture was wholly wanting in any of the Western nations. As with cotton so with iron; industry in Britain was at a very low ebb, alike in mining and in manufacture.

The connection between the beginning of the drain of Indian wealth to England and the swift uprising of British industries was not casual: it was causal. Mr. Brooks Adams says:

> 'Very soon after Plassey, the Bengal plunder began to arrive in London, and the effect appears to have been instantaneous, for all authorities agree that the "industrial revolution," the event which has divided the nineteenth century from all antecedent time, began with the year 1760. Prior to 1760, according to Baines, the machinery used for spinning cotton in Lancashire was almost as simple as in India; while about 1750 the English iron industry was in full decline because of the destruction of the forests for

fuel. At that time four-fifths of the iron used in the kingdom came from Sweden.

"Plassey was fought in 1757, and probably nothing has ever equalled the rapidity of the change which followed. In 1760 the flying shuttle appeared, and coal began to replace wood in smelting. In 1764 Hargreaves invented the spinning-jenny, in 1779 Crompton contrived the mule, in 1785 Cartwright patented the power-loom, and, chief of all, in 1768 Watt matured the steam-engine, the most perfect of all vents of centralising energy. But, though these machines served as outlets for the accelerating movement of the time, they did not cause that acceleration. In themselves inventions are passive, many of the most important having lain dormant for centuries, waiting for a sufficient store of force to have accumulated to set them working. That store must always take the shape of money, and money not hoarded, but in motion.

'Thus printing had been known for ages in China before it came to Europe; the Romans probably were acquainted with gun-powder; revolvers and breech loading cannon existed in the fifteenth and sixteenth centuries, and steam had been experimented upon long before the birth of Watt. The least part of Watt's labour lay in conceiving his idea; he consumed his life marketing it. Before the influx of the Indian treasure, and the expansion of credit which followed, no force sufficient for this purpose existed; and had Watt lived fifty years earlier, he and his invention must have perished together. Considering the difficulties under which Matthew Boulton, the ablest and most energetic manufacturer of his time, nearly succumbed, no one can doubt that without Boulton's works at Birmingham the engine could not have been produced, and yet before 1760 such works could not have been organised. The factory system was the child of the 'industrial revolution,' and until capital had accumulated in masses capable of giving solidity to large bodies of labour, manufactures were necessarily carried on by scattered individuals, who combined a handicraft with agriculture.

'Thus isolated, and favoured by mines of coal and iron, England not only commanded the European and American markets, at a time when production was strained to the utmost by war, but even undersold Hindoo labour at Calcutta. In some imperfect way her gains may be estimated by the growth of her debt, which must represent savings. In 1756, when Clive went to India, the nation owed £74,575,000, on which it paid an interest of £2,753,000. In 1815 this debt had swelled to £861,000,000, with an annual interest charge of £32,645,000. In 1761 the Duke of Bridgewater finished the first of the canals which were afterwards to form an inland waterway, costing £50,000,000, or more than two-thirds of the amount of the public debt at the outbreak of the seven years' war. Meanwhile, also, steam had been introduced, factories built, turnpikes improved, and bridges erected, and all this had been done through a system of credit extending throughout the land. Credit is the chosen vehicle of energy in centralised societies, and no sooner had treasure enough accumulated in London to offer it a foundation, than it shot up with marvelous rapidity.

'From 1694 to Plassey, the growth had been relatively slow. For more than sixty years after the foundation of the Bank of England, its smallest note had been for £20, a note too large to circulate freely, and which rarely travelled far from Lombard Street. Writing in 1790, Burke mentioned that when he came to England in 175.0 there were not 'twelve bankers' shops' in the provinces, though then, he said, they were in every market town. Thus the arrival of the Bengal silver not only increased the mass of money, but stimulated its movement; for at once, in 1759, the bank issued £10 and £15 notes, and in the country private firms poured forth a flood of paper".

England's Unbounded Prosperity

Thus England's unbounded prosperity owes its origin to her connection with India, whilst it has, largely, been maintained—disguisedly—from the same source, from the middle of the eighteenth century to the present time. 'Possibly, since the world began, no investment has ever yielded the profit reaped from the Indian plunder'.

What was the extent of the wealth thus wrung from the East Indies? No one has been able to reckon adequately, as no one has been in a position to make a correct 'tally' of the treasure exported from India. Estimates have been made which vary from £500,000,000 to nearly £1,000,000,000. Probably between Plassey and Waterloo the last-mentioned sum was transferred from Indian hoards to English banks. There have been several cases which many know with details of individual 'embezzlements', as the phrase of that day expressed it. These will indicate the scale on which nearly every Briton in India enriched himself. Modern England has been made great by Indian wealth, wealth never proffered by its possessor, but always taken by the might and skill of the stronger. The difference between the eighteenth and the twentieth centuries is simply that the amount received now is immensely larger, is obtained 'according to law'; British money is seen to be invested, British goods are purchased and payment must be made for whatever one buys. Further, 'services are rendered':

'Could you not find the service in India itself, from among the Indian people?'

'We have never really tried, and do not intend to try'.

Apparently, everything is straightforward. But India has never said, she wants these things. Indeed, her opinion on the matter, even though she pays, is the last consideration to be regarded, and no one troubles to regard it.

Here and here has India helped us,
What have we for India done?

British Connection, Good and Evil

Later pages will show how much of good has come to India from the British connection; likewise, how much of evil. But, once for all, with the result writ so large and writ so indelibly before our eyes, let us cast away the now out-of-date morality which taught that ill-gotten wealth cannot bring blessing or prosperity with it. Considering what England owing to her appropriation of Indian moneys, counted for amongst the nations of the world during the whole of the nineteenth century, there can no longer be any doubt that 'out of evil good cometh', nor, perhaps, of the sequel, 'Do Ill that good may come'. With some of the money thus obtained England struck down the ancient industries of India, and, during a whole century, has done naught that is worthy to constitute India a land of varied industries.

These be hard and cruel words for an Englishman to write. Written, however, they must be so as to help to an understanding of the wrong which has thus been done to India—and, in a deeper sense, to England. With understanding may come a redeeming of the wrong;—may, more likely, may *not.*

England's conquest by trade being complete. India lying at the feet of her conqueror, the time had come for a further step. How was this new (yet ancient) country, its brow wrinkled with the learning of the ages, its people steeped in spirituality, its morals equal, if not superior, to those of the West, to be ruled? Were its peoples to become British citizens or British helots? There was not much delay in coming to a conclusion. Peoples who had allowed themselves so easily to be robbed, who, in the astute intellect of a Nuncomar could be outwitted by the subtler mind of a Hastings—what was there for such a people but subjection?

CONQUEST BY DELIBERATE SUBJECTION

India—not for India first, and then for England, but India for England, first and last 1783-1833

With the advent of Lord Cornwallis as Governor-General of India in 1786, were exhibited the first real glimmerings of a conscience as to the principles on which the newly-acquired territories were to be ruled. Philip Francis, it is true, had revealed some facts, but he was unpopular, and therefore his views were ignored. It was open to us to associate the people of India with us in the administration of Indian affairs. Recognising how much they knew and how little we knew of the complexities of rule in their own land, such a course seemed the commonest of common sense. Time has proved that the adoption of such a course would have been the noblest, as it would have been the most profitable, line of policy which could have been adopted. Through some strange psychological change in the mind of the inhabitants of India, or by the working out of some spiritual force, the time had arrived when a foreigner's domination became acceptable, nay more, seemed as if it were desired in fact if not in words. Strange to relate, this was as true of the martial races as of the peaceful peoples. Hindu and Muslim, Bengali, Sikh, Madrassi, Maratha,—they all for a time resisted the foreign domination, they fought fiercely, but, having been beaten, they all accepted defeat, and contentedly acquiesced in the rule of the alien overlord. History records in its annals no greater marvel of one race overmastering another in all matters alike of mind and body. The leaders of British thought in those distant days may be partly forgiven in that they did not discern the possibilities of the future. 'Put the people of India in a position of equality with us !' they asked; 'that would never do. If we let them co-operate with us, if we give them the same facilities to acquire knowledge and experience as we possess, as they gain such knowledge and experience they will use it to get rid of us'.

So it has not been. Never has there been a national revolt in India against British rule. There was, in 1857, a mutiny of mercenaries. Never has there been an uprising of the people. Nor, had another course been adopted than that which unhappily was taken with the soldiers, and had not our 'bad faith' with the Feudatory States been so manifest, would there have been even a revolt of the troops. England, when she obtained supremacy in India, had a golden opportunity to enrich India whilst bringing prosperity to herself. She threw it away. Deliberately, she threw it away. There were not wanting, even then, wise men in plenty to show the truer way. Nevertheless, the wrong course was taken. Not colleagues, but subordinates; not in their own land, rulers and chiefs, with reasonable ambition satisfied and a scope for natural and national energies provided—not these things for Indians. For them, of every caste and creed, the doom was fixed, they at home, among their fellows, were to become 'hewers of wood and drawers of water', with such employment in governmental service as would not be worth the acceptance of any Englishman, however poor. The decision was fateful, alike for India and for England. It was consciously taken. It has been accepted by the under dog in struggle; it has only been varied infinitesimally by the dog on top, accordingly as to whether he found himself in a good humour or not.

Nowhere, perhaps, has the policy of keeping the Indians under found such plain-spoken and emphatic demonstration as in an official document written by a favoured Madras civilian, Mr. William Thackeray. At the time when Lord William Bentinck was Governor of Madras—August, 1803, to September, 1807—Mr. Thackeray was a member of the Board of Revenue in that Presidency: that Board is a survival, an atrophied survival, to the present day. The great fight as to whether peasant farmers, with the government revenue periodically fixed, should be settled on the land, or whether landed proprietors and the permanent settlement such as Lord Cornwallis had established in Bengal, should be adopted, was the subject of consideration. The Governor was a strong advocate for the peasant farmer; the Revenue Board member was even stronger on the same side. In the course of many inquiries, and in the voluminous discussions carried on in the favourite Indian form on elaborate Minutes, each enough to fill a 200 page octavo volume, the foundation principles of Indian subordination and British supremacy were laid down most absolutely. Never, perhaps has the arrogance and cruelty of alien rulers towards their subjects been more nakedly and cynically announced. That which was essential for English greatness in its home land, and for every other people in their respective home lands, was to be withheld, deliberately withheld, from the Indian people in their own country. Without circumlocution and with a cynicism which belies the profession expressed at the same time that the happiness of the people was the sole object of the new conquerors, the subjection of many scores of millions of people for at least a century and may be for ever—(this world is to the strong and not to the amiable, to the brutal and not to the saintly)—was unconcernedly set forth in clear terms. The paragraphs in Mr. Thackeray's report which are the very negation of the charters in which nearly every civilised people find their rights enshrined, the paragraphs which have rendered futile Acts of Parliament subsequently passed, and even have made of none effect the Queen-Empress's Proclamation of 1858, deserve quotation in full. The argument is too interesting to be summarised, has been too fruitful in its baneful consequences not to be recalled and enshrined in twentieth-century literature, *verbatim et literatim*.

After arguing in vigorous terms against a landlord settlement—'one fat rajah supposes fifty-two ryots' (peasant farmers)—Mr. Thackeray remarks.

SUBJECTION BY TERROR

Lal Pultan-Mutineers Blown Away

The present second battalion of the 12th regiment appears, to have been raised some months before the "Mathews". It is the first raised battalion. This corps was at the battle of Plassey. It was named by the sepoys the Lal Pultan, or the Red battalion, and afterwards Gallis, from the name of one of its first captains. It was associated with the "Mathews" in all its early service, particularly at Masulipatam, Gheretty, etc.; but in 1764 it mutinied, on the pretext of some promises which were made to it having been broken. Having no apparent object, it was easily reduced to obedience; but Major Munro (afterwards Sir Hector Munro), who then commanded the army, thought a severe example necessary, and twenty-eight of the most guilty were tried by a drum-head court-martial, and sentenced to death. Eight of these were directed to be immediately blown away from the guns of the force then at Chuprah. As they were on the point of executing the sentence, three grenadiers, who happened to be amongst them, stepped forth, and claimed the privilege of being blown away from the right hand guns. "They had always fought on the right (they said), and they hoped they would be permitted to die at that post of honour." Their request was granted, and they were the first executed.

First Encounter between European and Native Troops

The force detached to the Carnatic in 1781 was commanded by Colonel Pearse. It consisted of five regiments, of two small battalions (500 men each) of Native infantry, some Native cavalry, and a proportion of artillery. This corps, which marched about 1,100 miles along the sea-coast, through the province of Cuttack, and the Northern Circars to Madras, arrived at that Presidency at a most eventful period, and their services were eminently useful to the preservation of our power in that quarter. Among the many occasions which this detachment had of distinguishing itself, the attack on the French lines at Cuddalore in 1783 was the most remarkable. The Bengal sepoys that were engaged on that occasion behaved nobly. It was one of the first times that European troops and the disciplined Natives of India had met at the bayonet.

A mutiny of a serious nature seems to have occurred in the regiment of European Artillery stationed at the Mount, Madras, on the 15th and 16th January, 1798. We have failed in procuring any details of it, but have only an account of the execution of the ringleaders in mutiny, which took place at the Mount on the 15th March, which was after all the parties concerned had been tried by court-martial. Lawrence and Connor were sentenced to death; the first three to be hanged in chains and Lawrence and Connor to be shot. When the first four had been disposed of, and the execution party were prepared to carry out the sentence on the two remaining prisoners. Lawrence and Connor who had been viewing the fate of the others, Major-General Brathwaite went up to them and announced the Commander-in-Chief's pardon. Lawrence fell senseless on the ground, Connor, after a moment's pause, dropped on his knees, and offered up thanks in loud and serious manner. In an order dated Choultry Plain, 15th March, the Commander-in-Chief dwelt upon the destructive consequence of an offence which is most flagitious that can brand the character of a soldier. He ordered that the two pardoned men should be struck-off the rolls of the Artillery, and sent out of the country.

"At a general court martial held at the cantonments near Chuprah, on twenty-four sepoys of Captain Galliez's battalion of sepoys, confined for being taken in actual mutiny and desertion, the court having duly weighed the crime alleged against them, found them guilty of the first and third articles of the second and fifth sections of the Articles of War: and therefore, sentenced them to be put to death, by being blown away from the guns, which sentence is approved by the Commander-in-Chief and is to be put in execution accordingly."

"Major Munro, on receiving the verdict of the court, immediately ordered four of the prisoners to be tied to the four

6-pounders, when four grenadiers of the party immediately stepped forward, and represented that as they had always occupied the post of honour in the field, they claimed the usual priority and right of place on this occasion. The Major complied with the request, the battalion men were untied and the gallant but misguided grenadiers occupied their places; at a signal from the Commander they were launched into eternity, and the fragments of their bodies scattered over the plain.

Major Munro of convicted Sipahis for the mutiny to proceed, when 16 more of the party were in like manner, blown away; the whole of them marching boldly up to the instrument of their execution and awaiting the final signal with firm and unmoved countenance. The remaining four were sent to Moneach, and there executed in a similar manner in the presence of two battalions that had recently evinced a mutinous disposition; and on the return of the Major to Bankipore on the 15th, he caused six Sipahis of other corps, who had also been convicted of mutiny, to be blown away from the guns at that station, in the presence of the assembled troops. The wholesome and well-timed display of resolution and I severity effectually and completely suppressed the spirit of insubordination that had been so long existing in the native army."

Bloody Bath at Vellore

In November 1805 an order was issued introducing a new type of turban, resembling hats worn by Eurasian drummers, for the native troops. Another order published in 1806 by the Company, laid down that "a native soldier shall not mark his face to denote his caste or wear ear-rings when dressed in his uniform, be clean shaven on the chin and preserve a uniform quantity and shape of the hair on the upper lip." Vellore in those days was a big military station quartering several battalions. In the massive fortress, interned were the members of Tipu Sultan's family after his defeat and death at Seringapatam six years earlier. When these orders reached Vellore, the Indian guards and sepoys objected strongly.

On July 11, 1806 at about two in the morning the sepoys of the main guard stationed near the fort suddenly attacked the

British troops and killed all but four who managed to escape. At about the same time an attack was made on all Europeans, present in Vellore. The British flag was pulled down and the Mysore flag was hoisted over the fort. Indians attacked with muskets, spears, swords and two six-pounders, most of which they had captured from the magazine, killing hundreds of Europeans. For about 40 hours, the Indians were again the rulers of the land from which they had been dispossessed. The European cavalry charged into the fort and other troops also rushed in. A bloody battle ensued but the Indians were overwhelmed by a large number of guns and men and a general massacre followed. Those who escaped through the sally port were cut down outside. Hundreds of Indian men, women and children were killed or blown away.

Namdhari Sikhs Hanged and Blown Away

The first organised struggle by the Sikhs for independence came in the form of Kuka Movement under Baba Ram Singh of Bhaini, district Ludhiana. The Kukas had divided the area of their activities into 22 *subas*, with their own means of communication, own postal arrangements, their own courts to decide cases; they discarded rails, British Courts and the foreign-made clothing. They were the first Indians to carry out non-cooperation with the rulers. Baba Ram Singh established contacts with the rulers of Nepal and Jammu and Kashmir. Mr. J.P. Warburton; who had closely watched the Kuka Movement since 1872, reported "that the movement from the beginning was manifestly directed against the existing government and in the recorded opinions of most competent authorities of that time, involved a serious menace to the peace of the individual districts". But the British being vigilant, came to know of these activities in time and were able to suppress it effectively. A large number of Kukas were arrested, and without making even a show of a trial, many, including children, were blown from guns; a number of them were hanged, many, including their leader Baba Ram Singh, were deported. Quite a number of them died while in confinement. Their properties were confiscated. "Blowing from a gun", was considered by the British as "an impressive and merciful manner of execution, well calculated to

strike terror into bystanders". However, the use of the term "merciful" to such a punishment was, in the opinion of Lord Napier, "a strange misuse of language". He called it "repugnant to humanity and a punishment unfit to be inflicted by civilised men".

—*Spokesman*

Aggressive Policy against Native Rulers

The aggression here referred to was the first attempt on the part of the Company to exercise authority over or dictate terms to the native rulers. With this intent Bombay was ordered to be fortified as strongly as money could make it, and "the Court of Directors pompously announced that they were determined to make war, not only on the Nawab of Bengal, but in the sequel, upon the Emperor himself. Nor was this sufficient," says the writer from whom we have quoted; "they actually ordered their general to seize the goods of the King of Siam, Bantam and Zombi as reparation for injuries received."

The Emperor Aurangzebe naturally became indignant at these threats, at several piratical acts of the English on the coast of Bengal, and still more so when he learnt that his governor at Surat had been insulted by the British authorities. Upon demanding from Child some explanation, the latter instead of entering on such, in his turn made numerous demands from the governor of Surat, who, thereupon on the 26th December, 1688, "seized and imprisoned the factors, Harris and Gledman, and ordered all the goods of the Company to be sold, and offered a large reward to anyone who would take Child, dead or alive." The general having failed by negotiation to obtain the release of Harris and Gladman, now exhibited his real character, and captured several native ships, besides forty vessels laden with provisions for the Mogul army. Besides which he behaved with great arrogance to his admiral the Siddee, "and told him plainly that if his fleet ventured to sea, he would assume their intentions as hostile and deal with them as enemies." Instead, however, of carrying out this threat, and adopting means for securing the safety of Bombay, he merely acted upon the defensive.

"With an unaccountable infatuation the English governor had neglected to strengthen the fortifications of Bombay, although the Court of Directors had so urgently reminded him that this was necessary; and on the 14th February, 1689, the Siddee landed at Sewri with twenty or twenty-five thousand men, and at one o'clock in the morning three guns from the castle apprised the inhabitants of their danger. Then might be seen European and Native women rushing with their children from their houses, and seeking refuge within the fort. Next morning the Siddee marched to Mazagon, where was a small fort mounting fourteen guns, which the English abandoned with such haste, that they left behind them eight or ten chests of treasure, besides arms and ammunition. Here the Siddee established his headquarters, and dispatched a small force to take possession of Mahim fort, also deserted. The following day the enemy advanced, and the General ordered Captain Penn with two companies to drive them back, but he and his little party were defeated. Thus the Siddee became master of the whole island, with the exception of the castle, and a small tract extending about half a mile to the southward of it. He raised batteries on Dongari Hill, and placed one within two hundred yards of the fort. All persons on whom the English authorities could lay hands were pressed into their service."

Thus passed the months from April to September, and provisions ran scarce; but when the monsoon was over, "the Company's cruisers, being able to put to sea, were so successful in capturing vessels and supplies belonging to the Mogul's subjects, that distress was alleviated." Still the danger was imminent. The Siddee's army had been increased to forty thousand fighting men, and the English troops which never amounted to more than two thousand five hundred, dared not venture to meet them in the field.

British Seamen Surrender to Mughal

Child now perceived that negotiation was his only resource, and that the most abject submission would alone assuage the Emperor's wrath. He accordingly despatched two envoys, named Weldon and Novar, to the Mogul court. They were treated with the utmost indignity, and after much suffering were admitted to the Emperor's presence as culprits, with their hands tied behind them. He listened to their entreaties, and at length consented to an accommodation, on condition "that all monies due from them to his subjects should be paid; that recompense should be made for such losses as the Moguls had sustained, and that the hateful Sir John Child should leave India before the expiration of nine months." Thus, terminated this unfortunate act of bombast, by which the Company, both in money and reputation, was a severe sufferer, as well in England as in India.

Harris, who with several other factors had been released after great sufferings, succeeded to the presidentship of Surat and governorship of Bombay. He was a weak, incompetent person, and was soon relieved of his appointment by Annesley Vaux, who after two years' service, was himself dismissed for violating the law against interlopers. In 1692, Captain (afterwards Sir John) Goldesborough was appointed Commissary General with absolute powers. His death in 1694 afforded an opening for the appointment of Sir John Gayer, a man of good character and ability, but whose efforts were frustrated by events beyond his control.

Conflict between Old and New Company

The conflicts between the old and new Companies now commenced, and were carried on with unflinching tenacity. Mutual opposition ensued, and after severe losses on both sides, a compromise was eventually effected. The new Company managed to secure the services of Waite, Pitt, Mather, Annesley and Bourchier, who had been servants of the old Company; they were men of great experience and integrity, and now embarked zealously in the establishments of their new employers. To the secessions were added in 1699, those of Mewse and Brooke, much to the consternation of the president, Sir John Gayer; and this defection was speedily followed by the arrival of Sir Nicholas Waite as president of the new Company, on the 11th January, 1700.

Gayer would not acknowledge Waite's authority, and for some time the greatest confusion reigned between the contending parties. This continued till the 28th of December, when Waite, incensed at Gayer's contumacy, determined "to strike a blow, which, it was hoped would be fatal to the old factory. This was no less than the seizure, in February 1701, of Sir John and Lady Gayer, several factors, their wives, children, soldiers and servants—in all one hundred and nine persons, who were kept in confinement for upwards of three years."

Notes and References

1. It is curious to note the names of the five vessels which first sailed for India. They were the *Scourge,* the *Susan,* the *Hector,* the *Ascension,* and a pinnace.
2. Tavernier was born at Paris in 1605, and died at Moscow in 1689. He travelled through Persia and Turkey and India six times. His .large fortune, with which he purchased the barony of Aubonne, was acquired in the East. The burial ground attached to the old Church of Surat, indicates the last resting place of successive generations of the servants sent out by the East India Company to administer its affairs in the provinces adjoining the Taptee.

Establishment of the Company in India

W.H. CAREY

The successful results of the two expeditions, viz., Sir Francis Drake and Thomas Cavendish fired the genius of the English nation, and led to the coalition of the company of merchant adventurers who first undertook to lay the scheme before the public of trading on an extensive scale with India. On the last day of the 16th century, the London East India Company was formed at the house of Alderman Goddard, or Founders' Hall, where the parties assembled determined upon measures to equip certain vessels "upon a purely mercantile bottom".

Charter Granted to London Merchants

Some four or five years before the death of Akbar (A.D. 1600) Queen Elizabeth granted a charter with certain privileges to a company of London merchants, just at the time that the Dutch East India Company was established, whose first attempt to trade on the Malabar Coast was nearly coincident with the arrival of the London Company's first ships at Surat. The privileges conceded to the London Company enabled them to purchase lands without limitation, and to have a monopoly of trade for fifteen years with the East Indies.

In the year 1600, the consent of the Government was obtained to equip a fleet of five ships for an Indian voyage. Captain James Lancaster commanded the fleet; and thirty-six factors, on salaries varying with their different trusts, accompanied it. On the 2nd of May, 1601, the vessels set sail from Torbay. After a prosperous voyage they landed at Acheen in Sumatra. The natives were tractable, and readily entered into a treaty of commerce; and for such articles or implements of iron ware as Lancaster's crew had with them, they offered in exchange those natural products of their island-pepper and benzoin, cassia and camphor, aloes, spices and fruits. Amicable arrangements having been concluded, the vessels set sail for Java. Captain Lancaster delivered his letters, and, leaving an agent behind, returned in 1603 to England, after making a considerable percentage of profits for his employers, the East India Company of adventurers.

In the year 1600 John Maidenhall, a merchant, was deputed to the court of Akbar. No records are left of the results of that embassy beyond the fact that he obtained a fireman, was well received at court, and that he returned in a few years to England, but that subsequently revisiting India, he died at Agra.

British Missions Sent to Jehangeer Court

It was during the reign of Jehangeer, that two missions were sent from England to his court: the first by the East India Company, conducted by Captain Hawkins, for the purpose of opening up a commercial intercourse with India; the second by the celebrated Sir Thomas Roe as ambassador from King James I. Hawkins after much difficulty arrived at Agra on the 16th April 1607, and being able to speak Turkish was most favourably received by the Emperor, who subsequently insisted on his marrying a young Armenian lady. He succeeded in obtaining the royal promise for an unlimited extension of the English trade; but being opposed by a violent party, the Jesuits, then possessed of great influence at the Mogul court, was at the end of two-and-a-half years obliged to quit Agra, without having effected any of the objects of his mission. The only advantage resulting from Hawkins' voyage was the promise alluded to respecting the establishment of a factory at Surat on the Bombay coast, he had already established on small footing in 1907.

Factory at Surat

The establishment of a factory at Surat was eventually effected by a daring mariner named Best, who despite the impediment and resistance offered him by the Portuguese, boldly proceeded in 1611 to the promised settlement; upon which the Emperor gave a fireman that provided for the residence of an English plenipotentiary at Surat, and an authority for his countrymen to trade fully, openly and without impediment.

Best, being as shrewd as he was determined, well knew that this concession was produced more through fear than any other cause, and therefore determined to avail himself of so favourable an opportunity, and demanded and obtained a ceremonious acknowledgement of his rights from the native authorities. He thereupon established the long desired factory; and having accomplished this returned home in 1613, having laid the foundation of assure and profitable trade.

The first impressions of Surat were not calculated to impress the English favourably with the wealth and the civilisation of India. Nearly half a century later, Tavernier, in that pleasant and graphic style which makes his travels so readable and interesting, described Surat as "a town with a wretched fort, with dwellings built of mud which resemble barns, shut in by reeds dabbed with wattle and mud." A century later, in manufacturing and commercial prosperity it rivalled Bombay, when Bombay had not yet attained to political or maritime importance.

Best was ably succeeded by Captain Downton, who upon his arrival at Surat in 1615, found but three factors, as they were then termed, who had been appointed by his predecessor; intrigue or interest had caused the dispersion of the remainder. Downton's measures produced much animosity towards him from European interests, and considerable native injustice. These coupled with the unhealthiness of the climate, caused his death in the ensuing August. He was a vigorous and talented man, and perfected the arrangement connected with the factory, or as it was then termed "the English house," which he placed under the management of a head factor named Kerridge.

A curious illustration of the rapid growth of an Indian town might be found in the rise of Surat. In 1530, when the Portuguese had first captured the town, its population was estimated at 10,000 only. In 1638 (1538), that population had increased to 133,544.

In the year 1657, so greatly had the town increased in importance, that the East India Company ordered that the administration of all its possessions should be placed under the direct control of the president and council of Surat.

Sir Thomas Roe on a Royal Mission

Until 1614 all transactions with native powers had been carried on by the Company's agent, but it was now resolved to try the effect of a royal mission, and Sir Thomas Roe was deputed as ambassador to the court of the Emperor Jehangeer. He sailed from Gravesend on the 6th March 1615, and arrived at Surat on the 26th of September. Thence he proceeded to Boorhanpore, where he was graciously received by the governor of the province. After a short residence with that prince, Sir Thomas advanced to the royal residence at Ajmer. He reached that city on the 23rd December, but did not obtain an audience of the monarch till the 10th January 1616.

The object of this embassy was two-fold: (1) to arrange a definite treaty; and (2) to recover a large amount of money alleged to be owing by the countries and ministers of the Emperor.

On delivering the royal letter sent by the English sovereign the Mogul Emperor received Sir Thomas Roe with as much consideration as it was in his nature to bestow on any ambassador; he offered to redress some of the grievances complained of, and ratified a treaty by which he conceded to the English nation the right to establish factories and to trade with any part of the Mogul empire, Surat and Bengal especially.

At his court Sir Thomas remained four years, and after successfully overcoming many impediments thrown in his way, he returned, having recovered all bribes, extortions and debts, from the countries and ministers of the court, and further obtained permission to establish another factory at Baroach.

The curious and interesting account left by him of the court and camp of the Great Mogul, forms one of the most important accessions to works on oriental literature and oriental politics. During his residence in the East, he made some valuable collections of ancient manuscripts, among which must be classed the Alexander MS. of the New Testament.

The vessel that conveyed Roe to his destination, was commanded by a "General" Keeling, who endeavoured to found a factory at Cranganore, but failed in his efforts, the factors availing themselves of the first favourable opportunity of escaping with their property to Calicut, where was established the factory, whose looms soon obtained an European celebrity, and which they retained, until British skill and capital removed the seat of manufacture from India to Manchester.

Portuguese Opposition

The feeling of jealousy engendered by the concession alluded to above on the part of the Mogul Emperor, was not allowed to remain long dormant. Open hostilities were soon commenced by the Portuguese, whose fleet burnt the town of Baroach. Another fleet commanded by the Portuguese Viceroy in person anchored off Swally. The naval engagements which followed, proved disastrous to the prestige which the Portuguese had already acquired; and the Mogul court, without offering any interference, looked with pleasure on the checks thus given to an enemy whose encroachments, and whose power they had alike learnt to view with anxiety, if not with dismay.

For several years after Best, Downton and Roe, we have no authentic documents upon which reliance can be placed; but this much is certain, that debauchery and peculation of the most flagrant character usurped the place of good government in Surat. The oldest despatch of the factory is dated July 26th, and it affords little information; but, from other sources we learn that the Company's agents were then negotiating with the Emperor of Golconda for an extension of their trade to Hindustan. Surat at this period had become a position of considerable importance, and was destined to be the point of radiation, whence the commercial spirit of Britain should thrust forward its then infantine powers.

About the year 1636, Methwold, who was president at Surat, returned to England, and was succeeded by Fremlin, and the latter by Francis Benton, whose monument in the cemetery at Surat bears testimony to his exertion, and declares, that "for five years he discharged his duties with the greatest diligence and strictest integrity." Then followed Captain Jeremy Blackman, whose appointment is dated 1651.

Dr. Fryer, a surgeon in the Company's service, visited Surat in 1674, when the English factories were in their zenith. The factors lived in spacious houses and in great style. The salary of the president, according to Fryer, was "£500 a year, half paid here, the other half reserved to be received at home, in case of misdemeanor to make satisfaction, beside a bond of £5,000 sterling of good securities. The accountant has £72 per annum, £50 paid here, the other at home. All the rest are half paid here, half at home, except the writers, who have all [been] paid here."

President of Company at Surat Appointed

Surat was governed by a Company's "agent" till the restoration of Charles II, when a President was sent out. At this time the Surat Government employed "forty sail of stout ships to and from all parts where they trade out and home; manning and maintaining their island Bombay, Fort St. George and St. Helens". The last agent at Surat was named Rivinton; he was succeeded by President Wynch, who lived only two years, and was succeeded by Andrews, who resigning, Sir George Oxendine took his place, and continued to hold the office till his death. It was during his presidentship that Sivajee plundered Surat. He was succeeded by the Hon'ble Gerald Aungier, who fought against Sivajee and repulsed him.

In 1615 a piece of ground was obtained at Armegaun, from the Naik or local chief, and a factory built thereon, which in

1628 was described as being defended by "twelve pieces of cannon and twenty-eight factors and soldiers".

Foundation of Madras Laid

The English having a valuable trade on the Coromandel Coast, were desirous of obtaining a territory which they could fortify. After several ineffectual attempts to obtain such land from the Moguls, they at length succeeded in buying a piece from a Hindu prince, the Rajah of Chindragheri, which was afterwards called Madras. This was in 1639. For the strip of land (six miles long and one mile wide) the English paid an annual rent of £600. There was a small island in the strip facing the sea; this was fortified by a wall and, fortress, to secure the residents against the predatory attacks of native horsemen.

In granting the land to the English the Rajah (Sri Ranga) expressly stipulated that the English town should be called after him, Śri Ranga Rajapatanam. The grant was engraven on a plate of gold. The English kept the plate for more than a century; it was lost in 1746 at the capture of Madras by the French. On the Naik of Chingleput coming into power, he ordered that the town should be called Chinapatanam; this name the English afterwards changed to Madras. To this day, however, the natives call it by the old name of Chinapatanam.

In 1653 Madras was raised to the rank of a presidency. Little or nothing is known of Madras in those early days previous to 1670. In 1672, however, we find Madras was an important place. The government was carried on in the same way as at Surat. The governor drew a yearly salary of £300; the second in council £100; the third £70; and the fourth only £50. Factors were paid between £20 and £40. Writers received only £10, and apprentices £5. But all were lodged and boarded at the expense of the Company.

Sir William Langhorn was governor of Madras from 1670 to 1677, and when he retired, he was succeeded by a gentleman named Streynsham Masters. In 1683 Mr. William Gyfford was made governor. At this period Mr. Josiah Child was chairman of the Court of Directors.

About 1688 there was a great change in the fortunes of Madras. The Sultan of Golconda was conquered by Aurungzeb and consequently the English settlement of Madras was brought under the paramount power of the Great Mogul. During the following ten years, there were great dissensions between the Mahrattas and the Moguls. In 1706 Daood Khan became Nawab of the Carnatic. Mr. Thomas Pitt was governor of Madras.

Trade Opened in Bengal

In 1636 the Emperor of Delhi, having a beloved daughter seriously ill was informed by one of the nobles of his court, of the skill exhibited by European practitioners of medicine, and was induced to apply to the president of Surat for aid in his extremity. Upon this Mr. Gabriel Boughton, surgeon of the ship *Hopewell,* was directed to proceed to Delhi, and render his professional services. "This he did with such success, that the imperial favours were liberally bestowed upon him, and in particular he obtained a patent, permitting him to trade, without paying any duties, throughout the Emperor's dominions." The benefits of this concession would probably have been very doubtful, had his good fortune not followed him to Bengal, where he cured a favourite mistress of the Nawab; who in gratitude confirmed all his privileges, which were thus employed: "The generous surgeon did not in his prosperity forget his former employers, but advanced the Company's interests, by contriving that his privileges should be extended to them. Having done so, he wrote an account of his success to the factory of Surat, and the next year a profitable trade was opened in the rich provinces of Bengal."

Company takes over Bombay

The natural advantages of Bombay did not escape the notice of the Company, who hoped to gain possession of it as early as 1627. "In that year", writes the Rev. Mr. Anderson, "a joint expedition of Dutch and English ships, under the command of a Dutch General, Harman Van Speult, had sailed from Surat with the object of forming an establishment here, as well as of attacking the Portuguese in the Red Sea. This plan was defeated by the death of Van Speult, but in 1653 the

President and Council of Surat again brought the subject under the consideration of the Directors, pointing out how convenient it would be to have some insular and fortified station, which might be defended in times of lawless violence, and giving it as their opinion that for a consideration, the Portuguese would allow them to take possession of Bombay and Bassein." This suggestion, which was submitted to Cromwell, remained unacted upon. But in 1661, the Portuguese Government, upon the marriage of the Infanta Catherina with Charles II, ceded the long-wished for island to England as the Infanta's dower. Accordingly a fleet of five ships, under the Earl of Marlborough, arrived in the Bombay harbour on the 18th September of that year, to take possession.

But the Portuguese were unwilling to resign a place so richly endowed by nature, and refused the English demands. Marlborough, not having the means of reducing the place, was compelled to leave the island and return to England. After Marlborough's departure the Portuguese permitted Cook (who commanded the few soldiers remaining of the body that had been brought out), to occupy the place, but subject to most humiliating terms. The government being dissatisfied with Cook's proceedings, Sir Gervase Lucas was appointed, in 1666, in his room, who soon brought the Portuguese into good behaviour, but he died on the 21st May of the following year. He was succeeded by Captain Gary.

The island not having proved commensurate with the expectations of the king, he made it over by royal charter to the Honorable Company, "in fee and common soccage, as of the manor of East Greenwich, upon payment of an annual rent of £10 in gold on the 30th of September in each year." On receipt of the copy of the charter in 1668, Sir George Oxen den, then president of Surat, was appointed governor of Bombay. The island was soon found to be of importance, its military strength was increased, and fortifications built to guard the harbour and the settlement.

In 1672 the island was invaded by the Siddees a powerful and dangerous neighbouring people, whose depredations were after a time put a stop to by force and arrangement.

Pomp and Show by the Bombay President

Some idea of the absurdities of the times may be drawn from the pomp with which the president used to move about. The Rev. Mr. Anderson, from whose work these details are obtained writes : "He had a standard-bearer and body-guard, composed of a sergeant and a double file of English soldiers. Forty natives also attended him. At dinner, each course was ushered in by a sound of trumpets, and his ears were regaled by a band of music. Whenever he left his private rooms, he was preceded by his attendants with silver wands. On great occasions when he issued from the factory, he appeared on horseback, or in a palanquin, or a coach drawn by milk-white oxen. Led horses with silver bridles followed, and an umbrella of state was carried before him." This pomp and extravagance the Directors wisely strove to check, and they distinctly informed their president that it would afford them much greater satisfaction were he to suppress such unmeaning show and ostentation. And the more effectually to compass their wishes, they reduced his salary to three hundred pounds a year, and dignified him simply with the title of Agent.

The expense of fortifying Bombay not having been covered by the revenue, the Company became burdened with debt, and determined to reduce the number of their military, and consequently the entire "establishment was reduced to two lieutenants, two ensigns, four sergeants, four corporals and a hundred and eighty privates. No batta was to be paid the detachment at Surat; the troop of horse was disbanded, and Keigwin, its commandant, dismissed the service".

Revolt by Bombay Population

Keigwin, who was a man of energy and decision, forthwith went to England, and remonstrated against such unjust and impolitic proceedings, and made such an impression on the Court of Directors that he was invited to return and lend the aid of his experience to the Company in their embarrassed position. He immediately complied, and would doubtless have arranged everything satisfactorily, but to his chagrin, in twelve months after his return, he found the Home authorities had revoked a portion of his official control, and reduced his pay to a miserable pittance. Disgusted with such treatment, and having a strong public sympathy, he declared his secession from the Company and that the inhabitants of Bombay were subjects only of the King of England. In this declaration he was supported by the majority of the residents. "When the intelligence reached England that Bombay had revolted and the president had not been able to reduce it to order, the King commanded the Court of Directors to appoint a Secret Committee of Enquiry. Upon their report His Majesty sent a mandate under his sign manual to Keigwin, requiring him to deliver up the island, and offering a general pardon to all except the ring-leaders. It was further declared that if Keigwin and his followers offered any resistance, all should be denounced as rebels and traitors."

At the same time a reward was offered for Keigwin and his associates. Harsh measures were however rendered unnecessary by the immediate recognition of the King's authority by the whole of the population. Keigwin having obtained a promise of free pardon for himself and supporters, surrendered the island to Sir Thomas Grantham on the 12th November 1684. "Such was a revolt which happily began and ended without bloodshed. Alarming as it was and dangerous to the existence of Anglo-Indian power, it forms an episode in our history of which we are not ashamed. Keigwin emerges from the troubled sea of rebellion with a reputation for courage, honor and administrative capacity: on the other hand, the clemency of the Crown and Company is worthy of all admiration." Some few cases of hardship were doubtless experienced, but upon the whole it was a bold sedition, nobly forgiven and terminated in a juster treatment of the officials, without compromising the integrity of the Company.

Upon the suppression of Keigwin's rebellion, Sir John Wyburn was despatched as deputy governor to Bombay. But John Child, the governor, finding the new deputy too independent to lend himself to the perpetration of the various schemes of aggression which had been concocted by Sir Josiah Child and his brother Directors at home, means were employed for depriving Wyburn of his appointment; but fortunately he did not live to experience that mortification.

KEY TO IMPORTANT TERMS

Accoutrements—The belts, which support the arms, pouch, or pouches, of a soldier; Military dress and arms.

Action—An engagement or battle between opposing forces; or some memorable act done by an officer, soldier or detachment.

Adawlut—A court of justice. Under the Muslim governments were four main courts:

1. **Nizamat Adawlut**—The Supreme Court of Criminal Justice, nominally presided over by the Nazim, or Viceroy of the province.
2. **Diwani Adawlut**—The Civil Court of the Diwan, the chief officer in charge of the revenue of the principality.
3. **Faujdari Adawlut**—The Court of the Faujdar or chief of the magistracy and police of a district; the subordinate, or District Criminal Court.
4. **Adawlut al-Qazi**—The Court of the Qazi, the chief judge of a town or district in civil causes and questions regarding Islam.

Administration, Military—Relates to the system observed in all governments for the guidance, direction and management of military affairs in each country.

Aerial—Pertaining to aircraft or air navigation; performed in or from aircraft.

Ahimsa—The Hindu doctrine of non-violence.

Ain-i-Akbari—A compendium of documents of Akbar's time (1556-1605) illustrating the Emperor's activities in each departments of the administration including military.

Arquebus—An ancient handgun, which was cocked with a wheel.

Arrack—A strong drink or distilled spirit.

Arsenal—A place of receipt and issue of guns, small arms and all other warlike stores.

Arthashastra—A Hindu text on political administration, especially that traditionally attributed to Kautilya, a famous minister of Emperor Chandragupta Maurya.

Bahadur—A hero, a warrior; under the Mughals, a title of honour given to the nobles of the court, usually associated with other titles. At the Delhi court the usual gradation of titles was (ascending) (1) Bahadur, (2) Bahadur Jang, (3) Bahadur-ud-Daulah, and (4) Bahadur-ul-Mulk. Under the British it was given to persons of respectable station and to distinguished native officers! Le. Khan Sahib, Sardar Bahadur.

Bakhshi—A paymaster under the Mughals, whose duty it was to keep accounts of payments on military tenures, such as those of Mansabdars and Jagirdars.

Battalion—The tactical unit of infantry to be efficiently handled and commanded in action by one officer, its strength being approximately a thousand men.

Cadet—A student being educated at a military college or school.

Camp-followers—The sutlers, petty tradesmen, servants and all others who accompany an army in the field.

Cannon—A collective name for guns, mortars and howitzers; A piece of artillery used to throw balls and other projectiles.

Civilian—A term which came into use in the 1760's as a designation of the convenanted European servants of the East India Company, and was later appropriated to describe the Indian Civil Servants. The members of the Company's Civil Service were classified for the first five years as writers, then as factors, then in the 9th year as junior merchants and thereafter as senior merchants. These names emerged from the early commercial character of the company's transactions, and were abolished in 1833.

Colonel, Colonel Commandant—An old British custom followed in the Indian Army. Each infantry and cavalry regiment is allowed to have a Colonel of the Regiment while each corps has a Colonel Commandant, usually a high ranking officer, his position is comparable to 'god father'.

Court-martial—A military tribunal appointed under the provisions of the Code of military law for the investigation and punishment of all offences committed by officers and soldiers. Summary court martial was introduced in 1880 in lieu of field general court martial and consisted of three or two officers.

Darbar (Durbar)—A court, an audience or levee, or executive government of an Indian State.

District—The zila or administrative unit of British India, at the head of which stood the collector and district magistrate.

Dragoons—Soldiers trained Originally to serve indifferently on foot or horse and thereby enabled on an emergency to act as cavalry or infantry. Marshal Brissac, in 1600, appears to have raised this kind of horsemen.

Enfield Rifle—It takes its name from the small arm factory at Enfield, England. It was originally a muzzle-loading arm, but was subsequently converted into a breech-loader.

Factory—A trading establishment or ware-house of the E.1. Company.

Farman—A mandate, an order, a patent.

Fauzdar, Fauzdari—In the 14th century a military officer, corresponding roughly to general of division, and directly under the general-in-chief command. In the 16th-18th centuries an officer-in-charge of the general administration of a portion of province.

Gentoo—(Derived from the Portuguese 'gentio', a gentile or Heathen).

Havaldar (Havildar)—One holding an office of trust, especially used by Mahrattas in ministerial matters. Under the British a sepoy non-commissioned officer corresponding to sergeant.

Howitzer—A piece of ordnance for throwing shells. Howitzers are shorter, lighter, and have less metal in them than smooth bore guns of the same calibre.

I.C.S.— The Indian Civil Service, which in 1858 succeeded the Company's convenanted service. It formed the main administrative service in India and its members provided most of the collectors, judges and heads of departments in both central and provincial governments; and also political agents and residents.

Jamadar—In the Indian army the title of the second rank of Indian officer in a company of sepoys, the subedar being the first; Now designated as naib-subedar.

Khallasi—An Indian sailor. This class of men came chiefly from Chitagong area. Also employed in large numbers in Arsenals, bordering on the seaside.

Kshatriya— The name of the second or military and regal group of castes, or a member of it; the warrior, the king.

Laboratory—A department of an arsenal for the manufacture and examination of ammunition and combustible stores.

Mahabharata—A great Indian War Epic. One of the world's greatest philosophic poems, the Bhagavadgita (Song of the Lord), is related to it.

Matchlock—Name formerly given to a small arm or musket. The earliest muskets were fired by means of a piece of slow-match applied by the hand to the touch hold. Later in the 14th century the priming powder was ignited by the match lighted by the trigger of the lock.

Naval Terms—Afloat=at sea; Bravo Zulu=well done; Cabins=officers' rooms; Galley=kitchen; Jimmy=lieutenant; Old man=captain; Plumber=engineer officer; Victuals=foodstuff.

Orderly Room—The court of the commanding officer, where charges brought against the man of his regiment are investigated, and sentence passed.

Peshwa—originally the chief minister of the Mahratta power; in the 18th century becoming prince of an independent Mahratta state. The Peshwa's power ceased with the surrender of Baji Rao to the British in 1817.

Presidency (and President)— The chief of a principal East India Company factory was styled 'President' in the 17th century and the area of his jurisdiction the Presidency.

Senapati—In ancient India, the commander-in-chief.

Shah—Bandar-Harbour master, and usually head of the customs. A Muslim port-official.

Siege Train—The men, guns and material collected together for the conduct of a siege.

Silladar—A horse-soldier who provides his own horse and arms.

Sipahi (Sepoy)—Indian name of soldier.

Sipah-salar—A commander-in-chief (Mughal period).

Subahdar (Subedar)—Viceroy; governor of a province. A local commandant. Under the British the chief native officer of a company of sepoys.

Topasses—A name used in the 17th and 18th centuries for darkskinned and half-caste claimants of Portuguese descent and Christian profession. Worked at times in the Company gun-rooms.

Zila (Zillah)—A division, a district. Under the British the area under the jurisdiction of a collector, or of a collector and magistrate combined, or in the Punjab of a deputy commissioner.

British Politico-Military Power in India

M. JOHN

While moving a vote of thanks to their Army in India, in the British Parliament in March 1819, Mr. Canning paid tributes to the superiority of the British arms and said, "Looking back to the period when our possessions there consisted only of a simple factory on the coast for the purpose of a permitted trade : and in comparing that period with the present, when that factory has swelled into an empire, when about one-third in point of extent and about three-fifths in point of population, of those immense territories are subject immediately to British Government: when not less than another fourth of the land, and another fifth of the inhabitants, are under rulers either tributory to the English Power or connected with it by close alliance . . . ." Other speakers too, complemented these armed forces in India and described European and Native troops as two main pillars of the British Empire. The East India Company's great successes in India depended mainly on is miliary forces. How these forces—European and Native were composed, trained and disciplined and what role they played in building a vast empire for the British Crown forms an interesting study. (Ed.)

I

EVOLUTION OF THE BRITISH INDIAN ARMED FORCES

A—The Beginnings

The Military history of British India dates back to the year 1607 when the English ship *Hector* and militarised men of the East India Company under Captain Hawkins, first arrived at Surat[1] (India) and commenced their trade. Generally this history falls into four periods—under the East India Company 1607-1708 A.D., the Presidency[2] Armies of Bengal, Madras and Bombay 1709-1894, the United Indian Army 1895-1920, and finally till 1947 when India gained independence.

In addition to the European soldiers and armed factors who arrived in India in ships from England, natives were enrolled as guards for the various factories of the East India Company at Surat, Masulipatam, Armegaon, Madras, Hooghly and Balasore in the first half of the 17th century for purposes of protection of merchandise and for defence. The military necessity for these guards were progressively felt and they were better armed, trained and disciplined. In the early days of the Company, its military element consisted solely of the officers and crews of the ships the factors.[3] Those factors like soldiers were imparted military training during the long and dangerous voyages to India which enabled them to handle arms, put up an organised defence and function like combatants and when necessary arose to enlist themselves as regular soldiers. They handled arms and ammunition in times of emergency and were like reserves for a second line defence. This provided them a good opportunity to gain military training, experience and discipline which eventually led some to attain high military positions. Lord Clive who later occupied the highest position in the Company's military ranks started his career as a writer.[4]

The Army

The foundation of the Indian Army was laid with the 'ensign and thirtymen' of Bengal, the 'peons'[5] of the Madras factories commencing 1624 and the small holding force of Bombay in 1662. In the early years of Company's trade and till the factories were fortified, the armouries were located in the vessels. The peons and other native guards wore their own dress, and had their own weapons.

In 1634, permission was given, by a *firman* of the Emperor Shah Jahan, to the Company to establish factories in Bengal with a fort at Piplee. Initially in Bengal the forces were limited to an ensign and 30 European soldiers the equivalent to the traditional corporal's guard of the British Empire—reinforced by 'Gunner' and his 'Crew'. In 1686 an expedition consisting of ten ships of seventy to twelve guns each was sent out from England against the Nawab of Bengal. In 1696, Charles Eyre, the Company's agent was given permission to defend his factory by fortification and Fort William was constructed in 1702 and completed in 1717. This Fort, thereafter, remained for two hundred years the seat of the government and the Headquarters of the army in India.

In 1625, the factory at Masulipatam was shifted to Armegaon where fortifications[6] were allowed to be erected by the Company for the first time in India. The garrison of Armegaon in September 1628 consisted of 12 pieces of ordnance and 28 soldiers, who were trained as infantry and to work the guns in time of need. In 1640 the factory was removed to Madras-patanam and then to the newly constructed Fort St. George. In 1644, 30 recruits and a considerable amount of ordnance and military stores were landed from England and 20 more recruits in the following year. During 1662-63 a large number of African, Portuguese and natives were engaged as labourers and trained in the use of arms. In 1690-91 a company of European artillery and a troop of horse, constituted a part of the garrison of Fort St. George and in the same years Fort St. David, near Cuddalore, was built.

The Bombay island was handed over to the Company by King Charles II on 17th March 1668 on an yearly rent of £10 in gold. The King's troops stationed at Bombay accepted their conversion to the service of the Company. The garrison consisted of 75 officers, 139 non-commissioned officers and men (all Europeans) and 54 Topasses besides 2 gunners and their 21 pieces of cannon. Certain increases were made in the Company's forces, notably in 1683, when the Bombay garrison was supplemented by the enrolment of 2 companies of Rajputs. Each company consisted of 100 men, commanded by their own Rajput officers; and this small force may be regarded as the first beginning of the Indian Army. But according to another version:

> "Technically—although not in spirit—the Indian Army can be traced back to the native retainers of the East India Company, who guarded its merchandise, and sometimes (but not always) increased the prestige of its officials. But its real ancestors are the sepoys of South India who fought under Clive and Wellesley, and the races who were once masters of Hindustan, and who afterwards served in the British ranks as volunteers."[7]

In 1675 orders were sent out to Surat, the seat of Company's government, that the civil servants[8] were to apply themselves to acquiring a knowledge of military discipline so that if there was any sudden attack, or if they were found better qualified for military duties than for mercantile work, they might receive commissions and have the pay of military officers.

In 1698 a new Company of Merchants known as English Company received its charter. The two Companies became bitter rivals but in 1708 they were merged into the "United Company of Merchants trading to the East Indies" better known as the East India Company.

The Navy

Experience gained during the third voyage compelled the Company to have a strong armed marine force to cope with the depredations of the Portuguese and the Dutch and the pirates on the Indian coasts. The Indian Marine Service was formed in 1612 which, from 1612 to 1686 was known as the East India

Company's Marine, from 1686 to 1830 as the Bombay Marine, from 1830 to 1863 as the Indian Navy, from 1863 to 1877 again as the Bombay Marine, from 1877 to 1892 as Her Majesty's Indian Marine and from 1892 to 1947 as the Royal Indian Marine.

In 1612, the Marine Force consisted of 4 warships namely the 'Dragon', the 'Hoseander', the 'James' and the 'Solomon' under the command of Captain Thomas Best. The first action was fought off Surat with the Portuguese having a fleet of 4 galleons and 21 armed vessels. After 3 days bitter fighting, the English emerged victorious. For three years Captain Best was engaged in almost continuous warfare. Credit goes to Captain Best for providing strong naval cover to the first factory of the English Company established at Surat.

As the trade and factories spread, the English strengthened their sea power by adding more warships to the Company's Marine Service. In that period it was a continuous sea warfare between the English and their adversaries, the Portuguese and the Dutch and the Arab, Malabar and Konkani pirates.

In 1668 when the East India Company took over Bombay from the Crown, Captain Young of the Marine was appointed as Deputy Governor. Mr. Warwick Pett, who was sent from England with a full supply of Marine stores and equipment for ship-building, built two small brigantines in 1670. In 1686 the seat of the Company's Government was transferred from Surat to Bombay. The Marine stores were shifted in the Bombay Castle, the Company's ships being anchored in Bombay Harbour. The Marine force became officially known as the Bombay Marine. An officer was regularly appointed each year as Admiral. The force at that time consisted of one ship of 32 guns, 4 grab ships mounting from 20 to 28 guns and 20 grabs and gallivats, carrying from 5 to 12 guns.

B—The Formative Period

During the Company's Times

One of the first measures taken in 1708 by the new United Company was the definite formation of three Presidencies, of Bengal, Madras and Bombay, each absolute within its own limits. The President[9] of each was also Commander-in-Chief of the military forces of the Presidency and was responsible only to the Directors at home.[10] Consequently, the armies of the three "Presidencies became distinct and separate from each other."[11]

By then the English had established themselves in three chief fortified places, the island of Bombay, Fort St. George, Madras, and Fort William at Calcutta. In the course of nearly 100 years, the mere unorganised handful of miscellaneous and ill-disciplined Europeans have been converted into a force consisting of small but organised military units. The presidential armies of those days were composed of Europeans recruited from England or collected locally, of half-caste Goanese Topasses and of Indian sepoys. The latter were mainly armed with their own native weapons, wore their own native dress and were commanded by their native officers.

Military arms, equipment and stores in large quantities continued to be supplied by the Board of Ordance at England to the Company's troops and also to the native purchasers. "In 1658 Cromwell granted to a Mr. Bolt licence to export to India 3 mortars and 2,20,000 rounds of shells for Aurungzeb", the Company at the same exporting large quantities of ordance stores to counteract Mr. Bolt's proceedings. Sir John Child once thought it highly advisable to cultivate the friendship of the Mughal's arch-enemy Shivaji and even supply him with ammunition, because he considered such friendship politically and commercially desirable.[12]

The Company supplied men, and military stores to the Mughals and local chiefs against the Dutch and the Portuguese but not the big guns.[13] Ordnance or big guns were however already being manufactured and positioned at various fortified places in India as is evident from the writing of early English travellers, namely, William Finch (1608-11), Nicholos Withington (1612-16) and Edward Terry (1616-19).[14]

With increase in their trade the Company gradually increased its armies in all the three Presidencies. By 1741, the Bombay army alone besides some 700 so-called sepoys, who attended on the civil servants of the Company in the capacity of peons, had a regular regiment consisting of 26 British officers, 166 warrant and non-commissioned officers, 1,276 rank and file and 27 followers.

In 1744 war broke out between England and France. The Company started thinking seriously to have a military organization in India to safeguard its trading interests and possessions. As fresh European soldiers were not available for service, the Company recruited, equipped and trained a large number of Indians to fight its battles against the French who had also a fairly big army of natives under their command.

Some far-reaching measures were adopted in 1748.[15] The armies were reorganised on European lines. Each Presidency got one company of artillery consisting of 5 British officers and 110 other ranks. A regular Ordnance Service for supply of military stores to the troops was also organised. Major Stringer Lawrence was named the first Commander-in-Chief of all the Company's forces in India both European and Indian. He took various steps to improve the organisation of the British Indian Army. He is called by some as "father of the Indian Army".

The war with France again broke out and in May 1754 at the request of Madras Government for help, Bombay despatched 3 companies of sepoys and 450 men of the European regiment. Simultaneously the first Royal troops including 39th Foot from England also arrived in Madras.

Shortly before the battle of Plassey, Clive reorganised[16] the Indian troops by giving them the shape of regular battalions. These battalions were commanded by the British officers and were equipped on the European lines. The first battalion organised on these lines was known as the 'Lal Pultan'[17] and was composed of 3 British Officers (1 captain, 2 subalterns), several British non-commissioned officers (1 sergeant-major and several sergeants), 42 Indian officers (1 commandant, 1 adjutant, 10 subedars and 30 jemadars), and 800 Indian rank and file, (50 havildars, 40 naiks, 10 buglers and 700 sepoys). The battalion was divided into ten companies. Gradually many more battalions were raised on this pattern. Clive first introduced the British officers into Indian army units.

Sir John Clavering,[18] the first Lt. Gen. as Commander-in-Chief of the East India Company's forces in India during 1774-77, introduced some more reforms such as complete renumbering of the sepoy battalions, first organised by Lord Robert Clive during 1757. In 1775 in Bengal, 21 regular battalions and one Parganna Battalion (the 24th) existed and all these were numbered consecutively by brigades. This facilitated in determining areas of supply and made smooth work of the British Indian Ordnance Board and the Arsenals and Magazines under it.

In 1796 the Indian Army was reorganised and the Bengal Army was the first to be 50 reformed. The infantry and cavalry were separated and their officers were placed on separate general lists. Infantry regiments were formed by linking existing battalions and amalgamating half battalions. There were British and Indian officers and the commanding officer was a Colonel. Each battalion had 2 grenadier and 8 infantry companies with a total strength of 1,600 sepoys. Similar were the improvements in the Madras and Bombay armies. In addition to infantry, cavalry and artillery regiments, they had a marine battalion each.

As the British authority became predominant, further expansion was considered necessary and in the process the Presidency armies were increased. In 1796 the Company had 17,956 Europeans and 84,232 Natives in its armies which increased to 30,423 Europeans and 246,125 Indians in 1825 and 36,409 Europeans and 187,067 Natives in 1830.

In 1824, the Indian infantry regiments, which had been formed by linking *two* battalions, were broken up again into single battalion regiments. In the same year, the number of the cavalry regiments was increased, partly by using regular regiments and partly by raising irregular troops. The irregular regiments were raised on the *Silladar*[19] system. Under this system the individual soldier supplied and maintained his horse, clothing equipment and arms (other than rifle), receiving in return a higher rate of pay that the non-*Silladar* soldier, whose needs were furnished by the Government.

In course of time, the East India Company acquired more territories and for their protection it increased the strength of the Army. The total strength of the Army on the eve of the Great Uprising (1857) was 38,000 Europeans, 276 field guns and 348,000 Indian troops with 248 field guns.

The Navy

Consequent on the transfer of the seat of Government and the Marine headquarters from Surat to Bombay in 1686, the marine matters began to improve. A regular supply of officer, men and equipment was kept up from England through the ships arriving from Europe to match the superior maritime forces of the Portuguese, Dutch and French and *for* protection against the attacks of pirates including the Arabian fleet which in 1715, consisted of one ship of 74 guns, two of 60, one of 50 and eighteen small ships from 32 to 12 guns each, and some "trankies" and rowing vessels of from 4 to 8 guns each.

In April 1717, the first important action, though unsuccessful, was fought by the Bombay Marine against Angaria's forces while attempting to capture the Caste Gheriah, the stronghold of Angaria.

In 1722 the Bombay Marine made a joint expedition with the Portuguese, the latter providing the land forces, against Alibeg, the marine force consisting of 3 ships under Commodore Mathews. Clement Dowing, a Lieutenant then in the service of the Bombay Marine, writes that the expedition failed due to the cowardice and treachery of Portuguese with many English officers and men killed or wounded. He adds further that after the failure of the attack, "the Commodore came on shore in a violent rage, flew at the Portuguese General and thrust his cane in his mouth, and treated the Viceroy not much better."

The English suffered more reverses and set-backs in the following years, Desertions amongst the European seamen became frequent. In 1724 an order was passed that the seamen should be kept two months in arrears of pay. A scheme for pension for the widows of officers and seamen who had performed distinguished service, was also approved.

In 1735 Lavji Nusserwanji Wadia, was brought to Bombay and started the work after establishing the Government Dockyard. The Bombay Marine now consisted of the 'Victoria' (Frigate), the 'Neptune' (Grab), the 'Prince of Wales', 'King George', 'Princes Caroline' and 'Rose' (Galleys), the 'Salamander' (Bomb Ketch) and several gallivats and boats.

During the year 1739-41 several additions were made to the fleet, amongst others two grabs, 90 feet long by the keel, 30 feet by the beam and 12 feet 8 inches in the hold to carry 20 guns (10 in a line) besides her prow guns. One sea going ship 90 feet by the keel, 30 feet by the beam and 14½ feet in the hold, to carry 11 guns in a line. Thus by 1741 the strength of the marine consisted of one ship of 44 guns, four ships of 28 guns, four of 18 guns and twenty large gallivats, employing nearly 100 officers and from 1700 to 2000 men. Because of peace prevailing in the following year, the post of Admiral was abolished and the number of officers in reduced establishment, consisted of 1 Superintendent, 8 Commanders, one of whom was styled Commodore, 3 First Lieutenants, 4 Second Lieutenants, 4 Third Officers and 6 Masters of Gallivats, besides Midshipmen.

In 1751 Captain James while conveying a fleet of 70 coasters from Bombay, was confronted with Angaria's fleet, fought and succeeded in saving his convoy and on his return to Bombay was appointed Commodore and Commander-in-Chief of the Bombay Marine.

In early 1756 a Royal Squadorn under Vice-Admiral Watson visited Bombay. It was decided to despatch a combined naval and military expedition against Tulaji Angaria's stronghold Vijayadurg by first attacking Gheriah. The combined expedition consisted of warships of Royal Navy. Bombay Marine and a land force of European and Topasses soldier under Colonel (afterwards Lord) Clive. After three days' bitter fighting the attack proved successful.

During the later part of the 18th century great improvements were made in the Bombay Dockyard, more graving docks were built, and the yard was fitted with every facility for building and repairing ships, Mr. Manackjee Lowjee being the chief builder. Ships built at Bombay were strong, handsome and well finished and compared better than those built in Europe. The 'Bombay' and the 'Swallow' were two such examples.

For a period of about 70 years till 1829, a Captain of the Bombay Marine was appointed Deputy of the Company, he flew the Company's colours at the peak of his flagship, but carried Mughal's flag at the main.

In 1766 the Company introduced a complete set of orders regarding discipline for the use of Commanders, which constituted the first body of regulations ever published for the Marine Service. (Bombay Government Consultations, 10 March, 1766). Later in 1771, pay of the seamen was formally regulated and the force was reduced and reorganised. In 1772 the first surveying expedition which went around and explored the coasts of Mekran, Sind and Katbiawar and a portion of Arabia and Persia was undertaken by the Bombay Marine. This later developed into Marine Survey of India responsible for scientific delineating the coast of India, Burma and the Persian Gulf.

In December 1775 a combined military and naval expedition was despatched from Bombay for the reduction of Mahratta stronghold of Thana. In 1780 the ships of Bombay Marine fought and co-operated in the battles against Hyder Ali. In 1782 the 'Bombay' squadron acted in concert with General Mathews on the Malabar coast and helped to capture Rajamandrug, Merju, Kundapur, Annanpur and Mangalore. In brief, there was hardly a naval engagement in Indian waters during the later half of the 18th century in which the Bombay Marine did not play a part. It rendered much help in co-operation with the ships of the Royal Navy at the capture of Pondicherry, Trincomalee, Jafnapatam and Colombo.

In August 1, 1998 the new regulations for the service were issued by the Directors. Relative rank with the officers in the Army, retiring pension for all officers, prohibition of private trade and the following duties were laid down: (1) The protection of trade, (2) Suppression of piracy and general duties as vessels of war, (3) Conveying transport and carrying troops if necessary, (4) The prosecution of Maritime surveys in the East. A civilian Superintendent was appointed at the head of the service. He was assisted by Master Attendant and the Commodore and two senior Captains. All formed a Marine Board to administer the service. The Superintendent was to rank next to Members of Council, the Commodore next junior to the Master Attendant to rank with a Colonel in the Army, Senior Captain with Lt. Colonel, Junior Captain with Major, First Lieutenant with Captain; Second Lieutenant with Lieutenant. In 1802 the perwnnel of the 'Bombay' consisted of the Superintendent, the Master Attendant, Commodore, Senior Captain, 13 Captains, 33 First Lieutenants, 21 Second Lieutenants and 37 Volunteers. In 1801, several vessels of the Bombay Marine bad participated in co-operation with the Royal Navy, in the Egyptian Campaign.

In 1808 Commodore Hayes was appointed Deputy Master Attendant and Secretary of the newly constituted Marine Board in Bengal and finally became Master Attendant. A Marine Survey Department was also established in Bengal in the same year. In 1810 the Bombay Marine helped in the capture of the Island of Mauritius and the conquest of Java.

In 1814 a table of precedence was fixed, the Superintendent of Marine coming immediately after Generals and Flag Officers (above the rank of Major General). The early part of the 19th century saw great activity in ship-building in the Bombay dockyard under Jamsetjee Bomanji; twenty-two war ships were built for the Royal Navy in the Bombay dockyard between the years 1800 and 1840.

In the years 1820-24 many alterations and improvements were made in the conditions of service, prospects and uniforms of officers. After the change of denomination of the service to that of Indian Navy in 1830, further changes were made in the uniform. The appointment of master attendant was abolished and a Controller of the Dockyard appointed instead. The period between 1834 and 1839 was again a period of change for the service due to the reduction of sail and the introduction of steam as the chief propelling power.

"In 1832 Marine establishment at Calcutta has no superior for utility and skill. The pilot vessels were schooner-rigged and adapted to the tempetuous weather which was so frequent of the sand beads. Officers were European who faced the difficult and dangerous navigation of the Hooghly. There came up light houses, floating light ships, buoys, etc. and telegraphic communication between Kedgeree and Calcutta.

At Madras, the Maritime was of course trifling in comparison.

At Bombay there is warlike Marine kept up for the protection of British commerce which consists of about one frigate, four 18-gun ships, six 10-gun corveties and brigs, two armed steamers and surveying ships, etc. The number of officers—12 Capts., 14 Commanders, 46 Lts., 71 Junior Officers, 4 Warrant Officers to each vessel and 500 European seamen. During the European wars, the Indian Navy distinguished itself in the battles.[20]

It was decided in]1838 to occupy Afghanistan. A squadron of the Indian Navy was employed to blockade the mouth of the Indus river and ships were also used for the conveyance of troops and stores. In the battle of Miani and capture of Sind in 1843, the ships took a leading part.

When Aden was captured in 1837 and made a portion of the British Empire, the Indian Navy took a prominent part in the operations. The title of Superintendent was changed to that of Commander-in-Chief of the Indian Navy by a Government order issued on 4th April, 1848.

In 1849 the broad pennant of the Indian Navy, which had been the same as that of the Royal Navy was changed, and henceforth the broad pennant of the Commander-in-Chief of the Indian Navy was to be a red flag with a yellow lion and crown in the upper canton nearest the mast. The following 10 years was a transition period from sail to steam as the chief motive power of the vessels.

From 1849 to 1856 the service attained high efficiency under its distinguished officers. In 1854 it was decided to amalgamate the small uncovenanted Bengal Marine with the Indian Navy.

The Indian Navy did not participate to any considerable extent in suppressing the Great Uprising of 1857. However, an Indian Naval Brigade consisting of 78 officers and 1740 men was formed and fought in D.P., Dacca and Assam. The first Victoria Cross awarded to an Indian Naval personnel was for bravery shown on land.

Air flying in India commenced in the twentieth century.[21] Civil aviation followed soon,[22] while Air Force in India had its beginnings in 1914.

Notes and References

1. "Surat is reckon'd the most fam'd Emporium of the Indian Empire, where all commodities are vendible. . . . And the river is very commodious for the Importation of Foreign goods, which are brought up to the city in Hoys and Yachts and country Boats". *Ovington* (1609). The seat of the Company's Government remained at Surat up to 1686.
2. On the 11th January 1613 the Mogul Emperor's firm and to establish a factory at Surat was delivered to Captain Best, the Company's representative. This was the origin of the Bombay Presidency. In 1625 a trading centre was established at Masulipatam (South India). In 1640 the

Company acquired the concession of Madras which became first independent position of the British in India. Such was the origin of the Madras Presidency. The Bengal Presidency originated when in 1634 by a *firman* of the Emperor Shah Jehan, permission was given to the Company to establish factories in Bengal with a fort at Piplee. *The Army in India and its Evolution.*

3. A word meaning simply commercial agent. At the bottom were apprentices, next grades upwards being writers, factors and merchants, senior merchants and agents. This classification of writers, factors and merchants ceased to exist in 1833.
4. "Mr. Robert Clive, Writer in the service, being of a Martial Disposition, and having acted as a Volunteer in our late Engagements, we have granted him an Ensign's Commission, upon his application for the same." *Letter dt. 2nd May, 1747 from the Council at Fort St. David to the Court of Directors.*
5. "The first Native foot soldiers in the service of the Government (East India Company) were known as Peons. In February 1747 there were about 3,000 of these men employed at Fort St. David, of whom about 900 were armed with muskets." *History of the Madras Army by* Lt. Col. W.J. Wilson.
6. "We fortify our Houses, have Bunders or Docks for our vessels, to which belong yards for Seamen, Soldiers and stores." Fryer.
   The armies of the native potentates had primitive artillery; and so it came about that the Company's factories had to be armed with ordnance, taken as a rule from their ships and mounted and manned by their sailors. Lt. Col. EWC Sandes, *The Military Engineer* in *India.*
7. F. Yeats Brown's *Martial India.*
8. As late as the year 1805, a writership in the service of the East India Company was thought to be as good as a seat in Parliament. It was mentioned in the British Parliament on April 25, 1809 that Lord Viscount Castlereagh in the year 1805 did deliver up into the hands of Lord Clancery a writership, of which he had the gift, for the purpose of exchanging it for a seat of Parliament.
9. The title 'President', as applied to the Chief of a principal Factory, was in early popular use, though in the Charters of the East India Company it first occurred in 1661. Sainsbury's *Calendar* mentions "Capt. Jourdnion, President of the English at Bantam" in 1614. "Speaking of the Dutch Commander, as well as the English 'President' at Surat, they go about with a great train, sometimes with people of their own mounted, but particularly with a great crowd or Indian servants on foot and armed, according to custom with sword, target, bow and arrows." *P. Della Valle.* (1623).
10. In early days of the Company, the Council at each Presidency exercised all military functions, including that of command and themselves dealt with every military matter including supplies of munitions till the middle of the eighteenth century when the post of Commander-in-Chief was instituted. Then, as territories were acquired, forces increased, and political, revenue and other business grew, Committees were formed which included officers and members of the Council. (Young).

11. Lack of adequate communication, nature of the country, characteristics of the peoples, their language and customs militated against the development of the Presidency armies and their administrative services on identical lines. (Young).
12. *Ledger and Sword,* Vol. I.
13. The only source of supply for the Companys' forces upto practically the last quarter of the eighteenth century for any sort of Ordnance was the home manufacturer (Young).
14. The early Indian-made guns were very crude, mostly of iron bars bound by iron rings *or* of iron cylinders with brass cast round them. They were clumsy and inefficient, and Orme says that even in the eighteenth century the natives thought it good if they fired a piece once in fifteen minutes. He also mentions that at Plassey in 1757 many of their guns were mounted on huge stage. The casting of brass cannon, however, was well established in those times in many other parts of India. The East India Company in 1770 issued direction that "the natives must be kept as ignorant as possible both of the theory and practice of artillery so that native powers are kept dependent on us for Ordnance." (Young).
15. On 17 June, 1748, the court of Directors in England issued Regulations for the formation of a regular company of Artillery, and establishment of regular Ordnance Service and Laboratories for manufacture of Ammunition. This revolutionary Regulation, applicable to the three Presidencies of Bengal, Madras, and Bombay transformed huge stocks of British military hardware from the gun-rooms of the ships onto the Indian land. Thereafter Artillery Companies, Ordnance Depots and Ammunition Laboratories, located mostly in forts were formed rapidly in the three Presidencies. The Company's troops up to this time were entirely English not partly Scotch or Welsh or Irish as is evident from an examination of the attestation forms in original lying in the Imperial Library. Out of these troops, no Catholic was employed or even admitted in the Ordnance Magazines or Ammunition Laboratories.
16. Clive's organisation was evolutionary, not revolutionary and in analyzing it one is led to reflect that, when two such conservative races as the British and Indian combine together to form a given institution, some traces of it tend apparently to remain for many years. *The Army in India and its Evolution.*
17. Or the Red Battalion probably from its dress. Originally in 1461 in England red was adopted for a small number of men, when a contingent for the army of the King-Maker, the Earl of Warwick, was sent from Rye dressed in Red coats. Henry VII, in 1485, instituted the Yeomen of the Guard as a kind of bodyguard, and they may be taken as a nucleus of the present standing army of the England. They consisted of picked men, and were armed, one half with bows, the other half with hand-guns. Their dress, as it continued subsequently was red. *Journal of the Army Historical Society.*
18. General Sir John Clavering, K.B. was the third son of Sir James Clavering, of Greencroft, Durham. He was born in 1722, and he married the Lady Diana, second daughter of the First Earl of Delawarr. He entered the Army in the Coldstream Guards; and in 1759 he served with marked distinction at the capture of Guadeloupe. He was then appointed Aide-

decamp to the King.—In 1772 he became Colonel of the 52nd Foot, and in 1776 he was created a Knight of the Bath. He attained the rank of Lieutenant-General in 1770. In 1773 he was appointed to the command of the Bengal Army, with a seat in the new Council in Bengal, and a salary of 10,000 a year. In 1777 he died in Calcutta aged fifty-five. He was "an honest, straightforward man, of passionate disposition, and mediocre abilities." *Dictionary of National Biography.*

19. "It is my opinion, that the arrangement with the Soubah of the Deccan should be, that the whole of the force should be *Silledar* horse." Wellington, III, 671 (1804).
20. *The Political, Commercial, Financial Conditions of the Anglo-Eastern Empire, 1832.*
21. The earliest civilian flights in India took place in Calcutta at the end of 1910. Captain Maxwell, Brigade Major of the 2nd Infantry Brigade was the first Military Officer to fly on 17 February, 1911.
22. As regards civil aviation in India, a temporary service between Karachi and Bombay operated by R.A.F. aircraft and personnel began in 1919. This was followed by air mail service between Bombay, Calcutta and Rangoon by three aircraft supplied by Messers Handley Page and Company which later helped considerably to lay the foundations for the Imperial Airways and other transcontinental air services. The first airship to leave England for Karachi—The R-IOI—crashed at Beauvais in France in October, 1930. Sir Sefton Brancker, a pioneer of civil aviation in India, was among those who lost their lives.

II

PRESIDENCY ARMIES : BENGAL, MADRAS, BOMBAY

The period 1796-1830 is considered very important in the history of the evolution of the Indian Army in general and the Presidency armies in particular. During this period two far-reaching reorganisations of the army, first in 1796 and the second in 1824, took place. The first general re-organisation of 1796 was reviewed and its various defects remedied by the 1824 re-organisation, to make it endurable for a long time. It is proposed to study in depth the state of Presidency armies during this period, and as these existed in 1830-32, after the second reorganisation. The following account is based on the evidence rendered by Major-General Sir J. Malcolm, Colonel Pennington, Colonel J. Munro, Colonel Stannus and other high ranking officers before the Select Committee of the House of Commons on the Affairs of the East India Company in 1831-32. (Ed.)

During the earliest days of the British Indian history which began in 1607 when the first British trading ship *Hector* arrived at Surat, the military element of the Company's personnel consisted solely of the factors themselves and of the officer and crews, of the armed trading ships, despatched from England to the Eastern seas. Subsequently as the English merchants started settling on the coastline land, they employed natives for guarding factories in their settlements. These first guard levies had no discipline and were armed with matchlocks bows and arrows, spears, swords or any other weapon they could get. They consisted of bodies of various strength, each under the command of its own chief, who received from Government the pay of the whole body and distributed it to the men. As time went on some improvement took place in discipline, while the best Indian officers were appointed as commandants. Muskets were issued in place of matchlocks and the men acquired some idea of drill.

Presidency Chief as C-in-C

The early English settlement was governed by the chief of

its principal factory who was designated President and a Council was formed to advise and assist him in his functioning as President. By a charter granted in 1661, the President and Council of each factory were entrusted with power of martial law for the government of the troops kept for its defence. The President was Commander-in-Chief of the forces belonging to the Presidency, which consisted, with few exceptions, of English soldiers sent out in the Company's ships, and on occasions of emergency, a few European mercenaries or deserters from the various French, Dutch and Portuguese settlements in India. In addition to these were a few half-castes, called Topasses and African slaves, the latter imported from the Company's stations on the east coast of Africa.

Origin of Presidency Armies

Whereas the English merchants transacted a good deal of business, they did a good deal of fighting too. For want of authority of a strong central government in the far-flung areas conditions in India were not stable. Prowling, looting and attacking by *Nawabs* and *Zamindars* and their armed men on the English and other European settlements were not uncommon. To safeguard their property and person, the English merchants armed themselves and also the natives, in their employment caned peons. Large quantities of big guns, shot, arms powder and other military stores were imported from England by the merchants for protecting their factories and fortifications. The Gunner and the Gun Room Crew were, in addition to their own duties, responsible for handling these military stores; they and even the storekeepers, factors, writers and merchants used to supply military stores to the Council, particularly in the Bombay Presidency, on substantial commission sometimes up to 30% on the cost of supplies. The Council dealt with these supplies normally through its Committee of Stores and Committee of Works.

Different Patterns

Consequent to the different sources of military supplies

each Presidency had a different pattern of general and technical stores such as tents, gun carriages, etc. Since each Presidency had a separate establishment for the management of stores nothing was given from the one to the other but as a private loan. In brief the general equipment of the Army in the three Presidencies varied very much. A Presidency deficient in military stores seldom got help from the other Presidencies.

An officer on his arrival in India took his chance whether he was appointed to an European or a Native regiment of a particular Presidency and in that Corps he remained until he obtained the rank of lieutenant-colonel, unless removed by augmentation of the army.

Different Pays of Sepoys

As regards difference in the pay and allowances of native troops of the Presidencies, Colonel John Munro stated in 1832: "Just before the conquest of Mysore there was very great difficulty found in procuring recruits and in maintaining the battalions of the Madras army in a complete state; the desertions were very frequent. This was the cause that induced the Madras Government, with the sanction of the Court of Directors, to increase the pay of the Native troops at Madras from five rupees to seven rupees a month; and this has produced a difference between the pay of Madras and Bengal sepoys which exists to the present moment. The Madras rates of pay were afterwards adopted at Bombay."

Presidency Forces

The table on the next twelve pages exhibits in detail the forces in the three Presidencies.

THE THREE ARMIES

The amount of force maintained at each Presidency, and in each year 1793 to 1830, was as follows :

The Three Armies	*Bengal*	*Madras*	*Bombay*	*India*
(1)	(2)	(3)	(4)	(5)
1793	34,922	39,895	13,612	88,429
1794	35,092	40,456	I 3,441	88,989
1795	34,313	42,198	13,213	89,724
1796	36,946	48,494	16,748	102,188
1797	40,323	52,184	16,494	109,001
1798	47,494	47,784	18,035	113,313
1799	55,760	52,556	21,163	129,489
1800	57,041	56,351	24,740	138,132
1801	58,909	85,696	11,271	155,876
1802	52,456	81,047	13,334	146,847
1803	52,853	72,278	15,010	140,141
1804	78,743	81,907	18,063	178,713
1805	88,068	81,832	21,665	192,565
1806	83,162	73,008	26,696	182,866
1807	80,619	72, 139	27,325	180,083
1808	81,375	71,233	28,310	180,918
1809	83,600	69,942	31,962	185,504
1810	87,840	71,455	29,919	189,214
1811	97,053	73.924	30,167	201,144
1812	101,619	69,353	28,485	199,457
1813	101,765	69,437	28,869	200,071
1814	99,775	66,389	28,274	194,438
1815	129,542	68,704	28,937	227,183
1816	130,935	70,998	28,950	230,883
1817	124,531	72,126	29,533	236,190
1818	136,128	73,517	33,595	243,2...0
1819	132,346	76,502	36,524	245,372
1820	132,914	88,430	35,951	257,295
1821	128,987	88,718	39,277	256,982
1822	129,239	77,664	38,337	245,240
1823	129,834	71,423	36,475	237,722
1824	136,096	69,446	37,885	243,427
1825	158,612	76,422	41,514	276,548
1826	157,561	83,829	49,755	291,145
1827	144,301	80,047	49,267	273,615
1828	135,810	75,473	47,745	259,028
1829	126,542	72,803	44,103	243,448
1830	112,598	70,730	40,148	223,476

Distribution of European and Native Troops—Presidency-wise was as under

Bengal Troops*	In 1813		In 1820		In 1830	
	Europeans	Natives	Europeans	Natives	Europeans	Natives
(1)	(2)	(3)	(4)	(5)	(6)	(7)
Bengal, Behar and Cuttak	2,368	21,622	3,931	27,246	5,440	16,776
Country between Behar and Oude, including Posts on the Banks of the Ganges	1,494	5,885	1,152	7.907	1,362	4,633
Oude	155	6,309	129	7,381	143	4,809
Dooab and Territory between the Ganges and the Jumna	4,521	12,975	4,516	14,072	4,795	14,124
Rohilcund	47	1,943	50	4,353	64	3,863
Acquisitions from Nepaul	—	—	33	4,209	41	3,552
Country west of the Jumna and North-west of Chumbul	765	19,688	664	17,065	2,233	15,987
Rajpoothana	—	—	237	9,970	357	9,102
Ceded Districts in the Nerbudda	—	—	390	13,745	246	6,167
Bundelcund	144	5,488	69	3,877	97	3,688
Malwa	—	—	285	3,942	340	4,693

(Contd.)

TABLE (Contd.)

Bengal Troops*	In 1813		In 1820		In 1830	
	Europeans	*Natives*	*Europeans*	*Natives*	*Europeans*	*Natives*
(1)	(2)	(3)	(4)	(5)	(6)	(7)
Assam, Sylhet, Chittagong and Arracan	18	1,103	12	1,679	84	4,776
Penang	21	1,620	24	1,508	—	—
Totals	9,553	76,633	11,455	1,16,954	15,202	92,170
	Exclusive of Troops at Java, Engineers, Escorts, Ordnance, Drivers, Conductors Staff, etc.		Exclusive of Engineers, Fort Marlboro' Local Corps, Ordnance Drivers, Escorts, Staff, etc.		Exclusive of Engineers, Escorts, Ordnance Drivers, Conductors, Staff, etc.	
Totals	6,150 15,703	9,429 86,062	218 11,673	4,284 1,21,238	399 15,701	4,727 96,897
Madras Troops**						
Nizam's Dominions	1,136	8,455	1,892	9,758	1,347	6,811
Rajah of Berar's ditto	—	—	678	8,035	816	4,001
Northern Circars	594	4,753	465	8,888	944	6,714

[illegible] Districts	1,002	7,588	1,020	3,936	1,069	4,472
Mysore	3,403	8,891	1,825	7,578	1,779	5,682
Carnatic	4,961	12,246	2,598	24,005	3,841	19,571
Portuguese Territories	464	'2,820	—	—	—	—
Malabar and Canara	1, 130	3,076	1,134	1,967	959	2,491
Travancore	493	2,909	1,019	2,039	169	2,455
Malay Peninsula	37	18	—	—	1,141	2,772
Candeish and Surat	—	—	48	2,217		
Poonah	20	575	46	2,645		
Southern Mahratta Country	—	—	352	5,538	75	2,456
Totals	13,240	51,331	11,077	76,607	12,140	57,425
	Exclusive of Engineers, Conductors of Ordnance Native Invalids, and Staff		Exclusive of Engineers, Conductors, Recruiting Derot, Staff, etc.		Exclusive of Engineers, Supernumeraries, Conductors, Staff, etc.	
Totals	350 135,90	4,516 55,847	256 11,333	490 77,097	841 12,981	324 57,749

(Contd.)

TABLE (Contd.)

Bengal Troops*	In 1813		In 1820		In 1830	
	Europeans	*Natives*	*Europeans*	*Natives*	*Europeans*	*Natives*
(1)	(2)	(3)	(4)	(5)	(6)	(7)
Bombay Troops***						
Cutch	—	—	59	3,431	116	1,135
Kattywar	—	—	19	420	32	1,208
Guzerat	1,053	5,890	755	4,070	1,260	7,938
Candeish and Surat	43	2,205	919	3,890	108	5,042
Bombay Island	3,383	6,828	2,474	5,879	1,441	3,873
Northern and Southern Conkan	24	1,197	72	4,670	66	3,997
Poonah and Sattara	253	7,836	1,169	6,789	3,580	7,889
Southern Mahratta Country		—	—	861	1,196	
Malwa			18	1,129	—	—
Totals	4,756	23,956	5,485	30,271	7,469	32,278
	Exclusive of Engineers, Conductors, Staff, etc.		Exclusive of Engineers, Conductors, Staff, etc.		Exclusive of Engineers, Conductors, Staff, etc.	
Totals	122 4,878	35 23,99 I	151 5,636	37 30,315	258 7,727	143 32,421

* In 1793 there were 5,440 European and 29,482 Native and in 1803, 7,627 European and 44,226 Native troops in the Bengal Presidency.

** In 1793 there were 9,981 European and 29,914 Native and in 1803, 12,765 European and 59,513 Native troops in the Madras Presidency.

*** In 1793 there were 3,347 European and 19,265 Native and in 1803, 4,548 European and 10,472 Native troops in the Bombay Presidency.

PRESIDENCY-WISE

The General and Other Staff in the Year 1832

Bengal	Madras
The Commander-in-chief. *(a)*	1 Lieutenant-general commanding the Forces. *(b)*
Military Secretary to ditto. *(a)*	Military Secretary to ditto. *(b)*
Persian Interpreter to ditto. *(a)*	Persian Interpreter to ditto. *(b)*
Aides-de-camp to ditto. *(a)*	Aides-de-camp to ditto. *(b)*
2 Major-generals in command of divisions of the Army.	2 Major generals commanding divisions of the Army.
2 Aides-de-camp to ditto.	2 Aides-de-camp to ditto.
Adjutant-general of His Majesty's Forces, Assistant Adjutant-general ditto.	Deputy Adjutant-general of His Majesty's Forces.
Brigade-major of His Majesty's Forces at the Presidency.	Brigade-major of His Majesty's Troops.
Quartermaster-general of His Majesty's Forces.	Deputy Quartermaster-general of His Majesty's Forces.
Inspector-general of His Majesty's Hospitals. Assistant to ditto.	His Deputy Inspector-general of His Majesty's Hospitals.
Surgeon to the Commander-in-chief. *(a)*	

(a) Also Commander-in-chief of the Company's Army, and allowed, in his joint capacity,—

1 Military Secretary.
1 Persian Interpreter.
3 Aides-de-camp.
1 Surgeon.

(b) Also Commander-in-chief of the Company's Troops at Madras, and allowed, in his joint capacity,—

1 Military Secretary.
1 Persian Interpreter.
2 Aides-de-camp.

(c) Also Commander-in-chief of the Company's Troops allowed, in his joint capacity, (please see next page)—

1 Military Secretary.
1. Interpreter.
2 Aides-de-camp.

Bombay

1 Lieutenant-general commanding the Forces. *(c)*
Military Secretary to ditto. *(c)*
Persian Interpreter to ditto. *(c)*
Aides-de-camp to ditto. *(c)*
1 Major-general in command of a divisions of the Army.
1 Aide-de-camp to ditto.
Brigade-major of His Majesty's Troops.
Deputy Inspector-general of His Majesty's Hospitals.

Bengal

1 Adjutant-general.
1 Deputy Adjutant-general.
2 Assistants Adjutant-general (head-quarters).
1 Assistant Adjutant-general of Artillery.
4 Assistant Adjutant-general of Divisions.
3 Deputy Assistants Adjutant general of Divisions.
13 Brigade-Majors.
5 Fort Adjutants (2 are Invalid Officers).
1 Town Major.

—
31
—

1 Quartermaster-general.
1 Deputy Quartermaster-general.
2 Assistants Quartermaster-general.
4 Deputy Assistants Quarter-master-general, 1st Class.
3 Deputy Assistants Quarter master-general, 2nd class.

—
11
—

1 Commissary-general.
1 Deputy Commissary-general.
3 Assistants Commissary-general, 1st Class.
3 Assistants Commissary-general, 2nd Class.
4 Deputy Assistants Commissary-general, 1st Class.
4 Deputy Assistants Commissary-general, 2nd Class.
12 Sub-Assistants Commi-ssary-general.

—
28
—

1 Auditor-general.
1 Deputy Auditor-gereral.
1 First Assistant Auditor-general.
1 Second Assistant Auditor-general.

—
4
—

1 Presidency Paymaster (an Invalid Officer).
7 Deputy Paymasters.
5 Paymasters of Native Pensioners and Family Money.

—
13
—

1 Judge Advocate-general.
7 Deputy Judge Advocates general.

—
8
—

1 Military Secretary to Government.
1 Deputy Military Secretary to Government.
1 Assistant Military Secretary to Government.

—
3
—

2 Stipendiary Members of the Military Board.
1 Secretary and Accountant to Military Board.
2 Assistants Secretary to Military Board.

—
5
—

Artillery Officer

1 Principal Commissary of Ordnance.
1 Deputy Principal Commissary of Ordnance.
6 Commissaries of Ordnance.
2 Deputy Commissaries of Ordnance.
1 Agent for Gun-carriages.
1 Superintendent of Foundry, Fort William (Engineer-Officer).

—
12
—

1 Secretary to the Clothing Board.
2 Agents for Army Clothing.

—
3
—

42 Department of Public
— Works; (of these 22 were Engineer Officers, 1 a Pensioned Officer, and 5 were not military-men).
16 Survey Department (4 were Engineer Officers).
12 Stud Department (I not a military-man, Chevalier De
— L'Etang).
59 In Political Civil, and Miscellaneous. Situations:
9 Residents and their Assistants.
11 Nizam's and such Service.
18 Political Agents and their Assistants.

21 Miscellaneous.
—

6 Aides-de-camp to Governor-general (3 were King's Officers; 1 was also Military Secretary).

1 Military Secretary to Commander-in-chief (King's Officers).

1 Persian Interpreter to Commander-in-chief.

3 Aides-de-camp to Commander-in-chief (King's Officers).

7 Aides-de-camp to General Officers on the Staff (Kings and Company's).
—
18
—
265 Total in Bengal.

Madras

1 Adjutant-general.

1 Deputy Adjutant-general.

1 Assistant Adjutant-general.

1 Deputy Assistant Adjutant general

4 Assistants Adjutant-general of Forces and Artillery.

6 Deputy Assistants Adjutant general of Divisions.

2 Majors of Brigade.

3 Cantonment Adjutants.

6 Fort Adjutants (1 at Fort St. George is also Superintendent of Gentlemen Cadets).

2 Staff Officers (Neilgherries and Cuddalore Depot);

1 Town Major.
—
28
—

1 Quartermaster-general.

1 Deputy Quartermaster-general.

1 Assistant Quartermaster general.

1 Deputy Assistant Quartermaster-general.

1 Deputy Quartermaster general of Nagpore Force.

2 Assistants Quartermaster-general of Hyderabad Force.

5 Deputy Assistants Quartermaster-general of Divisions.
—
12
—

1 Judge Advocate-general.

9 Deputy Judge Advocates-general of Districts.
—
10
—

1 Commissary-general.

1 Deputy Commissary-general.

7 Assistants Commissary-general.

8 Deputy Assistants Commissary-general.

12 Sub-Assistants Commissary general.
—
29
—

Artillery Officers

1 Principal Commissary of Ordnance, and Superintendent of Gun-carriages.
7 Commissaries of Ordnance.
3 Deputy Commissaries of Ordance.
1 Deputy Superintendent of Gun-carriages.

—
12
—

1 Deputy Surveyor-general.
6 Assistants Surveyor-general.

—
7
—

1 Auditor-general.
1 Deputy Auditor-general.
1 Assistant Auditor-general.
1 Deputy Assistant Auditor general.

—
4
—

1 Paymaster Presidency.
13 Paymasters of Divisions, Districts, and Forces.
1 Paymaster of Family Payments and Pensions.

—
15
—

1 Secretary to Military Board.
1 Deputy Secretary to Military Board.
1 Assistant Secretary to Military Board.

—
3
—

1 Secretary to Clothing Board.
28 Department of Public Works (all Engineer Officers except one).
1 Barrack-master, Fort St. George.
1 Superintendent Gunpowder Manufactory.

—
31
—

1 Military Secretary to the Governor.
2 Aides-de-camp to the Governor.
1 Military Secretary to the Commander-in-chief (King's Officer).
2 Aides-de-camp to Commander-in-chief (I King's Officer).
5 Aides-de-camp to General Officers on the Staff (King's and Company's Officers).
41 In Political and Miscellaneous Situations.
9 Residents and Officers under them.
23 Nizam's and such service.
3 In Persia.
5 Miscellaneous.

—
203 Total at Madras
—

Bombay

1 Adjutant-general.
1 Deputy Adjutant-general.
7 Brigade-majors.
1 Cantonment Adjutant (Belgaum).
3 Line Adjutants.
3 Fort Adjutants.

—
16
—

1 Quartermaster-general.
1 Deputy Quartermaster-general.
2 Assistants Quartermaster-general.
4 Deputy Assistants Quartermaster-general.

—
8
—

1 Commissary-general.
3 First Assistants Commissary general.
3 Second Assistants Commissary-general.
5 Third Assistants Commissary-general.

—
12
—

Artillery Officers

4 Commissaries of Ordnance.
4 Deputy Commissaries of Ordnance.
1 Agent for Gun-carriages.
1 Agent for Gunpowder.
1 Director of Depot of Instruction.

—
11
—

1 Auditor and Accountant of Military Store, Accounts and Returns.
1 Ordnance Assistant to Commandant of Artillery.

—
2
—

1 Auditor-general.
1 Deputy Auditor-general.
2 Assistants Adjutant-general.
1 Deputy Assistant Adjutant-general.
1 First Assistant Auditor-general.
1 Second Assistant Auditor-general.

—
5
—

6 Paymasters.

—

1 Judge Advocate-general.
2 Deputy Judge Advocates-general.

—
3
—

1 Deputy Surveyor-general.
1 Assistant Surveyor-general.
1 Assistant to Surveyor in the Concan.

—
3
—

16 Department of Public Works (all Engineer Officers).

—

1 Barrack-master (Bombay)

—

1 Superintendent of the Stud.
1 Military Secretary to the Governor.
2 Aides-de-camp to the Governor.

—
4
—

1 Military Secretary to Commander-in-chief.
2 Aides-de-camp to Commander-in-chief.
1 Interpreter to Commander-in-chief.

—
4
—

3 Aides-de-camp to General Officers on the staff.
12 In Civil, Political and Miscellaneous Situations.
5 Residents and Assistants.
2 Nizam's Service.
3 Guicowar's Contingent.
1 Holkar's Contingent.
1 Collector at Ahmednugger.

—
108 Total at Bombay.
—

ARMY OF BENGAL PRESIDENCY

The first battalion raised in Bengal were 10 companies of 100 men each, commanded by a captain, with one lieutenant, one ensign and one or two serjeants. Each company had a standard of the same ground as the facings, with a different device (suited to its subadar, or Native captain), of a sabre, a crescent, or a dagger. The Company's colours, with the Union in one corner, were carried by the grenadiers. The first battalions were known by the name of the captain by whom they were commanded, and though, in 1764, 19 corps received a numerical rank, corresponding with the actual rank of their commandants at that period, this did not prevent them from continuing to be known under their former appellation, or from assuming the name of a favourite leader. The 15th battalion, was raised in Calcutta in 1757, and called the "Mathews," from the name of its first commander. This corps was with Colonel Ford in 1759, when that able officer, with 346 Europeans and 1,400 sepoys, besieged and took by storm the strong fortress of Masulipatam, making prisoners a French garrison, who, both in Europeans and Natives, were nearly double his numbers. In 1763, in the wars with the Vizier of Oude, the "Mathews," which was with the force under the command of Major Adams, is stated, when the Company's European regiment was broken by cavalry, to have nobly supported His Majesty's 84th regiment.

In 1782, the "Mathews" was one of three Bengal corps who mutinied, under an apprehension of being embarked for foreign service; and though the conduct of those corps was remarkable for the total absence of that spirit of general insubordination and disposition to outrage by which mutinies of soldiery are usually marked, they were in the ensuing year broken and drafted into some other battalions.

Lal Pultan-mutineers Blown Away

The present second battalion of the 12th regiment appears, to have been raised some months before the "Mathews." It is the first raised battalion. This corps was at the battle of Plassey. It was named by the sepoys the Lal Pultan, or the Red Battalion, and afterwards Gallis, from the name of one of its first captains. It was associated with the "Mathews" in all its early service, particularly at Masulipatam, Gheretty, etc., but in 1764 it mutinied, on the pretext of some promises which were made to it having been broken. Having no apparent object, it was easily reduced to obedience; but Major Munro (afterwards Sir Hector Munro), who then commanded the army, thought a severe example necessary, and twenty-eight of the most guilty were tried by a drum-head court-martial, and sentenced to death. Eight of these were directed to be immediately blown away from the guns of the force then at Chuprah. As they were on the point of executing the sentence, three grenadiers, who happened to be amongst them, stepped forth, and claimed the privilege of being blown away from the right-hand guns. "They had always fought on the right (they said), and they hoped they would be permitted to die at that post of honour." Their request was granted, and they were the first executed.

This corps subsequently distinguished itself in 1776 at the battle of Korah. It had been known originally as the first battalion. It was afterwards numbered the 9th, from the rank of its captain. In a new arrangement of the army it was made the 16th, then the 17th. By the regulations of 1796, it has become the 2nd of the 12th regiment.

A detachment, composed of six Native battalions, a corps of Native cavalry, and a proportion of artillery, altogether amounting to 103 European officers, and 6,624 Native troops, was in 1778 sent from Bengal to the relief of the settlement of Bombay. During the five years that they were absent from their home, the men of this detachment conducted themselves in the most exemplary manner, and acquired distinction in every service in which they were employed.

First Encounter between European and Native Troops

The force detached to the Carnatic in 1781 was commandered by Colonel Pearse. It consisted of five regiments, of two small battalions (500 men each) of Native infantry, some Native cavalry, and a proportion of artillery. This corps, which marched about 1,100 miles along the sea-coast, through the province of Cuttack, and the Northern Circars to Madras, arrived at that Presidency at a most eventful period, and their services were eminently useful to the preservation of our power in that quarter. Among the many occasions which this detachment had been distinguishing itself, the attack on the French lines at Cuddalore in 1783 was the most remarkable. The Bengal sepoys that were engaged on that occasion behaved nobly. It was one of the first times that European troops and the disciplined Natives of India had met at the bayonet.

The rebellion of Cheyt Singh, the Rajah of Benares, in 1781, must be familiar to all acquainted with Indian history. The purpose in mentioning it, is limited to the object of showing the conduct of the Bengal sepoys under one of the severest trials of fidelity to which they were ever exposed.

Trust Well Rewarded

The numerous followers of the Rajah had risen upon two

companies of sepoys appointed to guard the house in which he was placed under restraint, and killed and wounded the whole of them. The rashness of an European officer had led another party to slaughter in the streets of Ramnagur. Mr. Hastings, who was at Benares when these events occurred, had only a few companies of sepoys to guard his person, and even these he had no money to support. He summoned corps from different quarters to his aid; but when we reflect on the impression which the first success of Cheyt Singh had made, and consider that by far the greatest proportion of the troops with whom Mr. Hastings had overcome the dangers with which he was surrounded were men of the same tribe and country as those against whom they were to act, and that the chief, who was declared a rebel, had long been considered by many of them as their legitimate prince, we must respect the mind that remained firm and unmoved at so alarming a crisis. The knowledge Mr. Hastings had of the sepoys led him to place implicit trust in them on this trying occasion, and his confidence was well rewarded. Their habits of discipline, and their attachment to their officers and the service, proved superior to the ties of caste and of kindered. Not an instance of defection occurred, and the public interests were preserved by their zeal and valour.

Composition of Bengal Army

I must offer some observations on the composition of the army of Bengal Presidency. The cavalry, which now consists of eight regiments, is comparatively young; its formation on the present establishment was only just completed when the Mahratta war of 1803 commenced. Their conduct, however, in the severe service that ensued has justly raised their reputation, and they at present form a most efficient and distinguished branch of the army to which they belong. The men are rather stouter than those in the same corps at Madras. The latter are almost all Mahomedans, and a considerable proportion of the Bengal cavalry are of the same race. The fact is, that with the exception of the Mahratta tribe, the Hindoos, are not, generally speaking so much disposed as the Mahomedans to the duties of a trooper; and the Mahomedans are apparently more zealous and highspirited soldiers, and it is excellent policy to have a considerable proportion of them in the service, to which experience has shown they often become very warmly attached. In the Native infantry of Bengal the Hindoos are in the full proportion of three-fourths to the Mahomedans. They consist chiefly of Rajpoots, who are a distinguished race among the Khiteree or military tribe. We may judge of the size of these men when we are told that the standard below which no recruit is taken is five feet six inches. The great proportion of the grenadiers are six feet and upwards. The Rajpoot is born a soldier. The mother speaks of nothing to her infant but deeds of arms, and every sentiment and action of the future man is marked by the first impressions that he has received. If he tills the ground (which is the common occupation of this class), his sword and shield are placed near the furrow, and moved as his labour advances. The frame of the Rajpoot is almost always improved (even if his pursuits are those of civil life) by martial exercises; he is from habit temperate in his diet, of a generous, though warm temper, and of good moral conduct; he is, when well-treated, zealous, and faithful.

In the year 1783 the artillery, consisted of a regiment of ten companies, each of 100 men, non-commissioned and privates, commanded by one colonel, two lieutenant-colonels, two majors, ten captains, ten captain, lieutenants, twenty lieutenants, and twenty lieutenant fireworkers, now called second lieutenants. The European infantry consisted of three regiments, each of ten companies, each company of 100 men; non-commissioned and privates, commanded by one lieutenant-colonel, one major, seven captains, one captain-lieutenant, twelve lieutenants, and eight ensigns. Neither the artillery nor European infantry were ever completed in men. The Native infantry consisted of eighteen regiments, each of two battalions, commanded by a major, and to each battalion a captain, with six lieutenants, and four ensigns. The engineers had one lieutenant-colonel, one major, three captains, six lieutenants, and six ensigns. The whole army was commanded in chief by a colonel with the rank of brigadier-general.

The army, so composed, was divided into three regular brigades, and an extra brigade posted at Futtyghur, to keep in awe the Nuwaub of Furruckabad and his turbulent Pathans; and each brigade was commanded by a colonel.

The staff of the army at that time consisted of an adjutant-general and his deputy, a quartermaster-general and his deputy, six majors of brigade, six barrackmasters, and one commissary-general, whose functions were then limited to the audit of accounts.

New Reorganisation

In the year 1785, Lieutenant-General Sloper was appointed Commander-in-Chief over all the British possessions in India, with a seat in the Council of Bengal; and about the same time orders were sent out to India for a new organisation of the army at all the Presidencies, by which the three European regiments of the Bengal army were formed into six, of eight companies each; and the eighteen regiments of Native infantry into thirty-six 'battalions, of 600 men each, commanded by a captain, having under him eight lieutenants, one of whom was appointed adjutant. The six European regiments and thirty-six of Native infantry were formed in six brigades, each brigade having one colonel, two lieutenant-colonels, and two majors. In the artillery and engineers no alteration was made. There were therefore in the Bengal army, as formed in 1786, seven colonels, fifteen lieutenant colonels, fifteen majors, ninty captains, sixteen captain-lieutenants, 386 lieutenants, and sixty-two ensigns or lieutenant fireworkers; total 591 officers, exclusive of general staff, for the command of 26,000 men; giving a proportion of nearly one officer to fifty men, and fifteen subalterns to one field officer; reducing, at the same time, six majors, six captains, seventy-eight lieutenants, and nearly 200 ensigns, including those who had been sent out cadets in the year 1781-82 and 1783, all of whom were placed on modified allowances somewhat better than half-pay.

At this period the army stations were Barrackpore, dependent on Fort William; Berhampore, Dinapore, and Chunar, within the provinces held by the East-India Company; and Cawnpore and Futtyghur provinces, under the paramount authority of the Nuwaub of Oude. These places were severally the head-quarters of brigades, where resided the colonels, having each an aide-decamp, a major of brigade, a paymaster or deputy-paymaster, which composed the whole staff attached to each brigade, with exception to the brigade at Cawnpore, to which the Deputy quartermaster-general was attached. There was a paymaster-general, a deputy paymaster-general, three pay-masters, and three deputy paymasters, appointed from the civil service to this department with the army; and for some time the commissary general was also appointed from the civil service.

The troops stationed at Barrackpore furnished two battalions of sepoys as guards for Fort William, where the headquarters of the artillery, engineers, and one European regiment were always fixed. These guards were relieved the first of every month. Two battalions were detached to Midnapore, then the extreme point to the south-west bordering on the Nagpore territory, and two were always at Barrackpore.

The brigade, the headquarters of which was at Berhampore, furnished one battalion to Chittagong, then the extreme point on the south-east, bordering on Arracan, one battalion at Dalla, and one at Dinapore.

From the Dinapore station one battalion was detached to Purneah, one to Kissengunge and one to Patna. Chunar detached two to Benares and two to Juanpore.

The stations in the Nuwaub's provinces had always two battalions on duty at Lucknow, which were relieved from Cawnpore every two or three months; and when the rivers subsided after the monsoon, two battalions, with a detail of artillery, took up a position a little beyond Anoopsur, in observation of the Sies, who under Bango Sing: the chief of Fennasir, occasionally made predatory incursion into the Nuwaub's provinces.

Camp Equipage and its Conveyance

At that time all the cattle required either for drought or carriage with the army were provided by contract, excepting in the Native infantry, for whom no camp equipage was provided; and then, as now, they found means to convey their own baggage and supply their own provisions out of their pay which, for the private soldier was seven rupees a mouth in quarter, and eight-and-a-half when marching. The European officers serving with the native force had an allowance proportioned to rank, out of which they found their own camp equipage, and cattle for the conveyance of that and their baggage.

The officers and soldiers of the European regiments were provided with quarters, and the latter with single rations by Government when in garrison or cantonments, and when marching with camp equipage, that was conveyed by the contractor's cattle. The camp equipage, as well for the officers as for soldiers of the European army, was also provided by contract, and of the very worst quality, neither sheltering them from sun nor rain, and the cause of greater loss of lives in every campaign than was ever produced by all other causes combined.

Such were the circumstances, as above described, under which the Company's army on the Bengal establishment existed from 1786 to 1795, during which period there was one regiment of His Majesty's foot in Bengal: first, the 73rd, relieved by the 76th, the latter being one of four regiments raised for the East India Company, to be supplied with officers in equal proportion from His Majesty's and the Company's half-pay officers.

New-modelling the Army

In 1795 an order for new-modelling the army was received from England, by which the artillery was formed into three battalions of seven companies each, having one colonel, one lieutenant-colonel, one major, seven captains, seven captain-lieutenants, fourteen lieutenants, and fourteen lieutenant fireworkers. To the engineers one colonel and one captain was added. At the same time five out of the six regiments of European infantry were reduced, and one regiments of 1,000 formed, of ten companies, having one colonel, two lieutenant-colonels, two majors, seven captains, twelve lieutenants, and eight ensigns. The thirty-six battalions were formed into twelve regiments of two battalions, each regiment having one colonel, two lieutenant-colonels, two majors, seven captains, one captain-lieutenant, twenty-two lieutenants, and eight ensigns: the officers to rise in their respective regiments to the rank of major, and after that in the line.

It was at the same time resolved to increase the army by a body of regular cavalry. There had been for some years two corps of Natives, about one hundred and eight each, commanded by captains with two subalterns to each, drawn from the infantry; and taking these as the nucleus, four regiments of six troops each, and sixty men a troop was formed upon them: having to each regiment one lieutenant-colonel, one major, two captains, one captain-lieutenant, six lieutenants and six cornets, with a full colonel to every two regiments.

Great Promotions and New Raisings

The orders issued for the new organisation produced great promotion in all the ranks of the army, all that were then colonels being promoted to the rank of major-general, the number of which in a few years was increased to forty; but four only were appointed on the staff of the Bengal Presidency, where there were two officers of His Majesty's service of the rank of major-general also appointed on the staff, although there was at that time only one regiment of foot, the 76th, at that Presidency, to which was added, in 1797, the 27th regiment of dragoons.

The major-generals on the staff had an aide-de-camp and major of brigade attached to them; and at the same time were added to the general staff of army an adjutant-general and a quartermaster-general, officers in His Majesty's service, the staff of the Bengal army still remaining as before stated; but from the peculiar constitution of that army the staff were retained on the strength of regiments, and military paymasters were appointed.

I have omitted to mention, that in 1795 a marine battalion was raised, and soon after detached on service to the islands; and the following additions to the Native infantry followed the new organization in rapid succession.

In 1797, shortly after arrival of Lord Mornington as Governor-General in contemplation of the war which soon followed with Tipoo Sultan, two regiments, the 13th and 14th, were raised.

In 1798, three regiments, the 15th, 16th and 17th, were raised.

In 1800, two regiments, the 18th and 19th, were revised.

In 1802, another marine battalion was raised, and, added to the former, were together numbered the 20th regiment.

In 1803, war with Scindia and the Nagpore Rajah being unavoidable, three regiments, the 21st, 22nd, and 23rd, were raised.

In 1804, Bolkar having joined the confederacy, four regiments, 24th, 25th, 26th, and 27th, were raised.

In 1815, being then engaged in war with Nepaul, three regiments, the 28th, 29th, and 30th, were raised.

In 1823, four regiments, the 31st, 32nd, 33rd and 34th, were raised. The cavalry, within the same period, had been increased to ten regiments, and the artillery to four battalions.

In 1824, orders were sent to the new-model army of Bengal, giving to each regiment of cavalry one colonel, one lieut.-colonel, one major, five captains, ten lieutenants, and five ensigns; converting the artillery into nine battalions; three of horse and six of foot; the engineers to be formed into two battalions; the European regiment into two regiments, and the thirty-four regiments of Native infantry into sixty-eight, each of the same strength as to officers as that of the cavalry regiments: thus adding to the cavalry five colonels, ten captains, and twenty lieutenants and reducing ten majors, and ten cornets; adding to the artillery five colonels, one lieutenant-colonel, one major, eighteen captains, and reducing twenty-seven captain-lieutenants; adding to the infantry thirty-five colonels, seventy captains, thirty-five ensigns, and reducing sixty-eight lieutenants. Subsequent to the Burmese war, six volunteer battalions, which were raised on that occasion, have been formed into regiments, and embodied with the rest to No. 74. Such have been the alterations and increase in the Bengal army between 1756 and 1832.

In the year 1830, there were extra corps, staff or department appointments, the duties of which were performed by officers withdrawn from the Native service.

ARMY OF MADRAS PRESIDENCY

The general history of the Native army of Fort St. George is short. Sepoys were first disciplined on that establishment in

1748; they were at that period, and for some time afterwards, in independent companies under subadars or Native captains. Mahomed Esof, one of the most distinguished of those officers, rose by his talents and courage to the general command of the whole; and the name of this hero, for such he was, occurs almost as often in the page of the English historian of India as that of Lawrence and Clive. As the numbers of the Native army increased, the form changed. In A.D. 1766 we find ten battalions of 1,000 men each, and three European officers to each corps. In 1770 there were eighteen battalions of similar strength, and in 1784 the number of this army had increased to 2,000 Native cavalry and 28,000 infantry; a considerable reduction was made at this period, but subsequent wars and conquests have caused great increase, and in 1826 the effective strength of the Native army of Fort St. George consists of eight regiments of cavalry, and twenty-four regiments or forty-eight battalions of Native infantry. There were besides several troops of horse artillery, some battalions of gun lascars, and a very large invalid establishment.

Cavalry Raised by Carnatic Nabob

The Native cavalry of Fort St. George was originally raised by the Nabob of the Carnatic. The first corps embodied into a regiment under the command of European officers, on the suggestion of General Joseph Smith, served in the campaign of 1768 in Mysore. From 1771 to 1776 the cavalry force was greatly augmented, but then again declined both in numbers and efficiency. The proportion that was retained nominally in the service of the Nabob, but actually in that of the Company, served in the campaigns of 1780, 1781, 1782 and 1783, and was formally transferred, with the European officers attached to it to the Company's service in 1784. The prospect of fortune which the liberality of an Indian prince offered attracted to this corps many active and enterprising European officers, and the favour which a Native court extended to its choicest troops filled the ranks of its regiments of regular cavalry with the prime of the Mahomedan youth of the Carnatic. When this corps was in the service of the Nabob of the Carnatic, though it was often very highly distinguished the intrigues of a venal court and irregular payments caused frequent mutinies. Since it has been transferred to the Company's establishment, a period of more than thirty years, its career has been one of faithful service and of brilliant achievement, unstained by any example, that I can recollect, of disaffection or of defeat. The two severest trials of the courage and discipline, of this corps were at Assaye and Vellore, in both these services they were associated with the 19th dragoons.

Subadar's Pride Hurt

In the campaign of 1791, when Secunder Beg, one of the oldest subadars of the Native cavalry, was riding at a little distance in the flank of his troop, two or three horsemen of Tippoo's army, favoured by some brushwood, came suddenly upon him; the combat had hardly commenced when the son of the subadar, who was a havildar or serjeant in the same regiment, flew to his father's aid and slew the foremost of his opponents, the others fled; but nothing could exceed the rage of the old man at his son's conduct; he put him instantly under a guard, and insisted upon his being brought to condign punishment for quitting his ranks without leave. It was with the greatest difficulty that Colonel Floyed, who commanded the force, could reconcile him to the disgrace he conceived he had suffered (to use his own expression) from his enemy "being taken from him by a presumptuous boy in front of his regiment".

Shaikh Moheedeen, a subadar of the bodyguard of Madras, who was one of the first officers appointed to the corps of Native horse artillery, recently raised on that establishment, accompanied me to Persia, and was left with a detachment of his corps, under the command of Captain Lindsay, to aid in instructing the Persians in military tactics. This small body of men and their gallant European commander were engaged in several campaigns in Georgia, and their conduct has obtained not only for the subadar, but, for all the men of his party, marked honours and reward, both from the Persian Government and their own. Their exertions received additional importance from the scene on which they acted, for it is not easy to calculate the future benefits which may result from the display of the superior courage and discipline of the Native soldiers of India on the banks of the Araxes.

The Native infantry of Madras is generally composed of Mahomedans and Hindoos of good caste: at its first establishment none were enlisted but men of high military tribes. In the progress of time a considerable change took place, and Natives of every description were enrolled in the service. Though some corps that were almost entirely formed of the lowest and most despised races of men obtained considerable reputation, it was feared their encouragement might produce disgust, and particularly when they gained, as they frequently did, the rank of officers. Orders were in consequence given to recruit from none but the most respectable classes of society, and many consider the regular and orderly behaviour of these men as one of the benefits which have resulted from this system.

Firm Allegiance

I find in the Madras Native army many instances of unconquerable attachment to the service to which they belong. Among these none can be more remarkable than that of Syud Ibrahim, commandant of the Tanjore cavalry, who was made prisoner by Tippoo Sultan in 1781. The character of this distinguished officer was well known to his enemy, and the highest rank and station were offered to tempt him to enter into the employment of the State of Mysore. His steady refusal occasioned his being treated with such rigour, and was attended, as his fellow prisoners (who were British officers) thought, with such danger to his life, that they, from a generous feeling, contemplating his condition as a Mahomedan and a Native of India as in some essential points different from their own, recommended him to accept the offers of the Sultaun; but the firm allegiance of Syud Ibrahim would admit of no compromise, and he treated every overture as an insult. His virtuous resolution provoked at last the personal resentment of Tippoo, and when the English prisoners were released in 1784, the commandant was removed to a dungeon in the mountain fortress of Couley Droog, where he terminated his existence. His sister, who had left her home, the Carnatic, to share the captivity of her brother, was subsequently wounded in the storming of

Seringapatam. She, however, fortunately, recovered, and the Government of Fort St. George granted her a pension of fifty-two pagodas and a half per month, or £250 per annum, being the full pay of a Native commandant of cavalry. A tomb was also erected at the place where Syud Ibrahim died, and Government endowed it with an establishment sufficient to maintain a fakeer or priest, and to keep two lamps continually burning at the shrine of this faithful soldier.

In 1804, the subsidiary force in the Deccan, commanded by Colonel Haliburton, was enclosed between two rivers, which became suddenly so swollen as to cut-off their supplies of provisions. It was a period of general famine, and the communication was cut-off with the grain dealers, from whom alone they could expect a supply. All the rice in camp was found to be barely sufficient for five days' allowance, at a very reduced rate, to the European part of the force. Issues to the sepoys were stopped, but while they were left to the scanty subsistence they might be able to procure for themselves, they were appointed the sole guards over that grain, from all share in which they were from necessity excluded. This duty was performed with the strictest care, and the most cheerful submission. Fortunately the waters subsided, and an ample supply prevented their feeling that extreme of famine, the prospect of which they had contemplated with an attention to discipline and a composure of mind which even astonished those best acquainted with their habits of order and obedience.

Constitution of Company's Army

The constitution of the Company's army has experienced frequent and important alterations. Previously to 1783 all Company's officers were commanded by King's officers of the same rank; an old captain of the Company's service, for instance, was commanded on duty by the youngest captain of the King's. The extreme injustice of this arrangement produced a strong remonstrance from the Company's army assembled in the camp at Cuddalore in 1783; and orders were won afterwards issued, granting to the Company's officers' rank and authority with the King's according to the dates of their commissions. From this period of time until 1796, the Company's armies had an independent constitution and system of promotion, that was altogether unconnected with the King's service, that produced a high military spirit and an efficient state of discipline, and that would have answered exceedingly well, if there had been no King's troops in the country; but the superior relative ranks held by the King's officers gave rise to feelings of jealousy and discontent in the minds of the Company's. During this period of time, that is until 1796, the officers of each branch of the Company's army at every Presidency rose by succession in one general line from ensign to colonel; at Madras, and the Madras army may be taken as a specimen of the others, the infantry consisted in 1976 of four regiments of Europeans, having each one colonel, one lieutenant-colonel, one major, ten captains, twelve lieutenants, and eight ensigns; and of thirty-six battalions of sepoys, having each one captain-commandant, six lieutenants, and four ensigns. The infantry was formed into six brigades, having each a lieutenant-colonel and a mojor. The officers of the infantry accordingly amounted to four colonels, ten lieutenant-colonels, ten majors, seventy-two captains, two hundred and sixty-four lieutenants, and one hundred and seventy six ensigns, all rising in succession in one general line. This was an independent constitution. There were, it is true, no general officers, and far too few field officers and captains; but the system worked extremely well until the great increase that took place in the number of King's troops, and the number of superior officers attached to them, produced continual supersessions over the Company's. A captain commanding a battalion of 1,000 men was subject to be commanded on duty by a captain commanding a company of Europeans. The King's troops had, it is true no general officers, in India, with exception of the Commanders-in-chief; but still the relative superiority of their rank over the Company's was a serious grievance to the latter.

Remedying the Evil

In order to remedy this evil, a new arrangement was made in 1796 of the Company's armies. The infantry at Madras was formed into two European and twelve Native regiments, the latter of two battalions each, with an establishment of officers, of one colonel, two lieutenant-colonels, two majors, twenty-two lieutenants, and eight ensigns. A separate establishment of general officers was allowed to each Presidency. The officers, instead of rising as formerly in a general line, were promoted regimentally to the rank of major, and then rose in a general line to the rank of colonel, which they acquired on obtaining a regiment. They were, besides, made eligible to be included in the King's brevet promotion; and indeed the only general officers whom they have ever had, excepting the few at first appointed, have been those made by the King's brevet. This plan, although marked by some anomalies, worked sufficiently well for the Company's officers, because the advantage of obtaining the rank of full colonel with a regiment was in some degree a compensation for the extreme slowness of promotion in comparison with the King's officers, before they arrived at that rank. But in 1805, a change highly injurious to the Company's officers was effected. The King's officers complained of being superceded by the promotion of the company's officers to the rank of colonel, on obtaining their regiments by succession; and it was ordered, that the Company's officers when advanced to regiments should have the rank of lieutenant-colonel-commandant only until they should acquire the rank of colonel by the King's brevet. This arrangement, which still (in 1832) virtually exists, has been extremely detrimental to the Company's army, and makes their promotion to the higher ranks depend alone upon the brevets issued by His Majesty to his own troops; and these brevets, calculated for the wants and circumstances of one army, are frequently unsuitable to the state of the other.

Since 1796, the armies of all the Presidencies have been increased by successive and considerable augmentations; and in 1823, another change was effected in their internal organization and system of promotion. The regiments consisting of two battalions were constituted into separate regiments of a single battalion, with a colonel or lieutenant-colonel-commandant at their head, and the promotion from the junior rank to that of major took place in these separate corps. This was in every view an advantageous arrangement for the officers and the army.

The Staff

The staff at the several Presidencies is extremely well organized, and has received successive improvements. The duties of the adjutant-general and quartermaster-general of the army correspond with those assigned to the same officers in England. The due allotment duties to these two principle branches of the staff has, however, been only a recent arrangement, as for many years the adjutant-generals at all the Presidencies engrossed the functions appertaining to the Quartermaster-general's department. There is a commandant of artillery and a chief engineer for the superintendence of the internal detail of these arms. An auditor-general, appointed by the Government, and immediately under its orders, is charged with the control of the army accounts, and in general discharges that important duty with great ability. At every Presidency there is a Military Board, analogous in some respects to the Board of Ordnance in England, and composed of the commander-in-chief, the adjutant-general, quartermaster-general, chief engineer, commandant of artillery, and auditor-general, for the superintendence of the supply, distribution, and custody of the military, ordnance, and provision stores. The Commissariat department has acquired great efficiency during the last few years. Formerly, in time of peace, the paymasters in the several districts, who were civil servants, were employed in furnishing the cattle, provisions, and certain descriptions of military stores required for the use of the troops in marches, or service in the interior. When a general war took place, separate commissaries were appointed to the Cattle, the Provisions, and the Ordnance departments. Those officers, without previous experience, or establishments of well-trained servants, found great difficulties in the execution of their duties; and the military operations were exposed to, and often suffered, great disasters, from the inefficiency of the system under which they acted. Since the introduction of a separate and permanent Commissariat establishment for peace and war, a degree of activity of hitherto unknown has been imparted to this important branch of the service; and the rapidity of the movements of the troops during the last Mahratta war affords a proof of the goodness of the principles by which it is regulated. In the several divisions of the army suitable staff establishments are attached; and the whole of the arrangement of this department seems to be efficient and satisfactory.

Distribution of Army

The distribution of the army has been directed by just views, in conformity to the nature of the country, and to the changes effected in our situation by the conquests and acquisitions of territory that have been made. At Madras, the army is formed into divisions; at the principal stations bodies of troops are maintained in a state of readiness to act with promptitude against internal commotion, or to join the rest of the disposable forces in the event of a general war. These remarks apply chiefly to the local distribution of the army with respect to the internal service of the several Presidencies; but there is another and more important view of the distribution of our military force in all India, considered as a whole. The actual state of our political and military power in India renders it requisite to regard our defence of that country as a whole, and to regulate the distribution of our forces accordingly; for whatever serious danger might threaten anyone point must necessarily be repelled by the combined effort of the whole of our disposable force. The distribution of our armies should be regulated on the principle of enabling us to collect the greatest possible mass of force with the greatest possible expedition at any given point. In this view the central position of the Madras army gives it great advantages; for the mass of its force could be moved to either of the extremities of our line of defence in half the time that would be occupied in moving a force from one extremity to the other. This applies especially to the defence of the coast, but it applies also to the defence of the extreme northern forntier; for the Madras troops, if they could not arrive there as soon as those in Upper Provinces of Bengal and Bombay, could at least replace the letter, and render them more available for instant movement.

ARMY OF BOMBAY PRESIDENCY

It was at Bombay that the first Native corps were

disciplined by the English. Regular sepoys are noticed in the account of the transactions of that part of India some time before they were embodied at either Madras or Bengal. A corps of one hundred sepoys from Bombay, and four hundred from Tellicherry, is mentioned as having joined the army at Madras in A.D. 1747, and a company of Bombay sepoys, which had gone with troops from Madras to Bengal, were present at the victory of Plassey. The sepoys at Bombay continued long in independent companies, commanded by subadars or Native captains. As the possessions and political relations of that settlement were enlarged its army increased. The companies were formed into battalions under European officers; and during the war with the Mahrattas, A.D. 1780, we find the establishment consisting of fifteen battalions. These, at the termination of the war with Tippoo, 1783, were reduced to six, and one battalion of marines. In 1788, its numbers were augmented to twelve battalions. In 1796, it was reformed into an establishment of four regiments, of two battalions each, from which it has been progressively raised, by the acquisition of territory and subsidiary alliances, to its present establishment of nine regiments of Native infantry, of two battalions each, one battalion of marines, and a small corps of Native cavalry.

The men of the Native infantry of Bombay are of a standard very near that of Madras. The lowest size taken is five feet three inches, and the average is five feet six inches, but they are robust and hardy, and capable of enduring great fatigue upon very slender diet.

Bombay Army Composed of all Classes

This army has, from its origin to the present day, been indiscriminately composed of all classes, Mohamedans, Hindoos, Jews and some few Christians. Among the Hindoos, those of the lowest tribes of Mahratta and the Purwarrie, Soortee and Frost sects, are much more numerous than the Rajpoots and higher castes. Jews have always been favourite soldiers in this army, and great numbers of them attain the rank of commissioned officers. It is probably owing to the peculiar composition, and to the local situation of the territories in which they are employed, that the sepoys of Bombay have at all periods been found ready to embark on foreign service. They are, in fact, familiar to the sea, and only a small proportion of them are incommoded in a voyage by those privations to which others are subject from prejudices of caste. But this is only one of the merits of the Bombay Native soldier: he is patient, faithful, and brave, and attached in a remarkable degree to his European officers. There cannot be a class of men more, cheerful under privation and difficulties; but desertion in early stages, is very frequent among the recruits of this army.

In 1797, the Bombay army consisted of the following corps: viz. one European regiment, eight Native infantry regiments of two battalions each, a Native marine battalion, available for general service, with a battalion of artillery and corps of engineers amounting in the whole to 18,000 men and upwards. The establishment thus possessed a respectable numerical force when compared with its limited extent of territory, which was then confined to the provinces of Malabar and Canara, the islands of Bombay and Selsette, and I believe, a small district in the neighbourhood of Surat. Since the year 1803, repeated augmentations have been made to the army, which at present consists of a brigade of horse and two battalions of foot artillery, three regiments of Native cavalry and one European, and twenty-six regiments of Native infantry of one battalion each; but the complement of Native corps is at present so much reduced, and the actual strength of the army so little increased, that there can be but a very small body of troops disposable for emergencies, after making a reasonable allowance for the garrisons and outposts throughout the establishment. The following appears to be the present distribution of the army. In the Deccan, that is say, in the Poona, Sattarah, Sholapore, and Ahmednuggur districts, are stationed one regiment of cavalry and five of infantry. These troops are scattered over a wide tract of country, and there is consequently not more than a single regiment at anyone station, with the exception of Poona, where a small force is collected, consisting of two Native battalions, in addition to a regiment of dragoons and one of infantry of His Majesty's troops. In Guzerat there are one cavalry, one European and five Native infantry regiments, three of which latter corps are stationed at Baroda and one at Ahmedabad, the remainder being contoned at Deesa, a station on the north-west frontier.

Four Native infantry regiments are stationed in the Southern Mahratta districts, of which two are at Kulladgee, one cavalry and three infantry regiments in Kattywar, three infantry regiments in Candeish, two in the Concan, two in Bombay garrison, and one in Cutch, complete the number of regular regiments composing the Bombay army.

British Model

The organization of these troops is modelled on that of the British army, each regiment being divided into companies, with a complement of European and Native commissioned and noncommissioned officers and regimental staff. The only peculiarity in the constitution of Native regiments is, that of native commissioned officers, under the designation of subadars and jemadars, who rank below all European officers, and are selected from those havildars or serjeants considered best qualified for promotion. This class of men possess but little influence in their corps, the men being taught to look for promotion exclusively to their European officers; the rank, however, is useful as holding forth the strongest inducement for good behaviour throughout the inferior gradations, but as further incentive ceases on attaining the rank of jemadar, it is found that few Native officers long retain the active and zealous qualities that contributed to their advancement.

The employment and designation of the general staff are similar to that of the British army, nor does the system of conducting the departments of the adjutant or quarter-master-general appear to require any alteration whatever. With regard to the Commissariat department. I can only vouch for its efficiency, of which I have had most convincing proofs on field service, but of its economical merits, or the manner in which its details are conducted. I am unable to speak from personal experience; on these points, however, there can be no difficulty in obtaining the fullest information, as there are many officers of that department now in England, particularly Lieutenant-colonel Bellasis, late Commissary-general at Bombay, and Colonel Hull, formerly Deputy Commissary-general to the Deccan division of the army. The Ordnance and Store department is exceedingly well supplied and conducted.

Exemplary Fidelity

During the progress of the war with France, subsequent to 1803, several parties of the marine battalions of Bombay sepoys were captured on board of the Company's cruisers and carried to the Isle of France, where they were treated in a manner that reflects no credit upon the local government of the island, when the Isle of France was captured, they met with that notice which they had so well merited. The Government of Bombay granted to every individual who survived his captivity a silver medal, as a memorial of the sense which it entertained of his proved fidelity and attachment.

Four years ago, when the commanding officer of a battalion on the Bombay establishment was proceeding along the Banks of a ravine, with eight or ten men of his corps, to search for some lions, which had been seen near the cantonment of Kaira, in Gujarat, a royal tiger suddenly sprang upon him. The ground gave way, and the tiger and Major Hull rolled together to the bottom of the ravine. Though this fall prevented the latter from being killed by the first assault, still his fate seemed certain; and those who know, from having witnessed it, the terror which the attack of this fierce animal inspires, can only appreciate the character of that feeling which led every sepoy who was with him to rush at once to his succour. The tiger fell under their bayonets, though not before it had wounded two of the assailants most desperately; one having lost his leg, and the other been so lacerated as to be rendered unfit for future service as a soldier. These wounds, however, were deemed trivial by those who sustained them, when they saw that the officer whom they loved had escaped unhurt from his perilous situation.

In 1797, Captain Packenham, in his Majesty's ship 'Resistance', accompanied by some small vessels of war belonging to the Company, took possession of Copong, the chief Dutch settlement on the Eastern Isle of Timor, lieutenant Frost, of the Bombay marine, commander of the Intrepid cruiser who was to be appointed Governor of Copong, had taken a house on shore, where he expected Captain Packenham to meet the Dutch Governor, and make arrangements for the future administration of the place. The Malays had formed a plan, by which it was settled that the moment Captain Packenham landed to attend this meeting, they were to rise and murder all the Englishmen on shore. Fortunately something occurred to induce Captain Packenham to defer his visit; but he sent his boat, and its reaching the beach was the signal for the commencement of the massacre. Nearly twenty persons were slain. A large party had rushed to Lieutenant Frost's house. The head of his surgeon had been struck-off and his own destruction seemed inevitable, when two sepoys of the Bombay marine battalion, whom he had landed from his vessel, exclaimed to him, "Save yourself by fight, we will fight and die" : at the same time exposing themselves to the fury of their assailants, and giving their commander time to escape to a boat. The sepoys, after a resistance as protracted as they could render it, were slain, and their heads, exposed on pikes, explained their fate to their lamenting companions on board the Intrepid. Captain Packenham took prompt and ample vengeance of this treachery; he opened a heavy fire upon the place, under which he landed an efficient force, which defeated the Malays, who fled after losing 200 men.

III

BRITISH POLITICAL POWER THROUGH INDIAN TROOPS

Major. General Sir John Malcolm

In 1748, Regulations with far-reaching effects for forming a Company of Artillery, organising an Ordnance Service responsible for handling military equipment and stores in each Presidency and establishing Ammunition Factories were issued to the Bombay, Madras and Bengal Presidencies of the East India Company by the Court of Directors from England. In the same year Major Stringer Lawrence arrived at Fort St. David and took up the appointment of first Commander-in-Chief of all the Company's forces in India both European and Indian. He employed large bodies of Indian troops because the then contending European powers realized that military and political victory would be with the side which succeeded best in raising and developing its native forces.[1] *In 1683, two companies of Rajputs, each consisting of 100 men had already been enrolled in Bombay, and this force may be regarded as the first beginnings of the modern Indian army. Initially the Indian sepoys were mainly armed with their own native weapons, wore their own nath'e dress and were commanded by their own native officers. In 1757 Clive reorganised the Indian troops under his command by forming them into regular battalions with a small nucleus of British officers. He armed and dressed the men somewhat resembling that of Europeans. The first battalion thus organised was nicknamed "Lal Pultan". Thereafter Clive's military successes caused large increase in the native armies and his organisation of native battalions with British Commandants and British Company Commanders developed in all the three Presidencies of Bengal, Madras and Bombay. (Ed.)*

Among the many political considerations likely to affect the future prosperity and political security of the British Empire, there appears hardly one of more magnitude than the attachment and fidelity of the Indian troops of our army.

The great proportion of the inhabitants of India are devoted to peaceful occupations, and are consequently, to a certain degree, unable, if they were willing, to defend that government, to which a sense of benefit may have rendered them well affected. The object of our laws and institutions is to repress if not destroy those habits which distinguish the military tribes subject to our rule: but such changes, to be safe, must be gradual; we cannot otherwise expect to escape the dangers and convulsions with which they are likely to be attended. As long however, as we can repose on the fidelity of our native army, we are safe from internal danger; but every disquietude must assume an alarming appearance, when associated with disaffection in that army; nor can we obtain relief by an accession of European force, for the very means which would give us security for the moment, would aggravate the evil as they would tend to lessen the efficiency, and weaken the attachment of those native troops, by whose courage and fidelity alone we can preserve India. As the truth of these observations will hardly admit of dispute, we can contemplate no measures of more importance than those which are calculated to incite and confirm the obedience and allegiance of the native crops employed in our service. The rigid principle of economy, and the precise forms of our civil rule, should both yield to the establishment of this corner-stone of our strength; as, without it, the vast fabric which has been raised with such pains must totter to its base at every tempest with which it is assailed.

The native army has undergone many changes from its origin to the present day.

When the British government first established itself in India, military tactics in Europe were in a less advanced state than at present, and the caution with which a few Europeans, endeavouring to conciliate the natives of India to fight their battles on a foreign shore, were obliged to act, prevented the introduction of any part of those tactics which could in the least interfere with their prejudices, habits, or religion. A jacket of English broad cloth, made up in the shape of his own dress, the knowledge of his manual exercise, and a few military evolutions, constituted the original sepoy; and with this qualification, and his English fire-arms, he was found to possess an incalculable superiority over the other natives of India, who, ignorant of the first principles of discipline (which enable men to act in a body), were easily defeated, however great their numbers, by a small corps of their brothers, armed, disciplined, and directed, by the art, intelligence and energy of European leaders.

It was natural that the early sepoy should share in that feeling of pride which his superiority in discipline obtained him over his countrymen; and the native officers in the employment of the Company were gratified not only by the opportunities which they had of acquiring military distinction, but of improving their fortunes. There were but few European officers in the first sepoy battalions. A captain, an adjutant, with a serjeant to each company, was the original establishment. Commands frequently fell to Soubahdars and Jemadars; and the comparative laxity of discipline, as well as the general corruption of the times, enabled the whole of the native army, from the Soubahdars to the sepoy to derive pecuniary benefit from the nature of the services on which they were occasionally employed.

This system, which had, undoubtedly, many defects, had also much to recommend it; for though the European commanding officer, who acted without check in the exercise of a great trust, generally made his corps a source of pecuniary advantage, in which he was aided by the native commandant, who shared in this indirect emolument; yet both had a strong interest in the character and conduct of the corps, to the men of which they were almost always kind and generous.

An increase of their European officers, a great alteration in their dress, and an improvement in their discipline, made material changes in the constitution of the native corps, and these took place through several causes. The native princes had trained sepoys European tactics; and to maintain a superiority over them, it became necessary that the native army of the Company's government should make further advances in the military art, which they were enabled to do, not only from the great improvements which had taken place in that science in Europe, and from the example furnished by some of the King's regiments sent to India, but from the number of officers of liberal education and respectable character, whom a prospect of advantage had at this period drawn to the service of the Company. According to the opinion of many able officers, it was under this system that the men became most attached to their officers, and the native army attained as great a degree of efficiency as it has ever known.

The native officers continued under this system to enjoy great respect and regard. This circumstance chiefly owing to the European commanding officer, who, from his station, and the emolument attached to it, enjoyed a consideration and consequence which enabled him not only to confer distinction by his personal favour and regard, but to keep in complete check and control the younger officers of the service, and to direct their minds to a moderate and indulgent conduct towards all the natives; but particularly to those who, from their gallantry or long services were entitled to respect and attention, and which it was proper to show them on every ground of policy as well as of generosity.

The native service underwent another great change in the year 1796, when new regulations were introduced, which a train of events, connected with the comparative rank of the Company's officers with those of His Majesty serving in India, had rendered indispensably necessary. By these regulations, two battalions of native infantry were formed into one regiment, to which the same number of officers were allowed as to a regiment in the King's service. Regimental rise to the rank of major was, at the same time, introduced; and this, it was hoped, by attaching the officers to corps, would confirm and strengthen reciprocal confidence and connexion between the European officers and the sepoys, which had ever been deemed the most essential principle in the constitution of the native army.

If the nature of our power in India requires as it certainly does, the exclusion of the native officers from the exercise of high military command, and that gate to distinction is barred by policy, others should be opened. In the strictest conformity to those principles upon which the native army is formed, we might lead the minds of these troops to expect comfort and distinction in civil life, as the reward of approved military service; and by directing their ambition to the natural and seductive object of acquiring importance in their tribe, and enjoying some privileges, however trivial, which, under certain regulations, might descend to their children, we should not only discover a motive sufficiently powerful to supply the place of that which a jealous but wise policy obliges us to withhold, but place their fidelity beyond the power corruption. If such measures were adopted, the native service would become popular and respected; it would be embraced with eagerness by men of the first families in the country; and in the course of years we might expect the attachment of our subjects to be greatly improved by a spirit of active allegiance, which would be generally diffused by veterans and their descendants, whose claim to their rank or land was founded in the gratitude of a state whom they had served with fidelity and distinction.

The men who form the native army of the Company are almost all sober, and of good conduct in private life. Drunkenness, as a general vice, is indeed, unknown; and notorious immorality is rare. But their virtues are more of a passive than an active nature. They consist more in forbearance, from fear of offending against their civil institutions and the rigid tenets of their religion, than from any sense of the beauty of virtue, or the deformity of vice. These men appear, in many cases, hardly to consider themselves as free moral agents; they often blindly resign their judgement to the law of usage, the dictates of their priest, or the influence of their superiors in caste or station; and, under such influence, they change, in an instant, their mild, inoffensive, and pliant character, for that of the most determined obstinacy and savage ferocity.

All the natives of India, but particularly those of military classes, are fond of show and of high titles; and they often seem to prize the semblance, almost as much as the reality of power. It is indeed surprising to see the consequence which they attach to every mark of outward respect, especially when bestowed by their superiors; and, partaking of the character of his countryman the native soldier of the Company, intelligent and quick in his conception, full of vanity and a love of pre-eminence, if not of glory, is of all men the most sensible to attention or neglect. Though the climate disposes him to inertness, and his frame is seldom very robust, he may be flattered and encouraged to make the most extraordinary exertions; while harshness or cruelty serves only to subdue his spirit, and sink him into apathy, if it does not rouse him to resentment.

It may be stated as the result of the fullest experience, that the native troops of India depend more than any in the world upon the officers who command them: when treated by these with notice and kindness, and when marked consideration is shown to their usage, they become attached, and evince, on all occasions, a zeal and valour that can hardly be surpassed; but when they have not confidence in those who command them, when they are made secondary, or treated in any manner indicating a want of reliance of them; much more when any of their commanders betrays ignorance or contempt of their prejudices or religion, they become spiritless or discontented. This is the natural consequence of their condition, as mercenaries of a nation with whom they have no ties beyond those that compel them to a cold performance of their duty, and such as they form with their immediate officers; but able leaders, who understand how to infuse their own spirit into those they command, find no difficulty in making what impressions they desire on the minds of men, whose education and sentiments predispose them to participate in every feeling associated with military fame and distinction.

The employment of native troops associated with Europeans, is a point that merits the most serious attention. The ablest of those commanders who have led them to victory, however, impressed with a just sense of the superior courage and energy of a British soldier, have carefully abstained from every act that could show the least want of confidence in the native part of their force, or convey to the latter an impression that they were viewed in secondary light. By mixing them in every operation with English troops, they have succeeded not only in exciting an emulation and pride in the minds of the native soldiers, which greatly added to their efficiency, but diffused a spirit of cordiality and good feeling, not more calculated to promote the success of their immediate operations then the general interests of the empire.

It would occupy too much pace to enter into a fuller detail of the plan best calculated to animate the zeal and confirm the fidelity of our native troops; but if the importance of these objects is acknowledged, there will be no difficulty in devising the means for their accomplishment.

The necessity of creating and maintaining a superior class amongst the natives is recommended by every consideration of wise and generous policy: and assuredly there is no measure more calculated to aid in obtaining this end than that of conferring on the veteran, who has gained reputation in the army, rank and consideration in his native district, so as to render him an object of respect to his countrymen, who will see in his services to the state a legitimate claim to favour and distinction, whatever may have been his former condition. This mode of reward is quite accordant with the usage of all Asiatic states, and its adoption by us would be congenial to the habits and feelings of the whole population.

Government Essentially Military

Sudden changes in any system of administration are unwise, and it would be sufficient, if this plan were approved, to make its gradual introduction imperative. The details would be adapted to local circumstances, but no deviation should be allowed as to the fundamental principles on which it is grounded. These are political and connected with our very existence in India. Our government of that country is essentially military, and our means of preserving and improving our possessions through the operation of our civil institutions depend on our wise and politic exercise of that military power on which the whole fabric rests. This is a recognised fact; but unless a conviction of its truth is continually impressed on the minds of those placed at the head of the Indian administration, it will be in vain to attempt plans which will meet with every obstacle that partial and local views, a desire or personal influence and power, or attachment to established system, can devise or create to impede and defeat their execution.

Note and Reference

1. An English, whilst on a hunting party, hastily struck a peon, for improperly letting loose a grey hound. The peon happened to be a Rajah-pout, which is the highest tribe of Hindoo soldiers. On receiving the blow, he stared back with an appearance of horror and amazement and drew his poignard. But again composing himself, and looking steadfastly at his master, he said, "I am your servant, I have long eat your bread"— and having pronounced this, he plunged the dagger into his own bosom. In those few words he surely pathetically expressed, "The arm that has been nourished by you, shall not be employed to take away your life; but, in sparing yours, I must give up my own, as I cannot survive my dishonour." Cranford's *Sketches of the Hindus* (1792).

APPENDIX

ENACTMENTS PERTAINING TO INDIAN MILITARY LAW
ACTS OF BRITISH PARLIAMENT

Calender year	*Regional year*	*Short title*	*Part concerned*	*Subject*
(1)	*(2)*	*(3)*	*(4)*	*(5)*
1793	33 Geo. 3, c. 52.	The East India Company Act, 1793—known as the Charter Act of 1793.	Ss. 25, 33, 42, 43, 62-64.	Ss. 25, 33 relate to the appointment of Commander-in-Chief in India; ss. 42, 43 to the making of war; and ss. 62-64 to the receipt by officers of remuneration beyond their salaries.
1802	42 Geo. 3, c. 85.	The Criminal Jurisdiction Act, 1802.	S.I.	Provides for the indictment in England of officers charged a $ such with misconduct abroad. The first section only has been referred to.
1809	49 Geo. 3, c. 126.	The Sale or Offices Act, 1809.	So much as is unrepealed, except, s. 13.	Is directed against traffick in appointments under Government.

(Contd.)

APPENDIX (*Contd.*)

(1)	(2)	(3)	(4)	(5)
1812	52 Geo. 3, c. 156.	The Prisoners of War (Escape) Act, 1812.	So much as is unrepealed.	Provides more effectual punishment for aiding prisoners of war to escape.
1832	2 & 3 Will. 4, c. 53.	The Army Prize Money Act, 1832	Ss. 2, 29.	S. 2 render distribution of prize money subject to His Majesty's directions, and s. 29 provides for the case of conjunct naval and military expeditions.
1833	3 & 4 Will. 4, c. 85.	The Government of India Act, 1833 known also as the Charter Act of 1833.	Ss. 39, 65, 73 75, 78-80.	Ss. 39, 65 give Governor General in Council supreme control in India, and s. 73 empowers that authority to make articles of war for Native troops. Ss. 74, 75, 78, relates to patronage and removal of officers. S. 79 prohibits the departure to Europe of Commander-in-Chief in India. S. 80 enforces obedience to Secretary of State for India.

1840	3 & 4 Vict., c. 96.	The Post Office (Duties) Act, 1840	Ss. 53, 54.	Conferred privilege of penny postage on soldier's letters.
1847	10 & 11 Vict., c. 85.	The Post Office (Duties) Act, 1847	S. 7.	Provides for recovery of foreign postage on soldier's letters.
1853	16 & 17 Viet., c. 95.	The Government of India Act, 1853- known also as the Charter Act of 1853.	Ss. 32, 35.	S. 32 relates to leave. S. 35 fixes salary of Commander-in-Chief, India.
1858	21 & 22 Vict., c. 106	The Government ment of India Act, 1858.	Ss. 30, 33, 35-38, 54-56.	Provided for transfer from East India Company to Crown. S. 54 requires intimation to Parliament of order for making war; S. 55 restricts applieation of Indian revenues to military operations out of·India; and Ss. 57, 58 relate to army service.

INDIAN ENACTMENTS

Calendar year	*Description and Number*	*Short title*	*Part Reproduced*	*Subject*
(1)	*(2)*	*(3)*	*(4)*	*(5)*
1804	Bengal Regulation X.	The Bengal State Offences Regulation, 1804.	So much as is unrepealed.	Provides for establishment of "martial law" in times of emergency in Northern Central India. There is similar law for the Madras—See Madras State Offences Regulation, 1808—but none for the Bombay, Presidency.
1806	Bengal Regulation XI.	The Bengal Transport and Travellers' Assistance Regulation, 1806.	Do	Provides, in conjunction with Bengal Regulation VI of 1825, for progress of marching troops in Northern and Central India. For Bombay there is similarly Bombay Reg. XXII of 1827; and for the Punjab special provision is made

				by Punjab Act I of 1903. See also s. 5 of Reg. XIV of 1887, s. 6 of Act III of 1889, and s. 55 of Reg. I of 1894.
1808	Madras Regulation VII.	The Madras State Offences Regulation, 1808.	Do	See remarks regarding Bengal Reg. X of 1804.
1817	Bengal Regulation XX.	The Bengal Police Regulation, 1817.	S. 30	Requires police to report circumstances indicative of danger to public peace, and to apprehend persons wearing uniforms without authority.
1817	Madras Regulation VIII.	The Madras Revenue Recovery (Military) Proprietors' Regulation, 1817.	So much as is unrepealed.	Makes special provision to prevent sale for arrears of revenue of lands belonging to Native officers or soldiers in the Madras Command.
1825	Bengal Regulation VI.	The Bengal Troops Transport Regulation, 1825.	So much as unrepealed.	See remarks regarding Bengal Reg. XI of 1806.

(Contd.)

APPENDIX (*Contd.*)

(1)	(2)	(3)	(4)	(5)
1827	Bombay Regulation XXIII.	—	Do	Provides for progress of marching troops in Bombay. *Cf.* Bengal Reg. XI of 1804.
1856	Act XI	The European Deserters, Act, 1856.	Do	Provides for recovery and arrest of European deserters concealed in ships or on shore. See, too, s. 54 of the Code of Criminal Procedure, 1898, and s. 155 of the Army Act, and *cf.* as regards Native deserters Arts. 185 and 186 of the Indian Articles of War.
1857	Act XI	The State Offences Act, 1857.	Do	Provides for speedy trial and punishment, by special commissioners, of persons charged with heinous crime in disturbed areas.

British Flattery and Deceipt

T.A. Bhai

The Britishers conquered India more with their deceptive methods than with their sheer military power. Camouflaged moves, underhand policies and crafty designs were employed by them to acquire one by one and rule territories of India. This is especially true in the case of the Punjab where double-faced deception of the British laid foundation for annexation of the land of five rivers. We quote below two writings in original by Englishmen under the headings, 'The Entertainment' and 'The Attack' which appeared in the year 1838 during the life of Maharaja Ranjeet Singh. It shows that simultaneously with the lavish entertainment and presentation of precious diamonds and horses offered to the Punjab ruler, the British were making preparation for subjugation of the Punjab.

THE ENTERTAINMENT

The Sutledge Camp, Dec. 4, 1838—Last evening, at half-past five, a splendid entertainment was given by the Miss Edens to the Maharajah Ranjit Singh, his sons, prime minister, and principal officers of State. An immense compound was formed in the usual way, in the rear of the durbar tents, the inner walls of which were illuminated by a profusion of flambeaux affixed to wood-work, and scaffolding raised for the occasion. Many portions of the ground too, being covered with innumerable *cheragus*, fancifully disposed, resembled a sheet of flame; while fire-works, consisting of skyrockets maroons, blue lights' Roman candles, Catherine wheels, and all the etceteras of pyrotechnic skill, 'flared up' in bold defiance of the stars, and the utter wonderment of the assembly. Immediately in the front of this display, and exactly in the rear of the durbar tent, was a spacious awning, duly carpeted, and illuminated by candelabra placed on the ground. Around this soft parterre, sat all the magnates, and the select few of our fair country women, who have been brought by accident courage, curiosity, or conjugal devotion, to the remote quarter of the empire. The Hon'ble Miss Eden was on the left of the Lion of the Punjab, in front of whom sat or squatted his interpreters, duly superintending the frequent supply of fiery liquids. On the right of the Maharajah was the Governor-General Lord Auckland and next to His Lordship, Mr. W.H. McNaghten, the Hon'ble Miss F. Eden, Sir W. Cotton, etc.; amongst the guests who occupied the remaining seats, we noticed, Mrs. W.H. McNaghten, Mrs. Churchill, Mrs. Mitchell, Mrs. Beresford, Mrs. and Miss. Sale, Miss. Stevenson, Mrs. Havelock, Mrs. Gavin Young, Mrs. Craigie, Mrs. Wymer; Rajah Dhian Singh, the handsome prime minister, and his son, the Maharajah's favourite; Rajahs Kurruck Singh and Sher Singh, the sons of Runjeet Singh; Sucheyet Singh, the Pelham of the Punjab Court,—a remarkably good-looking and elegantly dressed personage;—the famous Hindoo Rao; and a great many more. Behind the rows of chairs were clustered the usual picturesque medley of British and Punjaubee *militaries* and *diplomats*, occasionally relieved by the sombre and somewhat unsatisfactory toggery of sundry Ditchers and Mofussilities, who have ventured themselves into these 'entres vast and deserts idle!'—After a few complimentary effusion a bevy of *bayaderes* was introduced, and under the direction of select orchestra of three fiddlers and a tom-tom wallah, chaunted the praises of the Maharajah and his ally and nautched for an hour by the Ferozepore clock. The ladies were reported to be Cashmerians and tip-top people in their way.

After the nautch, the Maharajah was presented with precious diamonds and horses, and then took his farewell, which was the signal for the dispersion and the guard of honour.

The Attack Plan

The death of Runjeet Singh (an event probably not very remote) will give rise to three great parties: first, that of the legitimate son Kurruck Singh; secondly, that of Sher Singh; thirdly, that of Duhan Singh, the favourite. Possibly two of these parties will unite; at all events great confusion and anarchy must arise, and every petty chief will turn marauder, and encroachments will take place in the territory of the protected states: the Indian Government will have the choice of either taking possession of the Punjab, or keeping up an army of 10,000 men on the left bank of the Sutledge.

The Fort at Loodianah is in its present state quite untenable; its front should be put in efficient repair, and the fort should merely be considered as a depot for detachment stores: a wall should be also built round the town of Loodianah.

The Punjab, if attacked, should be invaded by the fords of the Sutledge, and the fort of Ellore taken at once by the gate, or by escalade. It is a more brick Seraie, and light guns would even make a breach: when the army once crosses the Sutledge, there is no other obstacle to impede its march but the Beah river, which, in the cold season, is fordable in many places, and is said to be 150 yards in breadth; the fort of Gobind Ghur would soon fall, and the capture of this place and Lahore would for ever subvert the power of Runjeet; and all the Jageerdars of the Punjab would gladly submit, to the British dominion.

As a defensive post Loodianah is well chosen, as by falling back on Umballah, the troops from Karnaul and Soobathoo would unite with the Loodianah detachment. It is obvious that, as a mere advanced post a battalion of eight companies at Loodianah, would be unable to take the field, and it would be more politic altogether to abandon the post and retire to Kurnaul than to leave such a handful of men to entice an attack from so powerful and warlike a people as the Seikhs.

It certainly seems anomalous that the Indian Government should leave its only assailable frontier open to attack, and concentrate at Meerut (an inland station to the east of the Jumna) two European corps, when the Sirhind division consists (excepting Artillery and one King's corps) wholly of natives.

Karnaul should perhaps have as well an European Cavalry corps, and a native one be stationed at Loodianah; this would enable the Government to concentrate in ten days 8,000 men on the Sutledge. Much have been said about the post of Ferozepore; as an offensive position it is a good one, but its occupation would lead to a remonstrance from the Seikh ruler; and as a defensive post, it is a bad one, for two reasons: 1st,—no native army ever will cross there, as the river is not fordable; 2nd,—the position is at once turned by the enemy crossing the Sutledge at any of the numerous fords near Loodianah. There are no less than eleven ghauts between Loodianah and the Hurree Ferry, where the Beah river joins the Sutledge, and there are the ghauts between the Hills and Loodianah; there are numerous fords in the vicinity of these ghauts, passable from the month of November until the month of April; "if therefore the British force was removed from Loodianah to Ferozepore, every facility would be afforded to an invasion of the protected states, as instead of the fords of the Sutledge being equally divided on the flanks of the British position, the whole of them would be on its right flank.

—(*The Civil and Military Review,* Vol. I, No. 10).

A FAKE COMMERCIAL TREATY

"On maturer reflection Ellenborough had decided that Russia's designs in Central Asia were to be feared not so much because she might directly attack British India but because she might rouse the native states in North-West India. Ellenborough therefore planned a mission to Runjeet Singh, ostensibly to carry presents to him and to make a commercial treaty, in reality to gather information about Lahore, the Sikh power and the navigation of the Indus. The mission to Runjeet Singh was carried through".

—*Board of Control (Commissioners) Secret Drafts,* Vol. 7, 13 Jan. 1830, p. 271.

Anglo-Sikh Wars of Freedom from British Rule

ARTHUR D. INNES

This was the most desperate series of battles that the British ever fought in India. In 1839, Ranjit Singh had died. His son followed him and his grandson was murdered. Another son, during these anarchical conditions, succeeded, but was soon murdered. There remained only a child of five years, Dalip Singh, whose mother, now became Rani of Lahore, the power behind the throne being two Dogra Hindus from Jammu, Dhian Singh and Ghulab Singh. Dhian Singh was murdered, and Ghulab Singh betook himself to Jammu, power passing to Lal Singh and Tej Singh. These ministers were no substitute for Ranjit Singh. The Sikh army, 60,000 strong, was completely out of hand. Unless Lal Singh and Tej Singh could find some means of distracting attention from themselves their days were numbered. Provocations also came from the British side, and the Sikh army crossed the Sutlej into British territory. "As it was the Sikh Army crossed the Sutlej with the confident expectations of a triumph and career, whether shrewder of the Sirdars may have thought. Once at least, during the conflict they were within an ace of victory which would have set all India in a blaze. They were beaten but they half believed that they were not fairly beaten".

First Sikh War with Exceedingly Stubborn Fighters

The situation was dangerous. The Governor-General has on 13th December declared WAR. Not only were the Jat Sikhs, who formed the bulk of the Khalsa army, exceedingly stubborn fighters, but Ranjit Singh had succeeded in turning them into disciplined regular infantry, armed, trained and uniformed as a close copy of the Company's sepoys. This was achieved by employing French and Italian officers who had served under Napoleon. There was no question of sweeping such men away at the first shock, and the sepoys of Oudh, who lacked the fighting power of the men of Wellesley and Lake, were definitely afraid of them. For this reason a disproportionate amount of the fighting and casualities fell on the British troops. The Sikhs had, moreover, a numerous artillery, comprising many heavy guns and served with the utmost determination. All that they lacked was resolution on the part of their commanders, which was not surprising in view of the risks those commanders ran from their own men, and it is probable that this mainly led to their defeat.

Mudki and Ferozeshah—British Guns Silenced

The first fight took place at Mudki, on the British side of the Sutlej, on December 18th, 1845. Gough, who was accompanied by the Governor-General, Sir Henry Hardinge, himself an old soldier and therefore inclined to interfere on occasion in military operations, attacked the Sikhs in a belt of jungle and succeeded in driving them back, though with heavy loss to his own men. The Sikhs retired to a strong position at Ferozeshah, a short distance in the rear, where three days later, late in the afternoon, Gough again attacked them. The Sikh Artillery was more powerful than Gough's and fought with the utmost courage. The attack was delivered in the teeth of a tempest of "grape". An Indian officer who was present wrote: "This was fighting indeed; I had never seen anything like it before. Volleys of musketry were delivered by us at close quarters and returned as steadily by the enemy. In all former actions I had been in one or two volleys at close distance were all that the enemies of the Sirkar (Government) would ever stand; but these Sikhs returned volley for volley, and never gave way until nearly decimated. They had their regiments placed between their guns and behind them; their fire was temple, such as no sepoy had ever been under. The British guns were almost silenced and the ammunition waggons blown up. I saw two or three European regiments driven back by the weight of the artillery fire; it was like the 'rains' they fell into confusion; several sepoy regiments did the same. One European regiment was totally swept away; and I now thought the Sirkar's army would be overpowered, and fear filled the minds of many of us.

"When it was almost dark, a loud shout was heard, which did not sound like that of the Sikhs; a roaring noise of cavalry came next and the Third (Light) Dragoons rushed right through into the enemy's entrenchment and rode over and cut down their gunners. This charge was so sudden, and the cavalry charging right into batteries such an unheard-of thing, that for a few moments the Sikhs left their guns in perfect amazement.

"It now became quite dark and the Sirkar's Army left-off fighting, but the Sikhs continued firing wherever they saw a light. The force I was with as commanded by General Littler Sahib, and lost its way in the darkness. For fear of marching right into the Sikh camp, we were ordered to lie down. This night was nearly as bad as some of those in Kabul; we dare not light a fire for fear of enemy's round-shot, no water was to be procured, and we had nothing to eat but what few 'chuppaties' some men had put in their haversacks. The Sahibs said this was real fighting, and that the Sikhs were noble enemies: still they looked anxious, wondering what the morning would bring forth."

There was every reason for anxiety, for only the army of Lal Singh had been fought; the remainder of the Sikh forces, under Tej Singh, had been watching Littler, who had slipped away and joined Gough just before the battle. Tej Singh might soon be expected and Gough was in no case to fight another battle. However, with great determination he had advanced again in the early morning on the Sikh camp and captured it, together with seventy guns. No sooner was this accomplished than the army of Tej Singh was seen approaching. Gough, with hardly a charge left for guns and muskets, stood at bay, and after a period of suspense Tej Singh drew-off. British supremacy in India had been within an ace of destruction.

Aliwal and Sobraon—British Forces Skillfully Managed

The battle of Aliwal, fought on January 29th, 1846, was a smaller but much more skilfully managed affair. Sir Harry Smith, had been sent with a small force to cover the transport of Gough's siege-train, when he came into contact with a superior force of Sikhs near the village of Aliwal, on the banks of the Sutlej. Realizing that they had their backs to the river and could not easily retreat, Smith at once attacked. The Sikh resistance was broken down, the most notable incident being a most daring charge by the Sixteenth Lancers. It is characteristic of the spirit of the Sikh infantry that they did not merely stand to wait the Lancers' attack, but actually advanced to meet them. But Smith's handling of his troops had been too skilful for the Sikhs, and they were driven across the river under the fire of the British guns, with heavy casualties and the loss of over fifty cannon. Aliwal was a badly-needed success of the right kind, for it showed that with proper management and skill the Sikhs could be thoroughly defeated.

Traitor Sikh Sardar—British Capture Punjab

The Sikhs now fell back on Sobraon, their last position on the British side of the Sutlej, again making the mistake of standing with the river immediately in their rear. On February 10, 1846, Gough attacked them with the main army. His siege-train had now come up, but not sufficient ammunition. The guns had soon to cease fire, but Gough attacked with the bayooet. The infantry burst through the Sikh entrenchments and were followed by the cavalry, the Third Light Dragoons again distinguishing themselves. The bridge of boats across the river was broken down, and the whole mass of the enemy driven pell-mell into the stream. Over eight thousand Sikhs perished and sixty-seven guns were taken. The challenge of the Khalsa had been met with success. British losses in these four battles were over nine thousand men, more than half falling on the few British units present, who had to do the bulk of the fighting. To quote again from the Indian Subadar: "The Khalsa fought as no man ever did in India before, but it was evident that their leaders knew not how to manage an army; when they have decided advantages in their hands they failed to make any use of them; their Cavalry never came near the battlefield that I ever heard of; and when I was at Lahore I heard many Sikhs loudly proclaim Sardar Tej Singh to be a traitor . . . . In a few days the British army marched on Lahore, and the whole Punjab was at the command of the mighty Company Bahadur (= 'brave' a title of respect) whose superior military skill and tactics none could withstand and whom it was useless to attempt to resist, without the risk of heavy loss.

The Punjab, a British Protectorate

Every effort was made, now that the challenge of the Khalsa had apparently been overcome, to avoid the formal annexation of the Punjab. A Council of Regency was set-up on behalf of the Maharaja Dalip Singh, comprising four Sikh chiefs and four British officials. Colonel Henry Lawrence was appointed as first Resident at Lahore, and was aided by men like John Nicholson and Herbert Edwardes. Everything looked hopeful, and Hardinge, now, together with Gough, a Peer, assured Lord Dalhousie, on handing over to him in January 1848, that it would not be necessary to fire a gun in India for seven years to come. But he was wrong. The pride and power of the Khalsa was : not yet completely broken, and they were determined to fight again at the first favourable opportunity.

The Revolt at Multan—British Sikh Governor Murdered

Mulraj, the semi-independent governor of Multan, had been giving trouble, and in April 1848 a new Sikh governor was sent to take his place, accompanied by Mr. Vans Agnew and Lieutenant Anderson. On April 18 these officers were attacked and wounded by Mulraj's men, and on April 20 were done to death. Mulraj now threw a challenge and the south-western comer of the Punjab was in revolt. Herbert Edwards, though a lieutenant, was in charge of the wild Pathans of the Derajet beyond the Indus, who, although included in the Sikh dominions, had some feelings against Sikhs. He instigated the tribesmen to arms, twice defeated Mulraj, and shut him up in Multan. It was the hottest season of the year in the hottest part of India, and Gough was reluctant to send troops. At last, in September, a British force, together with a Sikh contingent, appeared before Multan. On September 14 these Sikhs went over to Mulraj, and the British had to fall back to the south to await help from Bombay. This was the signal. Everywhere the Sikhs sprang to arms, to fight and turn out the Britishers out of India.

Ramnagar, Chillianwala and Gujarat—Sikh Terms for Peace Rejected by British

Gough, marching from Lahore, fought Sher Singh, the Sikh commander, on October 22 at Ramnagar on the banks of the Chenab. Both sides lost heavily and the Sikhs fell back on Chillianwala, near the River Jhelum, to await reinforcements. Here, on January 13, 1849, Gough attacked them. The Sikhs' position was in dense jungle and very strong. The preliminary cannonade was Ineffective and the assault disjoined. The Sikhs suffered equally heavily as the British and lost several guns, but they also captured several guns and several colours. Then it came on to rain and further fighting was impossible. In the interval Multan was captured by the British, and the Sikh reinforcements came up, bringing with them various political officers who had fallen into their hands. One of these was sent with the Sikh proposals for terms. The terms were rejected and the Sikhs moved to Gujarat. Second and final war close to the banks of the Chenab. There, on February 21, 1849, came the final trial of strength. The Sikhs had 40,000 men and Gough 35,000, and also for the first time he had a more powerful artillery, including the long eighteen pounders which had been used to batter down Multan. There was no premature assault, and throughout the morning the British artillery steadily replied the fire of the Sikh guns. Then the British lines swept forward, and the Sikhs were driven into overwhelming flight. The pursuit was continued relentlessly; Rawal Pindi, Attock and even Peshawar falling into the hands of the British.

Power of Khalsa Broken

The power of the Khalsa was broken at last, and the Sikhs everywhere laid down their arms. A witness of the surrender at Rawal Pindi relates: "One old fellow I noticed in particular: he stood for a long time looking wistfully at his arms and the pile before him, and evidently could not make up his mind to give them up. At last the officer on duty came up and touched him on the shoulder and ordered him to move on; he then threw down his sword and matchlock with a crash, 2nd turned away saying with tears in his eyes, 'All my work is undone now'." It is surprising to think that this was not altogether true of the bravest opponents British ever met in India, for it was these Sikh soldiers, previously in arms against them, who were one of their strongest supporters in the crisis.

The attempt to control the Punjab as a protectorate had failed, was given up, annexed, and with it the "Koh-i-Nur" (The mountain of light), which Shah Shuja had formerly possessed and which he had been to willingly surrender to Ranjit Singh. It was sent to England and is now set in the Imperial Crown. The Punjab was placed under a Board of Administration directed by Henry Lawrence, his brother John (famous in India as "John Larence") and Robert Montgomery. The long struggle by the British to gain India was at an end.

Supremacy but not Security

The whole of the coastline of India, from Karachi to Tenasserim, was now under British control, and there was no state in India able to resist them. But to achieve that conquest an immense Indian army, 200,000 strong, had been called into being. What if that army seeing but 40,000 British soldiers in the whole of India, were to deem itself the real master of the country? The British arms could, by their might, snatch unthinkable gains in a situation where Indian rulers fought among themselves, not rather than unitedly facing the foreign adventurers. The new rulers from England won battles which their superior military strength, shrewed strategy, adventurous spirit and strong urge to become rich but were not aware of the undercurrent of strong: feelings, resentment and anger of the Natives which ultimately erupted in the Great Uprising of 1857.

Mudki

With flashing eyes that gleamed with sullen ire,
With lips compressed revealing inward fire,
With darkly shaded and portentous brow,
With dignity that made inferiors bow,

With lion heart, unused to bend or fawn,
A chief, a warrior a hero born,
An Indian, a Sikh, in short—a man!
In stepped—his Lila's glory—Sardar Kahn.

I saw, the sun so brightly shining
O'er the *blue Indus' wave,*
But ere't was on that wave reclining,
How may found a grave!
I saw on Mudki's plains advancing
The *stern, invading foe;*
By twilight dim their swords were glancing
In grim imposing show.

In the preceding article from copy to crown, the British author has not mentioned 'Sikh' while other communities have been given about this discrimination the en speaker of Lok Sabha (Parliament) writer.

Though insignificant in numbers, the Sikhs have always made contribution out of all proportion to their population. It is a pity that very few Sikhs have taken the trouble to record facts as they happened.

Leaving aside Gurus' period and Maharaja Ranjit Singh's rule, the subsequent acts of bravery and valour of the Sikhs have not been done full justice. Some accounts recorded by a few Englishmen in an objective manner need to be collected in an authoritative manner.

It is an irony of fate that the Sikhs' contribution is either being deliberately suppressed, at least minimised much, or innocently ignored.

The Sikhs suffered most during 1947 partition and resultant migration. They were hunted out from West Pakistan, and accepted with suspicion and mistrust in India. The sufferings of the Sikhs did not end with partition. New battles had to be fought for the protection of Punjabi language and script.

No body has cared to bring out the composition of British army of Indians that fought under the foreigners to defeat the real indigenous rule of Punjabis before the annexation of Punjab in 1849. It is only the bard, Shah Mohd., who had given an indication of the real position in his verse: "It was a fight between the Punjabis and all the fighting army recruited by British from all over India". Almost all that is being eulogised as the war of independence of 1857 had helped the English to destroy the Sikh kingdom.

During the British Rule, the Sikhs were recruited in larger numbers, of course. But this was only natural because the English had personal experience of the toughness and endurance of the Sikhs.

*Maharaja Duleep Singh under British Protection in Mussoorie**

PRINCIPAL JAI DEV SINGH

Looses Identity, Faith and Empire

By virtue of the Treaty of Lahore (March 29, 1849) Maharaja Duleep Singh was to "reside at such place as the British Government of India may select". Many proposals regarding the future residence of the dethroned King were discussed at various stages. Hardwar, Allahabad ('*being places of High Sanctity*') were considered but dropped. Finally Maharaja Duleep Singh was moved

*Adopted from author's article 'Maharaja Duleep Singh in Mussoorie'—1981.

out of the Punjab and taken to Fatehgarh, the head quarters of Farrukhabad district (UP) in 1850 A.D. along with Rani Dukhnoo, the widow of Maharaja Sher Singh and their son Prince Sehdev Singh.

It was in the later half of 1851 that a decision was taken to the effect that the Maharaja's summer residence was to be at Mussoorie. The Maharaja was 'greatly delighted at the prospect of spending the hot weather of 1852 in Mussoorie and preceding winter months in Agra, Delhi, Hardwar and Dehradun.'

Mussoorie in those days, quite different from today, was sparsely populated and majority of the inhabitants were whites.

It was spread over 182 acres of a thickly forested hill with natural water springs, pictureque surroundings, salubrious climate and most suitable for "a quiet and retired life" with plenty of opportunities for "active outdoor exercise".

The Maharaja lived in the Castle, at the top of the hill. His bed-room was plastered and flored with a particular kind of mortar which would not absorb heat and was further kept cool with tall pine trees all round the Castle. Outside his bed-room the Maharaja had planted a number of Champa trees, the fragrance of which when in bloom would spread over the entire estate. Under-neath the residence of the Maharaja was bored a narrow tunnel, a kind of basement with two openings at both ends where in the Maharaja often used to play, 'hide and seek' with his friends and it also served the purpose of keeping the bed-room cool. It was under heavy and strict guard from where every activity of the Maharaja was watched and every word he uttered could be heard throughout the day and night.

There were number of other buildings meant for School, Boys Boarding House, Natural History Museum, Library, Music and Band School, the artistists' gallery, the dispensary, a huge stable for horses and elephants, and eyrie and barracks for large number of servants. Sufficient space for a playground on the Manor House, a part of the Estate, was levelled to play cricket in which the Maharaja took great delight. This playground was down below the Castle and its other end was linked through a narrow lane with the road leading to Landour. At the end of this lane was posted an Indian force to guard the entrance and exist to the playground.

The lay-out of the residence was such that neither the Maharaja could ever move out of his residence nor could anybody seek entry without notice. The security was further strengthened by the fact that all private residents of Mussoorie needed a permit to live in the civil station and in the cantonment areas only Government employees resided. The object of having Duleep Singh's residence in Mussoorie was to enable him to pursue his studies more effectively as the British Government was committed to train the boy in such a manner as that 'when the date of his majority arrives he may take possession of the heritage which has been secured to him a well principled and accomplished gentleman versed in the knowledge which usually is sought by the higher ranks in the East and instructed also in the English language and literature.

Mr. Walter Guise—a man of mild manners, neither qualified nor having any experience of teaching was picked up from road-side in Meerut to be the tutor of the ex-Sikh King. Mr. Guise taught English language, Maths, Literature, History, Geography and Science. A class of 8-10 students was formed and apart from the Maharaja and Princes Sehdev Singh, others were all English boys.

Maharaja Duleep Singh gave money out of his personal funds for setting up a dispensary in Mussoorie and also for the construction of roads. The City Board passed resolutions of thanks and the city fathers personally went over to the Maharaja to express their gratitude. The Maharaja also organised a Natural History Museum which had very valuable collections of specimen including some rarities.

Maharaja Duleep Singh right from his childhood was interested in painting. In 1849, when his kingdom was being grabbed, he was busy with his painters constantly employed to draw and paint all species of hawks for a book to be brought out in Persian. Mr. Beechey, a painter of international fame, was employed to encourage His Highness in this fine art. Mr. Beechey painted a portrait of the Maharaja while in Mussoorie which was presented to Lord Dalhousie at Calcutta.

But the most interesting character who caused remarkable changes in the tender mind of the Maharaja was Bhajan Lal, a Brahmin by birth and Christian by training in an American mission at Farrukhabad. He was employed first as a domestic servant, but was later installed as a confidential personal attendant and finally was raised to the status of a tutor.

Lady Login amongst several other English ladies used to be a centre of attraction. Their dress, manners, customs and etiquette were a novelty for Duleep Singh as he had been brought up in Brahminical way of living in his infancy. A child is easily influenced by the environments around him and so must have been Duleep Singh. He must have found the Christian way of living far superior to his own, more particularly when he was made to live in the company of English boys of his own age, who would often make a mockery of his personal style of life.

In Castle Hill Estate other families and his play-mates would eat at tables laid out in a fashionable style. The menu used to be English preparations and boys often remarked 'you can learn English language only if you eat English food and adopt English way of life'.

Duleep Singh like any other child would often like to immitate others around him. He was fascinated by the way people got ready and dressed themselves so well and by the sanctity they attached to going to church, in Landour on certain days of the week to attend the mass or other services at fixed hours. He would be left behind to be with servants and would feel lonely. He was often tempted to go to church with others. But they would refuse to take him along. His desire became acute and for this state of mind a single distinctive factor had made its contribution—**the desire of the new masters to convert him to Christianity.**

Lord Dalhousie and all others who handled the closing ceremony of the Khalsa Raj had one thing in their mind: to convert the Sikh Ruler and take him to England. This would mean that the British Empire would not have any claimant in Punjab and it would pave the way to enlarge the extent of Christian brotherhood in India. But according to Lord Dalhousie no such thing was to be done with which it might appear that there was any kind of "interference with the boy's religious faith". On the expression of this fear by Lord Dalhousie—Sir J.S. Login found out an alternative. "I trust however that God helping we shall be enabled as written epistles" to manifest the spirituality and benevolence of Christian life if we can not otherwise preach to him". Sir J.S. Login calculated well in advance that if at all Maharaja Duleep Singh could be converted it can be done within a short time before he achieves a kind of maturity.

But the most crucial role was given to Bhajan Lal (a Christian at heart) who may be called the hero of the conversion drama which was played under the direction of Lord Dalhousie. Sir J.S. Login gave a book—'English Instructor' and Lady Login gifted the Maharaja with a book entitled—'Boys Own Book'—Both these contained certain lessons on Christianity and Sir J.S. Login left it to the open mind of the young lad either to read those or not. But Bhajan Lal made him read those just for the sake of knowledge. One day this loyal servant carried a copy of the Bible to the Maharaja who was tempted to buy it. Bhajan Lal offered to present it to the Maharaja if he was able to read chapter which the Maharaja did. From henceforth Bhajan Lal would daily read a chapter from the Bible to the Maharaja. The story is told by Bhajan Lal himself—sometimes Bible, sometime a few tricks (Legerdomain) then sometimes out of 'Boys Own Book' but I am sure I never heard any Englishman talking or reading any of their religious things". This was found to be enough Evidence by Lord Dalhousie to sanction the request for conversion.

As an easy annexation had been ordered on frivolous grounds so also the Maharaja was converted to be a Christian at the age of 16½ years. Lord Dalhousie not only 'rejoiced' at this great change. "With so much satisfactory evidence of the reality and genuineness of his conviction" but also regarded as a "very remarkable event in History and in every way gratifying". Sir J.S. Login was given a pat by Lord Dalhousie—"under the circumstances of preculity, of great delicacy, and of great difficult, I have been most of satisfied with the judgement and discretion, the prudence and kindly tact which have been exhibited by yourself". Lord Dalhousie sent specific instructions that Baptism ceremony should be performed as silently as possible and no new name should be given to the Maharaja, instead he be made to retain his original name.

Soon after the Punjab was annexed to the British Empire, Sir Henry Lawrence, the resident Governor of Punjab and Mr. Mansel advised Lord Dalhousie that Duleep Singh be sent to England at once but Lord Dalhousie was not "fond of suggestions". Now that Maharaja Duleep Singh was converted and the British had a firm hold over his kingdom.

Sir J.S. Login wrote to Lord Dalhousie that on reaching England, Maharaja was thinking of 'entering one of the Public Schools and taking his place among boys of his own age—only hoping he won't get many threshings'. Lord Dalhousie did not approve of the proposal and did not even agree, that he could join a university giving an inelination that the idea working behind the proposal to send Maharaja Duleep Singh to England was not to educate him but to make him 'quit India'. Even then the Maharaja himself and many others had hopes that Maharaja would come back and have a Jaghir in Doon Valley with his headquarters at Mussoorie where he will take up social work of spreading education and Christianity among his countrymen, which did no happen and the course of history took different turn.

LORD DALHOUSIE'S DESIRE TO DEFEAT SIKH GOVERNMENT AND ABOLISH THE SIKH DYNASTY

Lord Dalhousie acted directly on the principle—precisely the reverse of Lord Hardinge's—which avowedly guided his policy throughout his administration. In his own words, used on a subsequent occasion, it was his "strong and deliberate opinion that in the execution of a wise and sound policy, the British Government is bound not to put aside or neglect such rightful opportunities of acquiring territory or revenue as may from time to time present themselves." While the war was in progress, he wrote (February 1st 1849) to Henry Lawrence, "I do not seek for a moment to conceal from you that I have seen no reason whatever to depart from the opinion that the peace and vital interests of the British Empire now require that the power of the Sikh Government should not only be defeated, but subverted, and their dynasty abolished."

* Gen. Sir Charles Gough and Arthur D. Innes in their book "The Sikhs and the Sikh Wars", p. 215.

Dalip Singh : A Life in Struggle

KANWARJIT SINGH KANG

Not many may be aware of the peculiar circumstances that conditioned the struggle of Maharaja Dalip Singh, the son and successor to Maharaja Ranjit Singh, against the British.

Born in 1838, Dalip's father died when he was less than a year old. His childhood witnessed the strenuous battle for succession. Dalip was installed the Maharaja of Punjab in 1843 when he was only five. He was out under the charge of a tutor guardian, Dr. John Login. Dalip remained in Lahore till he was 12, after which he was went to Fatehgarh, a village in U.P. From there, he was taken to England in 1854, via Mussoorie.

A study of historical records has revealed that the events were manoeuvered by Lord Dalhousie, the then Governor-General of India. The Maharaja's entourage was dismissed and his connection with his roots severed. At 12, Dalip was projected as having become deeply religious and in his quest for truth was stated to be engaged in a comparative study of the *Guru Granth Sahib* and the *Bible* and finally discovered that the salvation of his soul lay in the *Bible*.

Lord Dalhousie wrote to Sir George Couper about Dalip's decision to embrace Christianity : "politically we could desire nothing better; it destroys his possible influence for ever".

Dalhousie further opposed Dalip's marriage to his Sikh finance, the daughter of Chatter Singh. He wrote to Dr. Login : "I do not wish to countenance any relations henceforth between the Maharaja and the Sikhs, either by alliance with a Sikh family, or sympathy with Sikh feelings." Dalip finally decided not to marry Chatter Singh's daughter.

Dalhousie also poisoned Dalip's mind against his mother, Rani Jindan, who had escaped from her prison in the fort of Chunar and was living in Nepal under political asylum. Dalip reached London in May, 1854, but when he heard that Jung Bahadoor of Nepal wanted to get rid of Rani Jindan, Dalip decided to sail for India. He was allowed but with the condition that he would not visit Punjab.

When Dalip reached Calcutta, several Sikh regiments that had returned from the China war besieged his hotel to see their Maharaja. Lord Canning urged the Maharaja to return to England at once. The Maharaja did just that but took his mother with him.

Jindan told her son that he had a claim to his private ancestral estate in Punjab. This prompted the Maharaja to study the *Blue Book* at the British Museum and preset his claim to his family estates, including ancestral properties and family jewellery.

Rani Jindan died in August 1863. After immersing her last remains in the Godawari, Dalip, on his way back to London, married Bamba Muller, daughter of a German businessman and an Abyssinian mother, at Alexandria. The couple settled at their new house in Elveden Estate in England.

Dalip continued to pursue his claims. He debated the issue publicly and wrote a lengthy letter to the *Times*, which was published. This was followed by an editorial to which Dalip replied. Dalip then decided to proceed to Punjab to obtain the details of his private property, but was not allowed.

The news about his intending visit to India and the restrictions imposed on him, reverberated in Punjab too. *The Tribune*, then published from Lahore, in its issue of August, 1883, wrote editorially : "It is true that the Maharaja has been in

England since a long time and has adopted English manners, customs and modes of life, but yet he could not have forgotten that he was born in this country and that he is the son of one of the most powerful of Indian Princes. Brilliant associations crowd round his infancy which all his education and foreign training may not have been able altogether to efface, and it is, therefore, natural that he should feel a longing to see the land with which those associations are so intimately connected.

Amidst all the gaieties of Eleveden Hall and the pleasures of and English-married life, it was impossible for him to forget that he was by birth a native of India. And that we think is reason enough to impel him to visit the country of his forefather."

Disillusioned, Dalip realised that he was in exile. He made up his mind to leave England forever. He left for India with his family in April 1886, but was not allowed to proceed beyond Aden. Thakur Singh Sandhanwalia, his cousin, met him there and persuaded him to return to his own faith which he agreed to, and the ceremony of *Pahul* was gone through in the presence of Thakur Singh and four other Sikhs.

Thereafter, Dalip resigned the stipend paid to him by the British under the Treaty of Annexation. From Aden, he went to Paris and contacted the Russian Embassy. He met Patrick Casey, an Irish revolutionary who introduced him to M. Katkoff, a renowened Russian journalist, who helped him visit Rusai. He tried to convince the Russians about his ability to stir political unrest for the British in India.

Unfortunately, Katkoff died. By now, Dalip was short of money. He sent his trusted lieutenant Arur Singh to India to raise money who collected Rs. 80,000 but was arrested. Meanwhile, Thakur Singh Sandhanwalia and Dalip's wife died. Even though Dalip had failed in his mission in Russia, he continued his campaign against the Raj and issued an appeal to his fellow Indians on June 25, 1889, for the cause of freedom.

Dalip died on October 22, 1893. Although Dalip's love of his country was revived quite late in life, he never forgave those who had cut him off from his heritage and cultural roots.

—Courtesy : The Tribune, 15 June 2007

Bhai Maharaj Singh

Trailblazer

PROF. GOBIND SINGH
M.A., LL.B., PH.D., LONDON

SAINT-PATRIOT BHAI MAHARAJ SINGH AND HIS MARTYRDOM FOR NATIONAL FREEDOM*

Bhai Maharaj Singh was a soldier in the Lahore Army which was defeated (1849) by the British armed forces including Bengal and Oudh recruits also and then disbanded the Lahore Army and annexed Punjab to the British Indian Empire. Leaving the short army life Maharaj Singh joined Dera of Baba Bir Singh whereas a boy he was schooled and began a new life mission of *Seva, Bhakti,* and management of *Langar*. This Dera was popular with people of not only Punjab but also U.P., Rajasthan and Jammu. The Dera Chief before his death appointed Maharaj

* "Once atleast, during the conflict (Anglo-Sikh War) they (Sikhs) were within an ace of victory which would have set all India in a blaze", writes Gen. Sir Charles Gough.

Singh as the Dera Chief who in a message to the rulers of Kabul, Tibet, Nepal urged them to unite for expelling the Britishers from Punjab and India.

Mr. Vansittart, British Deputy Commissioner, Jullunder Division who arrested Maharaj Singh for conspiring against British Authority later wrote : "The Bhai is not an ordinary man. He is to the natives what Jesus Christ is to the most zealous of Christians".

Bhai Maharaj Singh was despatched to Singapore and kept alone in four sides bricked cell and suffered all kinds of ailments and privations the most heinous and cruel punishments.

Later Commissioner Jullunder Division Mr. Mcleod paying tribute to the Bhai wrote : . . . hundreds and thousands of devotees visited him for his divine discourses and urged independence. He also arranges *Langar* (food) for them. "His life is an outstanding example of a Martyr, a devoted Khalsa (Sikh) who lived upto the Guru's ideal of the saint soldier, and gave up his life for the cause of freedom, justice and human dignity."

—(Ed.)

His life and martyrdom were glorious, and bloodless like fifth and ninth Sikh Gurus. He asked his followers not to take revenge and not harm Britishers as happened in several other revenged cases. He faced his six years persecution and ghastly sufferings for freedom and independence only without religious issue put in like other revolts and mutinies. However, his acute sufferings for six years caused resolve to take revenge in Punjab and UP which contributed to the scenario of Great Uprising. His death caused widespread anguish against the Britishers as witnessed in 1857 Uprising. Colonel Mallason, the author of "sepoy mutiny", wrote about the dominance of national factor behind the Uprising, after talking to various people in India.

The aggressive and imperialistic policy of the British government in India left no stone unturned to annex the Sikh empire after obtaining a foot-hold therein as a consequence of the First Anglo-Sikh War of 1846. Naturally the Sikhs, Hindus and Muslims of the Punjab were scared by the unfair tactics of the, British government in accepting minor Maharaja Daleep Singh as the nominal head of an administration virtually under the control of the British Resident. In this patriotic struggle against the occupation of the Punjab and the subservience of the Lahore Darbar, Bhai Maharaj Singh, a preacher and Sikh saint, played a vital and heroic role.

HIS PATRIOTIC MISSION

During the interim period between First and the Second Anglo-Sikh War (1846-49) there were lots of intrigues in the Lahore Darbar affecting Maharaja Daleep Singh's minority administration. Hira Singh Dogra, a minister of the Lahore Darbar wanted to punish Attar Singh Attariwalla, Prince Kashmira Singh and Prince Pishora Singh for their rebellious activities. These persons had taken shelter in Baba Bir Singh's *Ashram*. The Darbar Army decided to attack the Dera of Baba Bir Singh to arrest the above so-called 'rebels'. Baba Bir Singh ordered Maharaj Singh to purchase food and *Karah Parsad* for thousands of people. So large quantities of cooked food were kept ready for the soldiers coming with artillery and cavalry to arrest the wanted persons. Baba Bir Singh told the attacking force that these persons had taken sanctuary in his hospice but they were free to go if they wanted too. The commander ordered the attack and bombarded the place on 6 May 1844. Before his death, Baba Bir Singh appointed Maharaj Singh as his successor and care taker of his Ashram. But Singh who was regarded as a saint, and many others, were killed, but Maharaj Singh survived the ordeal.

Bhai Maharaj Singh became the head of a popular movement against British occupation of the Punjab. As the grip of the British power over the Punjab tightened, Maharaj Singh became suspect in the eyes of the British officials. At this time (1847) some Sikh Sardars and demobbed soldiers of the Lahore Darbar made a plot to murder the British Resident—Lt. Col. Henry Lawrence. Prema and Sardar Lal Singh conspired to attack him at a meeting fixed for 21 April 1847, in Shalimar Gardens, Lahore. This is known as the *Prema Conspiracy* case. It was alleged that Maharaj Singh had given moral support to the conspirators and as such the authorities ordered his arrest. He was so much respected and honoured as a saint that no one dared to disclose his where about in spite of the award for his arrest. However, his property, whatever, it was, was confiscated. For three years, he moved about in the Punjab and yet the police and the military force could not capture him. This fact is supported by the Governor-General Lord Dalhousie in a note *dated 30 September 1848*, mentioning : "The Zamindars (landowners), the people and the Chiefs openly displayed entire sympathy in the cause, and the Darbar officials and the 'Kardars' who were ordered to pursue him, followed him tranquilly and remained on the best terms with him." Fearlessly, Maharaj Singh moved from one village to another and even military areas stirring the masses to revolt against British rule and to save the *Khalsa Darbar* and the remnants of the Punjab army from destruction.

At this time (September 1848) occurred the Multan Revolt in which Diwan Moolraj and some Sikh Sardars like Sher Singh and Attar Singh protested against the aggressive and anti-Sikh policies of the British administrator. Bhai Maharaj Singh wanted to join the agitation led by Sardar Chattar Singh Attariwalla in Hazara against the British occupation of the Punjab. Maharaj Singh went to Rawalpindi by a circuitous route to get assurances of help in terms of men and money before the outbreak of this revolt, and he was fairly successful in this task.

Later Maharaj Singh went to Ram Nagar exhorting the Sikh soldiers to be vigilant against the plots of the British to divide the Sikh community and to annex the Punjab to their own territories. It is uncertain whether he took any part in the actual fighting in the battles of Chillianwalla and Gujarat. However, there is no doubt that he gave a lot of support to the Sikh cause. The greatest need of the Sikh army during these battles was the shortage of food and fodder. Maharaj Singh procured adequate supplies of these things from the neighbouring villages and arranged for their transport to the 'rebel' army.

Finding stay in the Punjab difficult after its occupation by the British forces in 1849, Maharaj Singh moved to Jammu. From Chambi he sent messengers to different parts of the Punjab asking the people to sabotage the British administration. He was equally keen on securing the person of Maharaja Daleep Singh, fearing that he might be exiled and then it would be difficult to continue the struggle for the liberation of Punjab. He made a plan for the abduction of Daleep Singh from Lahore, but it did not succeed.

Great Influence on the Sikh Soldiers

The British authorities knew his great influence on the Sikh soldiers who might be tempted to revolt. In this connection Sir Henry Lawrence, President of the Board of Administration of Punjab wrote : "Bhai Maharaj Singh, a Sikh priest of reputed sanctity and of great influence, the first man who raised the standard of rebellion beyond the confines of Multan in 1848 and the only leader of note who did not lay down his arms to Sir Walter Gilbert at Rawalpindi, was tampering with the Sikhs of the Punjab Cavalry Corps at Lahore". The authorities therefore promptly exiled Maharaja Daleep Singh to Farukhabad in United Provinces in April 1849.

General Revolt Planned

Then Bhai Maharaj Singh planned a general revolt in the Punjab. He moved to Sajuwal from July to October 1849, to organise attacks on the cantonments at Jullundar and Hoshiarpur. For this purpose, he motivated the local priests to persuade the people to help the rebel cause for the liberation of Punjab. He sent his personal friends like Bhai Kishan Singh and Nihal Singh to Kabul for obtaining assistance from the Amir of Afghanistan, Jwala Singh Rarewalla and Mitha Singh to Anandpur, Hari Singh to Ambala, and Dharam Singh to Lahore. Attar Singh, a descendent of the erstwhile rulers of Kangra, promised to supply armed soldiers and adequate food-grains. Maharaj Singh contacted many influential persons in Hajipur. He visited the Sikh soldiers at Hoshiarpur to reassure himself of their help. He checked the arrangements for assembling of sufficient forces at specified places in Mahjha, Malwa and Hazara. He fixed 3rd January 1850 for attack on the Jullundar and Hoshiarpur cantonments. He collected stocks of weapons and grain near Tanda. For checking all these centres, he used to hold meetings at night in secret spots.

HIS ARREST AND PERSECUTION

Maharaj Singh reached Adampur on the night of 28 December 1849 to hold a meeting with his trusted friends in a garden in the suburbs. Unfortunately a Muslim informer happened to see him pass by, and he immediately contacted Mr. Vansittart, Deputy Commissioner of Jullundar. The latter reached the spot with 20 soldiers and surrounded the garden. After arresting Bhai Maharaj Singh, his personal attendant Kharag Singh and other associates, he lodged them in the local jail. Many people gathered near the jail to hold a protest demonstration. With tremendous self-control and will to suffer, his message to them and his followers was to be remain non-violent and peaceful. But the authorities fearing public disturbance, placed Maharaj Singh and Kharag Singh under heavy guard. Then they were sent to Allahabad under military escort and sometime later to Calcutta where they reached on 12 March 1850. The Governor-General decided that Maharaj Singh be deported to Singapore along with his attendant Kharag Singh. Under a special British guard, Maharaj Singh and Kharag Singh reached Singapore on 14 June 1850.

Six Years in the Solitary Cell

He was lodged in the new Jail, but his solitary cell was completely bricked so as to prevent light and ventilation. He was not allowed to move out of this. For this reason, his health deteriorated. After a few months, he lost his eye-sight. Later he developed throat cancer and could not eat anything. Maharaj Singh felt resigned to the Will of God and spent most of his time in prayer and meditation. **For six years, he had not moved out of the cell or seen the sun or the sky. The end came on 5 July 1856.** His last message to his compatriots was : "Never submit to injustice, never surrender your arms, never compromise on principles". He gave up his life in the cause of holy war against the treachery and aggression of the British rulers who had destroyed and dismembered the last independent Empire in India. The British had thus deprived the Khalsa of its freedom and its future. Some of his letters addressed to Sikh soldiers show his fearless spirit and faith in the ultimate freedom and moral victory.

BHAI MAHARAJ SINGH
Outstanding Example of a Martyr

Seldom has an outstanding patriot and freedom-fighter suffered so much persecution and yet won compliments from his captors as Maharaj Singh did. His courage of conviction, his valour, his devotion to the freedom of the Punjab and his zeal for selfless service of the masses were admired even by his enemies. Mr. Vansittart who arrested him later wrote : "The Bhai is not an ordinary man. He is to the natives what Jesus Christ is to the most zealous of Christians. His miracles were seen by tens of thousands, and are now implicitly believed than those worked by ancient prophets". As such, he recommended "special treatment to be given to him on political considerations".

Bhai Maharaj Singh was a true Khalsa. He bore no ill-will to the British officials. Before his arrest, he warned his friends, not to injure any British administrator. When one of his supporters shouted that he would kill the Deputy Commissioner of Jullundar, Maharaj Singh rebuked him, saying, "You want to defame us. We shall never capture or harm unarmed people. Bring the Deputy Commissioner to me, and I shall tell him that the Sikhs are not the enemies of the British people. All that we want is the sovereign right to freedom, and if we get it, we shall have no grudge against your community".

Mr. McLeod, later Commissioner of Jullundur Division, paid a tribute to the wisdom, resourcefulness, courage and devotion of Bhai Maharaj Singh. He wrote : "The Bhai alone was never found without resources. Any number of persons who might resort to him, and hundreds and sometimes it is said thousands, did so, being write sure of obtaining from him their daily meal, for the purpose of providing which, he carried about him scores of cooks and *langris* (Chefs) and the requisite materials". His life is an outstanding example of a martyr, a devoted Khalsa, who lived upto the Guru's ideal of the said-soldier, and gave up his life for the cause of freedom, justice and human dignity.

—(*The Spokesman*)

Mutinies in the Indian Army

W.H. Carey

I

EUROPEAN MUTINIES

To those who think a mutiny of Europeans in India chimerical, we may notice that of a handful of men who seized the castle and island of Bombay in 1683, then our only possession, and kept it against the Company for two years, though still professing allegiance to the King; the mutiny of French troops, under D' Auteuil, in 1749, which changed Duplex's triumph into terror and consternation, and nearly nipped in the bud the grand design of bringing all India under the rule of France; the mutiny of the European part of the Bengal Army under Clive, in the face of an enemy, in 1766; that of the Madras Army in 1776 (in which the Commander-in-Chief took part), which deposed and imprisoned Lord Pigott; the all but mutiny of Bengal officers in 1795-96 and that of a large portion of those at Madras against Sir G. Barlow in 1809. These were only partial mutinies, and in circumstances particularly unfavourable to the malcontents; yet in all of them a little less firmness or a little less moderation and concession on the part of the Government, would have led to a contest that might have proved fatal to our Indian empire.

The formidable mutiny which was discovered in September 1766 among the officers of the whole Europeans Army alluded to above, we shall notice more in detail. During Lord Clive's residence at Moorshedabad, "the alarming advices arrived that almost all the officers of the Army had combined, under articles of the most solemn agreement, to resign their commissions by a fixed day unless their batta was restored and the orders of the Company were abrogated. To secure their measures without incurring the penalties of desertion, they fixed on a period when they had no pay in advance, and it was every moment expected our frontier would be invaded by a large body of Mahratta horse; flattering themselves that the necessity for their services at so critical a juncture must infallibly reduce the Board to submission", but they were mistaken. "It was immediately recommended by Lord Clive to the Board, when he transmitted the advices, rather to put all to the risk than suffer the authority of the Council to be insulted. The saving to the Company from the reduction of batta was now of trifling consideration when compared with the danger of yielding to the menaces of so unprecedented and mutinous an association. To preserve the authority of the President and Council, and crush an attempt that indicated the total subversion of Government, became now the object; in which sentiments the whole Board with one voice concurred with His Lordship. He proceeded, accompanied by General Carnac, to Monghyr, where the first brigade lay in cantonment, and happily arrived at the install when the whole body of Europeans was ripe for revolt. Their officers (the Lieutenant-Colonel, and two or three subalterns excepted) had to a man withdrawn themselves, and the soldiers, fired with the contagious spirit of mutiny, were on the point of following the example of their superiors, when His Lordship's presence and authority awakened them to a sense of their duty, and probably saved these provinces from all the horrors of rapine, desolation and military anarchy. The same violence of conduct prevailed amongst the officers of the 2nd and 3rd Brigades stationed at Allahabad and Patna, insomuch that Colonel Smith, who was posted on the frontier of Korah, remote from all assistance, and in the very face of a formidable enemy, was totally deserted by his officers in those lines he had drawn to Oppose the irruption of the Mahrattas." Mr. Long in his "Selections", from which we have taken the above, does not give us the sequel to this alarming mutiny.

A mutiny of a serious nature seems to have occurred in the regiment of European Artillery stationed at the Mount, Madras, on the 15th and 16th January, 1798. We have failed in procuring any details of it, but have only an account of the execution of the ringleaders in the mutiny, which took place at the Mount on the 15th March, which was after all the parties concerned had been tried by court-martial. The prisoners, Clarke, Stumbles, Banks, Forster, Lawrence and Connor were sentenced to death; the first three to be hanged in chains. Forster to be blown away from a gun, and Lawrence and Connor to be shot. When the first four had been disposed of, and the execution party were prepared to carry out the sentence on the two remaining prisoners, Lawrence and Connor who had been viewing the fate of the others, Major-General Brathwaite went up to them and announced the Commander-in-Chief's pardon. Lawrence fell senseless on the ground, Connor, after a moment's pause, dropped on his knees, and offered up thanks in a loud and serious manner. In an order dated Choultry Plain, 15th March, the Commander-in-Chief dwelt upon the destructive consequence of an offence which is most flagitious that can brand the character of a soldier. He ordered that the two pardoned men should be struck off the rolls of the Artillery, and sent out of the country.

II

NATIVE MUTINIES

Casual readers of the military history of India often fancy that the mutiny of 1857 was unprecendented. That it was so in magnitude is happily true; but other insurrections, refusals to obey legitimate authority; and attempts to subvert the power of the military commanders, had happened at various times and in various parts of both the Madras and the Bengal presidencies.

One of the regiments of the Royal service employed in India at this time (1763) was the 89th Foot. Its time being up, it was about to proceed to England, when news reached Bombay, where it was stationed, that Major Adams had died, that the forces of the Great Mogul were invading Behar, and that the Council of Fort William needed the services of Major Hector Munro, with all the troops that could be spared. Munro immediately hastened round to Calcutta, assumed the post of Commander-in-Chief, and proceeded to take the field.

On the 3rd August, 1764 a scheme was discovered for a rising of the sepoy troops at Patna and Monghyr; this was carried into effect on the 7th and 8th, a large number of the men taking their officers prisoners and walking off with their arms. The cause of the disaffection was, that they had not received the same amount of prize money which had been accorded to other battalions. After much difficulty the men were brought back to their allegiance.

This epoch is one of so much interest in the history of the Bengal Army, and it at the same time offers so many more proofs of the mutinous disposition upon which Captain Turner Macan and Sir Edward Paget commented before the House of Commons, that we must take from Captain Broome's book the following quotation:

> 'A mutinous spirit engendered in an army is only to be suppressed by a strong hand and the unflinching exhibition of a marked example. The orders and professions of Major Munro had but little effect in quelling the seditious feeling then prevading the greater portion of the Native forces, which previous impunity and conciliation had only served to foster. The two battalions stationed at Monearch, were for a short time in a state of actual mutiny, but were speedily brought back to a sense of their duty by the influence of their officers; several other outbreaks occurred at the other stationed, but none sufficiently marked or tangible to enable the Major to make such an example of them as he desired. At length on the

8th of September, a mutiny of a more serious nature occurred in the 9th, or Captain Galliez's battalion, the oldest corps in the service, then stationed at Manjee. Instigated by some of their native officers, they assembled on parade, and declared their intention of serving no longer, as the promises made to them had been broken; they however retained their arms and accoutrements, and imprisoned Captain Ahmuty and the other European officers and serjeants of the battalion; but they do not appear to have offered them any insult or other annoyance; and on the following day they released the whole, and permitted them to proceed to Chuprah, the nearest station.'

"On the arrival of the officers at Chuprah, an express was immediately sent-off to Major Munro; and Captain Wemyss, who was in command at the station, marched at once to Manjee, with the Marines and the 6th, or Captain Trevannion's battalion, the latter officer expressing his full reliance on the fidelity of his men. After two days of a fatiguing march, the whole country being under water, this detachment reached Manjee at daybreak on the morning of the 11th. Here they found the mutineers bivouacked in a mangoe tope, which owing to the heavy rains that had fallen, was completely surrounded by water. Captain Wemyss drew of his detachment facing them, and the mutineers being taken by surprise, and probably without any recognised leader, lost their self-possession, and after a short parley, agreed to surrender. Rafts were immediately constructed, and the whole battalion were made prisoner, deprived of their arms, and marched to Chuprah, where they arrived on the morning of the 13th.

"Major Munro, who, on receiving intelligence of this mutiny, had immediately hastened from Bankipore to Chuprah, taking with him the Grenadiers of the European battalion, was awaiting their approach. Having received a communication from Captain Wemyss, stating when he expected to arrive, and the 15th or Captain Stabels' battalion, drawn up ready to receive them. He immediately ordered Captain Ahmuty to pick out 50 of the ringleaders; and from these he again selected 24, whom he ordered to be tried at once by a drum head court-martial, composed of native officers of Captains' Trevannion's and

Stabel's battalions. He addressed the members of this court-martial, explaining to them the heinous nature of the offence committed, and the consequence of such conduct as regarded the whole service. The result of their decision is to be found in the following General Order of the 13th September, 1764 :

> 'At a general court martial held at the cantonments near Chuprah, on twenty-four, sepoys of Captain Galliez's battalion of sepoys, confined for being taken in actual mutiny and desertion, the court having duly weighed the crime alleged against them, found them guilty of the first and third articles of the second and fifth sections of the Articles of War: and therefore, sentenced them to be put to death, by being blown away from the guns; which sentence is approved by the Commander-in-Chief, and is to put in execution accordingly.'

"Major Munro, on receiving the verdict of the court, immediately ordered four of the prisoners to be tied to the four 6-pounders, when four grenadiers of the party immediately stepped forward, and represented that as they had always occupied the post of honour in the field, they claimed the usual priority and right of place on this occasion. The Major complied with their request, the battalion men were untied and the gallant but the misguided grenadiers occupied their places; at a signal from the Commander they were launched into eternity, and the fragments of their bodies scattered over the plain.

"A thrill of horror ran through all ranks; a murmur arose amongst the whole of the Sipahis, and Captain Williams who was present, states that there was not a dry eye amongst the Europeans, although they had long been accustomed to hard service and fearful spectacles; and amongst the Marines were two men who had actually been on the firing party at the execution of Admiral Byng, in the year 1757. The officers commanding the Sipahi battalions then came forward and represented that their men would not allow the execution to proceed any further; but Major Munro, a man of remarkably humane and considerate disposition, which qualities he evinced throughout the campaign, felt that he had a high and sacred duty to perform, on which the well-being of the whole army and the very Government depended, stiffling his own feelings, he determined to proceed in his duty at all hazards, he directed the officers of the Artillery to lead the guns with grape, and drawing up the Marines on one side and the Europeans Grenadiers on the other, he dismissed the officers to the heads of their battalions, and then gave the order for the whole of the Sipahis to ground their arms, at the same time directing the Europeans and Artillery to fire upon any who refused to obey. This display of resolution and firmness had its due effect; the battalions instinctively obeyed the word of command, and the Major moving them a short distance from their arms, placed the Europeans and guns in the interval, and then ordered the execution to proceed, when 16 more of the party were, in like manner, blown away; the whole of them marching boldly up to the instrument of their execution and awaiting the final signal with firm and unmoved countenance. The remaining four were sent to Moneah, and there executed in a similar manner in the presence of two battalions that had recently evinced a mutinous disposition; and on the return of the Major to Bankipore on the 15th, he caused six Sipahis of other corps, who had also been convicted of mutiny, to be blown away from the guns at that station, in the presence of the assembled troops. This wholesome and well-timed display of resolution and severity effectually and completely suppressed the spirit of insubordination that had been so long existing in the native army."

Every recruit on enlisting into a native regiment is required to take an oath that he "will never forsake nor abandon his colours," and that he "will march wherever he is ordered, whether within or beyond the Company's territories". It had been the practice of Government to consider this oath, when not otherwise explained at the time of enlistment, as not in itself binding the soldier to proceed on service beyond sea, and, therefore, whenever regiments had been raised for service beyond sea, no man had been drafted or enlisted into them but at his own consent, and with a full and clear understanding of his engagement to serve beyond sea when required to do so.

An expedition on foreign service having been determined on, in 1795, a battalion of Native Infantry was thought sufficient for the service. On this determination being made known, the 15th Battalion Native Infantry immediately volunteered its services to proceed to any part of India. The high sense entertained by the government for this evidence of their zeal and good feeling was publicly made known both to officers and men. But this was only preliminary to an open revolt of the battalion, which was thereupon disbanded, by the following order :

> '*Military Department 26th October*, 1795. The Commander-in-Chief having laid before the Governor-General in Council a statement of the mutinous conduct of the 15th Battalion of Native Infantry-Resolved, that it be declared that the said Battalion had been broken with infamy, and its colours burned.'

"Resolved, further, in order to prevent misrepresentation or misconception of the transactions which have taken place in regard of the 15th Battalion, that the following declaration be published in General Orders, and that, for the more ready and general notification of them, they be translated into the Persian and other country languages, and copies of them circulated to the several native corps and dispersed by the Collectors through their respective districts.

"The 15th Battalion of sepoys having been broke with infamy, and its colours burned, the Governor-General in Council thinks proper to make known to all the Subadars, Jemadars and Sepoys in the Company's Army, the cause of the severe punishment which has been inflicted on this battalion.

"The public service requiring that troops should be sent to Malacca by sea, the battalion, on the proposition of their officers voluntarily offered themselves to embark; the proposition was repeated to them at three different times, as they might thereby have full leisure to deliberate upon it, and from their determination, and they again repeated their acquiescence.

"The Government, sensible of the prejudices of the Hindoos against a voyage by sea, and ever attentive to them, expressed their approbation at the zeal of the 15th Battalion in voluntarily undertaking service which was left to their option to accept or decline; convenient ships were prepared for their accommodation, and every precaution was used to provide food and water, under inspection of officers and men selected and deputed by the battalion to superintend the provisions.

"To the astonishment of Government, after many days, the battalion, without any reason whatever, retracted the acquiencence which they had voluntarily and deliberately given. This was a most shameful desertion of their duty as soldiers; but their subsequent conduct was such as to leave them without any title to forgiveness. They went for many days in a state of actual outrageous mutiny, and when required by Colonel Erskine to lay down their arms, had the audacity to fire on the 29th Battalion.

"For this conduct, the battalion has been punished in the manner mentioned.

"The Governor-General in Council deems it incumbent on him to take notice of the good conduct of the 29th Battalion, and he requests the Commander-in-Chief will be pleased to render the acknowledgement of the Government to Captain Breadly on an occasion so creditable to himself, and to desire him to notify to his battalion the sense which the Governor-General in Council entertains of their fidelity in the recent instance they have afforded of it.

"Resolved, that the Commander-in-Chief be requested to render to Lieutenant Colonel Erskine, the acknowledgement of Government for his mainly and judicious conduct in the application of the full powers entrusted to him for suppressing the mutiny of the 15th Battalion at Midnapore.

"Resolved that Captain L. Grant, who has evidently been acted upon in the whole of his conduct in this affair, by an earnest zeal to fulfil the wishes of Government, be directed immediately to raise a new battalion to be denominated the thirty-seventh; leaving number 15 at present a blank in the numbers of the native corps."

The above order was followed by another on the same subject by the Commander-in-Chief, under date the 5th November, 1795 :

> 'The resolution of the Governor-General in Council, of the 26th of October, are to be most minutely and clearly explained to every native corps in the service of the

Company. To assist the officers in making their communications, copies of their translations in the Persian and other oriental languages which will be forwarded to the several battalions, are also to be read and explained on the public parade, where they are to be delivered over to the Subadar, to be explained to their respected companies at leisure, until every individual understands them.'

"In addition to the acknowledgement which the Governor-General has ordered to be rendered to the 29th Battalion in general, the Commander-in-Chief thinks it right to notice particularly the conduct of the men who turned out volunteers to accompany the 15th Battalion, and after remaining with that corps several days, returned quietly to their own battalion, when the breaking out of the mutiny of the 15th Battalion took place, and he desires that his approbation of their behaviour on that occasion may be made known to them in the most expressive terms.

"It will occur to the officers of the army that the punishment of officers and men of the 15th Battalion will by no means be complete nor proportionate to their guilt, if any of them should again return into the service. The Commander-in-Chief therefore, most positively directs that none of them be received into any of the battalions of the Company's Army except as should, by express permission, be incorporated into the new battalion; and he calls upon the officers commanding native corps to exert their utmost care and vigilance to prevent their obtaining admission by the means of any imposition, and that they will attend to the first article of the section of recruits published in the general orders of September 1786, which will effectually guard against the introduction of any of the mutineers of the 15th Battalion, as well of desertion on all occasions.

For, as the slightest observations will readily discover a trained soldier from a new recruit, the Commander-in-Chief most positively directs that no man be enlisted who has served as a sepoy, without producing a discharge from the corps he last served and which discharge, on his admission into the service, is to be taken from him and deposited with the records of the Battalion. The truth of falsity excuses that discharge are lost or destroyed are easily discovered by a reference to the Commanding officer of the Battalion which the man who offers himself for service says he belongs to.

"Instructions will be given to Captain Grant regarding the raising of the new Battalion."

In 1825, three native regiments, stationed at Barrackpore, near Calcutta, were under orders for the Burmese war. With a caste prejudice against the sea, and a prescient dread of the Burmese climate, the sepoys demurred and refused to embark. The 47th Native Infantry became openly mutinous. The Commander-in-Chief, Sir E. Paget, marched two Europeans regiments and some artillery to the station during the night; paraded the 47th, the next morning, and ordered them to lay down their arms. They disobeyed. The guns opened on them and they broke and fled. It did not appear that the sepoys had contemplated active resistance, for though in possession of ball cartridge, hardly any had loaded their muskets. Sir E. Paget was much blamed for resorting at once to the extremist measure; but the events of 1857, which began at the same station of Barrackpore, threw a truer light on the gravity of the crime of military mutiny.

Besides the above following may be noted in few words:

> In 1822, the 6th Madras Cavalry mutinied at Arcot; in 1844, the 34th Bengal Infantry at Ferozepore refused to march to Scinde, and the 64th Bengal Infantry mutinied at Umballa, unless their pay and allowances were increased. In 1845, the 6th Macras Native Cavalry mutinied at Jubbulpore and the 47th Madras Native Infantry mutinied when ordered to Scinde. In 1849-50 several regiments of Bengal native infantry stationed in the Punjab either broke into open rebellion or were prepared to do so.

A—The Mohomedan Rebellion

To the commencement of the late persian campaign we would ascribe the first stir made by those who had been foremost in the struggle. It was then,—at the close of the last and beginning of the year 1857,—that the elements began to be agitated. The news of the capture of Herat in January had scarecely come upon us, when the tocsin of war sounded from China. Oude and our Nepaul frontier required the most careful attention. Our new Burmese possessions were cources of great anxiety. The dominions of the Nizam—the Decan, Gwalior, Rajpootana, and the Sonthal district, all demanded the most unflinching resolution and the constant backing up of troops. The natives appeared to have been alive to the weakness of our military power—the deficiencies in every branch of the army, especially as regarded its numerical force in Europeans. The conference of friendship with Dost Mohomed Khan also placed us in an awkward position, and seems to have opened up a hornet's nest around us.

When our conquering troops had fought the battle of Mohamra on the plains of Persia, there was found in the deserted tent of the Shahzada, a manifeste by the Shah of Persia, duly signed, but without date, to the following purport :

> 'Whereas the British Government, through the power acquired by the conquest of India and the advantages thereby gained, has framed its politics and has pursued a course of aggressions, to the end that all the East should be added to its dominions, and for the purpose of accomplishing this and advancing the performance of it, the British Government attempted the conquest of Afghanistan; and although nevertheless, it caused great destruction and mischief in the countries of Afghanistan, and took possession of Lahore, Peshawar, and several other dependencies of that country; and this is the proceeding and politics of this Government to obtain complete dominion in Persia; they try to prohibit the intercourse with the Sirdars of Afghanistan who are our neighbours and co-religionists, and have always been our allies; and this is with a view to open to themselves a road to Persian soil, so that whenever they wish they could advance their troops from every side into Afghanistan and all the countries bordering on Persia; and even, if they possessed the power, to reduce the Government of Persia to the state of the Rajahs of Hindostan, and to destroy the religion of Islam in Persia, in like manner as the religion of the

Musselman of India. And in order to carry out this design, the British have commenced invading the kingdom of Persia; they have occupied themselves in deceiving the vulgar, and through deceit and bad faith, and in improper mode of proceeding, whilst our Government have never resented it; and presuming upon our supposed weakness, they have carried their ill-practice and bad faith to such an extent, that they have tried to seduce persons in the employ of the Persian Government to enter the service of their Embassy, and also endeavour to bring Princes and Moonshees of the Kingdom under their authority; and they have employed stratagems and artifices, so that by false pretences and improper proceedings, they have tried to bring to pass that which they desire, and by degrees all their machinations have come to light. Unexpectedly they brought troops to the soil of a power of Islam, and having thus gained a footing, took possession of one of the Forts of Islam which was on the sea shore, and was only held by a small number of troops as its fixed garrison; and thus no army being present they occupied it, and when they saw that if they advanced from the sea shore they would flounder about like fish on dry land, they have stuck there; for they know that if they advanced the blows of the sharp swords of the heroes of Islam would not leave breath in the soul of one of them.'

"But His Majesty the Shah-in-Shah has taken advantage of his breach of faith of the British Government to make manifest his royal will and pleasure; and his orders have gone forth that countless armies are to be assembled on the boundaries of every country; and victorious troops have been directed towards the frontiers to drive out the enemies of the faith, and scatter the rubbish and direct along the shores of Arabia (for 'God giveth the victory to whom he pleases'). And now in obedience to the words of the Prophet, to him who doeth injury up to him in like manner as he does injury to you? Let all the people of Heran consider it incumbent upon them to follow the precept, 'slay in the name of God those who wish to slay you,' and let the old and the young the small and the great, the wise and the ignorant, the ryot and the sepoy, all without exception arise in the defence of the orthodox faith of the Prophet; and having girt up the waist of valor adorn their persons with arms and weapons: and let the Ullema and preachers call upon the people in the Mosques and public assemblies and in the pulpits, to give in a Jehad in the cause of God, and thus shall the Ghazis in the cause of the faith have a just title to the promises contained in the words of the Prophet, 'Verily we are of those who fought in the cause of God.'

"But whereas the victorious army of the .State have not drawn the sword upon the enemy, we have not permitted the eager multitudes to leave their homes and in the directions of Firs, we have appointed the Ameer Ool Umra Mirza Mahomed Khan Kasheekchi Bashi, and Meer Ali Khan Shooja Ool Moolk and several other generals and commanders with 25,000 men; and in the direction of Mohumerah the Prince Nawab Shusham 001 Dowla with 20,000 fine troops; and in the direction of Kirman, Goolam Hussain Khan, Tipahdar and Jaffer Koola Khan Meer, Pun-i-jah, with regiments and Cavalry of Kurrachee Daghi, and Axerbiyham and Kirmani to the number of 20,000 men; and in the direction of Cutch and Meekram towards Scinde, and from the direction of Afghanistan the Nawab Ahsham 001 Sultanut with 30,000 men and 40 guns, abundantly supplied and equipped; and the Afghan Sirdars (viz.) Sirdar Sultan Ahmed Khan, Sirdar Shah Doolah Khan, Sirdar Sultan Ali Khan and Sirdar Mohomed Allum Khan, who have been appointed by his Majesty, have been ordered towards India and they are hopeful that by the blessing of divine aid they may be victorious.

"And it is necessary, that the Afghan tribes and the inhabitants of that country, who are co-religionists of the Persians, and who possess the same Kuran and Kiblah and laws of the Prophet, should also take part in the Jahad and extend the hand of brotherhood, and on receiving these glad tidings act according to the words of the prophet, 'Verily all true believers and brothers', and 'also make manifest the decree of God'. 'Verily the Almighty will weigh the wicked in different scales from the pure,' and for the purpose of settling the quarrel, it is necessary that not only a small number of true believers should stand forth in the defence of the faith, but that the whole should answer our call, and this should also be made known to all the people of Afghanistan, that the Persian Government has no intention of extending its conquests in that direction, except to the government of Candahar, which should be given over to Sirdar Rahim Dil Khan, and the family of Sirdar Kohun Dil Khan, and the Governor of Cabool and its dependencies should be vested in its chiefs, and they should join in the Jahad against the enemies of Islam, and be of the number of those 10 whom the Prophet saith 'the grace of God dwelleth in the number of those who fight in Jahad'; and we are hopeful that after the publication of this proclamation, Dost Mohomed Khan, Ameer of Cabool, who always was desirous that the Persian armies should extend their conquests to Affghanistan, and who wished to be strengthened by their alliance, should also unite with us against this tribe of wanderers from the path of righteouness, and that he should become one of the leaders of the faithful in this Jahad, and that he should become a 'Ghazi' in Hindostan, for he cannot wish for the friendship of a tribe of whom the Prophet saith, 'Verily they do not love and neither do ye love them; nor can be wish to sell his faith for a wordly price and this proclamation is published for the information of all true believers, and please God the followers of Islam in India and Scinde will also unite with us and take vengeance upon that tribe (the British) for all the injuries which the holy faith has suffered from them, and will not withhold any sacrifices in the holy cause ?"

In the passages italicised it is plainly stated—1st, that the Mussulmans of India (the Shah proclaims it) had cause for fear in the matter of their religion, from the bad faith and deceitful mode of proceeding adopted by the British by invasion and annexation. 2nd, that the war he was about to enter upon was a religious war, and that all good Mahomedans should arm in defence of the orthodox faith of the Prophet and slay and exterminate in the cause of God. 3rd, that armies had been equipped and appointed to march on India for the assistance of the faithful residing there. 4th, combination is recommended and a general rising. 5th, all true believers are informed that this war has been waged for the purpose of taking vengeance on the

British for all the injuries which the holy faith has suffered from them.'

The complicity of the ex-King of Oude in the rebellion was proved by several documents found at his house and others bearing his signature. Immediately after the annexation of the Kingdom of Oude to the British territories in India, which occurred in March 1856, the ex-King commenced a correspondence with the King of Delhi, proposing to induce the whole Indian army "to join as one body, rise on a day to be hereafter fixed, massacre their officers, and all Europeans indeed all Christians, within their reach; invite all native princes to join, and after expelling the British troops, whom they might not succeed in murdering, restore the Hindoo and Musulman principalities, that existed before the advent of the Western and hated Feringhees, under the general sovereignty of the KING OF KINGS at Delhi.

The sepoy; by the injudicious acts of successive Governors-General and Commanders-in-Chief, had been taught to think too highly of himself—to believe that he was the chief pillar of the State—the mainstay of our power in India. The bonds of discipline were too much relaxed and finding that the government had taken all power into their own hands, the sepoy cared nothing for his officer, upon whom his welfare no longer depended, and became from various causes discontented and then disaffected. This feeling was fostered by the ex-King of Oude and his minister, the subtle and crafty Ali Nukee Khan. The sepoys, highly credulous, like all natives of India, and ready to believe any the most monstrous tales, had their attention drawn to the various ways in which we had interfered with their religious practices; the stoppage of infanticide; the prohibition of suttee; the prevention of self-immolation under the care of Juggunnath; the proselytising efforts of our missionaries, and the gradual spread of civilization; and the sepoys became alarmed. The Brahmins, of whom there were great numbers in our ranks, found their influence decreasing from year to year, and their alarm and discontent worked on the minds of the rest. Then Lord Dalhousie made every sepoy pay postage for his letters which had hitherto gone free under his commanding officer's signature. The roads and ferries were no ranger free to him as before, except when travelling on duty. He had to pay toll like other people. These taxes were not only particularly galling to the pride of all, but irritating and burdensome to the bulk of the men, whose pay was only seven rupees a month, out of which they had to feed and clothe themselves. In 1852, when the 38th Native Infantry refused to go to Burmah, Lord Dolhousie left them unpunished, and showed the native soldiers very clearly what power was in their hands, and how safety they might defy the Government. With all this material for revolt ready laid, there wanted but the spark to light the flame. This was supplied by the unpardonable carelessness of an official in Calcutta.

Addenda

A-i

Year 1795, Mutineers of the *15th Battalion of Native Infantry,* Nellore.

Trial and Punishment—Summary

Minute of Council in the Military Department, 26th Oct. 1795

The Commander-in-Chief having laid before the Governor-General in Council a statement of the mutinous conduct of the 15th Battalion of Native infantry, resolved, that it be declared, that the said battalion has been broken and its colours burnt.

First charge. Refusal to go to Malacca beyond the territorial limits of India across the sea, to fight the wars of the British outside India.

Second charge. When required by Colonel Erskine to lay down the Arms, had the audacity to fire on the 29th Battalion.

Proceedings of the Court Martial and Punishment

1. Subedar Rogonant Singh: Sentenced to be blown away from the muzzle of a cannon.

2. Subedar Bakah Singh:	To be blown away from the muzzle of a cannon.
3. Subedar Busrage Singh:	To be blown away from the muzzle of a cannon.
4. Jamadar Omrow Geer:	To be blown away from the muzzle of a cannon,
5. Jamadar Yacoof Khan:	To be hanged by the neck until he be dead.
6. Jamadar Adhuny Singh:	To be blown away from the muzzle of a cannon.
7. Jamadar Kussaul Singh:	To be hanged by the neck until he be dead.
8. Jamadar Pursuttum Singh:	To be hanged by the neck until by the neck until he be dead.

Later on the sentences were reduced. They were dismissed from service with infamy.

A-ii

Year 1849, 19th June. *Case of Open Rebellion against the* British Government established in the Mysore Territory

Prisoners' names: (1) Veera Mudekerry Naick, (2) Chetoany Runguppah Naick, (3) Saingunnah alias Ungalab Naick, (4) Pursaram Naick, (5) Jungalah Naick, (6) Rungapah Vakeel, (7) Bidray Louchmah and other 14 followers of Veera Mudekarnee Naick.

First Charge.—The first six prisoners are charged with having on or about the 19th day of June 1849, in the Talook of Hasdroog Halalkera in the Chittledroog division of the Mysore territory, assembled and led a band of armed men and others engaged in open rebellion against the British Government established in Mysore territory.

Second Charge.—The first five prisoners are charged with having on or about the 4th June 1849 at Chittledroog Division of the Mysore territory enlisted and collected several persons, some of whom were armed with a design to commit rebellion against the British Government establisbed in the Mysore territory and on or about the same day had accompanied the said persons and proceeded to array themselves in open hostility to the said government, and so continued on such hostility until they were captured by the troops sent against them on the 19th of the said month of June 1849.

The 6th Prisoner abetted the other prisoners . . . against the British Government.

Fourth Charge.—Drawing and writing highly seditious proclamation . . . addressing the various classes of people to subvert the rule of the British Government established in the Mysore territory.

Opinion of the Adawlat

1st. prisoner. Be imprisoned with irons but without labour for 10 years.

2nd. to be imprisoned with irons but without labour for 7 years.

3rd, 4th and 5th. To be imprisoned with irons but without labour for one year.

6th. Imprisoned with irons without labour for seven years.

7th. May be set at liberty.

The other 14 followers of Veera Mudekarnee Naick :

I. Burmal Naick, 2. Dulvayea Louinga, 3. Kaulah Naick, 4. Bommrh Naick, 5. Tulvar Chikka Ranga, 6. Gudda Runga, 7. Louchab, 8. Curssah, 9. Chourchegah, 10. Mayegah, 11. Goudhah Madocara, 12. Poojany Gheriah, 13. Hullo Trimaneah Gheriah, and 14. Gonnor Paul Naick.

First Charge.—To collect men with a view to making insurrection against the British Government in the Mysore territory.

Opinian of the Adawlat. 1st Prisoner. To be imprisoned in irons without hard labour for 10 years.

2nd, 3rd, 4th and 14th. To be imprisoned in irons with hard labours for five years.

5th to 13th. To be imprisoned in irons within hard labour for three years.

B—1857, AND EARLIER UPRISINGS

It is often said that the Great Uprising which started at Meerut on 10th May, 1857 to throw way the alien rule, was the first war of independence. This assertion, however, is not correct historically. Much prior to 1857, the Indian pratriotic forces had crossed and fought against Europeans to frustrate their designs for establishing British *raj* in India. Below is the story of some of those forgotten heroes who were pioneers in the freedom struggle.

India in the eighteenth century resembled a vast military areа. Armed gangs of free booters rampaged the country side and even the soldiers employed in the service of East India Company were given the prize money or share in the plunderings. As the central authority was becoming weaker and weaker, local chiefs assumed more powers and then fought amongst themselves for more wealth and territories.

In the initial stages of the East India Company many Indians joined the Company's forces and were employed as guards for protecting its settlements and warehouses. As the Company extended its military sphere, these native guards were used for fighting purposes. Territory after territory and town after town were taken over by the British Trading Company and during this process, their sinister intentions became known to the patriotic sections of the Indian people and resistance started against the expansionist designs of the foreigners.

Much before the happenings at Velore in 1806, a dispute arose on 7th August 1764 at Patna and Monghyr between the Company's officers and the Indian sepoys over the sharing of prize money. A large number of the men took the officers prisoners and thus resisted the despatch of prize money to England. After much difficulty and shrewed tactics the men were brought back to duty. On 8th September same year, all the European officers of Captain Galliez's battalion were imprisoned by the native sepoys, as the promises made to them had been broken and their religious feelings injured. The tidings spread to some other battalions also, but with diplomacy the men were persuaded to release the officers and allow them to proceed to Chuprah, the nearest military station. The men were promised that their demands would be fulfilled within ten days.

Instead of meeting their demands, the Indian soldiers were surprised while resting in a mangoe tope with a severe and sudden attack by a regrouped force of Europeans. After some fighting the Indian soldiers surrendered and were immediately made prisoners and fifty of them tried by drum head court-martial and sentenced to be put to death by being blown away from the guns. When this execution started and four of the prisoners were tied to the four 6-pounders, four grenadiers of the party immediately stepped forward and demanded that as they had always occupied the post of honour in the field, they should be accorded the priority on that occasion also. Another group of four Indians came forward and insisted to be blown off first. Everybody amongst the prisoners was keen to be the first martyr. The British officers were in a fix but ultimately the honour went to the grenadiers who were blown away and the fragments of their bodies scattered over the plain. In a similar manner other prisoners were fired in groups of four.

In November 1805 an order was issued introducing a new type of turban, resembling hats worn by Eurasian drummers, for the native troops. Another order published in 1806 by the Company laid down that "a native soldier shall not mark his face to denote his caste or wear earnings when dressed in his uniform, be clean shaved on the chin and preserve a uniform quantity and shape of the hair on the upper lip." Vellore in those days was a big military station quartering several battalions. In the massive fortress there were interned the family members of Tipu Sultan after his defeat and death at Seringapatam some six years earlier. Indian troops stationed at Vellore had learnt with much horror and dismay, the looting, abuses and ransacking of Seringapatam after the fall of Mysore kingdom. Therefore when the above orders reached Vellore, the Indian guards and sepoys objected strongly, which they thought was a measure preparatory to enforcing conversion to another religion. It is therefore not surprising that such inconsiderate orders hated by both Hindus and Mohemadans, should have caused the smouldering discontent already existing into open uprising for installing the children of Tipu on the throne of Mysore.

On 11th July 1806 at about two in the morning the sepoys of the main guard stationed near the fort suddenly attacked the

British troops and killed all but four who managed to escape. At about the same time an attack was made on all Europeans present in Vellore. The British flag was pulled down and the Mysore flag was hoisted over the fort. Indians were attacking with muskets, spears, swords and two six-pounder guns, most of which they had captured from the Magazine, killing hundreds of Europeans. For about forty hours, the Indians were again the rulers of the land from which they were dispossessed by foreigners.

Badly beaten and humiliated the Company's European forces were regrouped at Seringapatam and were reinforced with many parties of crack troopers and guns. It was planned to make a surprise assault on the Vellore fort in the early hours of morning, Colonel Gillespie led the attack. Although surprised, the Indian armed men in the fort fought valiantly and inflicted heavy losses on the Company's forces trying to enter the fort by breaking through the gates which were strongly locked and barred. At this moment somebody in the fort had turned traitor, as a rope was lowered from the ramparts of the fort which hauled up Col. Gillespie and his party over to the ramparts. Col. Gillespie headed a bayonet charge to clear the way for opening a gate in which he succeeded. The European cavalry charged into the fort and other troops also rushed in. A bloody battle ensued but the Indians were overwhelmed by a large number of guns and men and a general massacre followed. Those who escaped through the sally port were cut down outside. Hundreds of Indian men, children and women were killed.

Colonel Gillespie, chiefly responsible for all the killings at Vellore, was in 1814 shot through the heart during the Nepal war when attacking the fort of Kalinga at Dehradun and was buried at Meerut. As if in retaliation and a spirit of revenge the Great Uprising in 1857 started in Meerut within a mile of the grave of Colonel Gillespie who at Vellore, fifty-one years earlier, had mercilessly butchered hundreds of innocent Indians. Tippu was killed in the month of May (4th) 1799 while fighting against the British forces. The Great Uprising of 1857 also started in the same month, a week later.

C—Pre-mutiny Revolts in Princely States of Orissa

Manmath Nath Das

During two decades before the Rising of 1857 there were revolts of considerable significance against the British in some of the princely states of Orissa. These revolts were of a prolonged nature, causing sufficient anxiety and alarm to the Government. The hill tracts of Orissa proved difficult for the movement of troops, and the rebel princes or their chiefs, supported by their people, could effectively defy the might of the British.

It was in the cold season of 1835-36 that the Goomsur rebellion broke out and the British troops entered into the Goomsur territory to put it down. According to a report from G.E. Russel to the Chief Secretary to the Government of Fort St. George, the extent of Goomsur from east to west was about 60 miles and from north to south about 48 miles[1] Besides the Raja of Goomsur there were several petty chieftains in this area who acknowledged no allegiance and paid no tribute to anyone. The British were nominally their masters for nearly seventy years, but their continued hostility finally resulting in rebellion led to military operations against them. According to the British testimony the country "suffered intensely in the operations of the war, many chief men had suffered capital punishment and the people were thoroughly cowed and at our feet."[2] The ruling family was deposed, and the British selected "an influential man named Sam Bissey" and made him the chief over the people.[3] But a few years later Sam Bissey himself took up the cause of the people and revolted. Captain Macpherson, an officer to the Ganjam Agency, "did not give Sam a chance of reforming his conduct, but procured his deposition, and the banishment of himself and two of his sons". The consequence was that the whole family became immediately the enemy of the British and were the first to join the people of Baud subsequently in their insurrection. By 1845-46 discontent had spread from Goomsur to Baud and from Baud to Angul. A formidable leader had appeared in the meantime in Goomsur, Chokro Bissey by name. On 27 December 1846, J.C. Macpherson Agent in the Hill Tracts of Orissa wrote the following to A.M. Mills, Superintendent of Tributary mahals, Cuttack, "I beg leave to state for your consideration my view of the position in which the Raja of Ungool, the Khomo of Band and Chokro Bissey of Goomsur at present stand with reference to the operations in which I am engaged. There is I conceive no doubt that the Angul Rajah in "support of his design to resist the Government which he apparently entertained up to the middle of October last employed every possible means to implore (?) the Khomo family in Baud and Chokro Bissey in Goomsur to excite disturbances in these zamindaries."[4]

The report of disturbances in Goomsur, Baud and Angul took the Governor of Madras by complete surprise. On 7 January 1847 he wrote to the President of the Board of Control, "There is no knowing in this country how long one is to be in peace. . . Goomsur, the former scene of insurrection, is now in a great state of ferment . . . I have been long complaining of the want of sepoys in the Northern Division. We are two Regiments at least short of the force we require for the common duties of the Division. We have just received information that our regiments in the Southern Maratha country can be spared On hearing of the insurrection, I sent an express to the Residents of Hyderabad and Nagpore to ask them each to dispatch a regiment into the Northern Division: the former to Vizianagram, the other through the Khond country by Meypoor direct to Goomsur. . . . I forgot to mention that a regiment had already entered the district on its way to relieve a regiment going over to Moulmein to relieve the regiment stationed there. So that in two months we shall be in force.[5] Our sepoys have been hard-worked during the Sutlej campaign and for some time previous. About a month later, the Governor complained. . . . Had I not met with the opposition I received here in Council, I should have gone to Goomsur, to see how matters really were. It is most lamentable to think that public business is to be subject to delay and opposition in the manner it is, and that one's time is to be employed in so profitless a manner."[6] The President replied back in March, 1847, "It appears now that the Goomsur affair is not quite settled; but I dare say it will soon be set at rest."[7]

At the beginning of 1847 the Raja of Angul was in open war with British. Informations were received that the Raja "crossed the Mahanadi with guns and troops plundering and burning the country."[8] The Government forces in the meantime were busy in putting down the rebellion in Goomsur, and in May, 1847, Governor-General Hardinge wrote to the President of the Board of Control, "The Goomsur disturbances are, I trust, nearly at an end. These operations are under the President-in-Council in conjunction with the Madras Government whose troops and officers are employed."[9] A little while ago the Governor-General had proudly declared that with the exceptions of the disturbances in the hill tracts of Orissa "general tranquillity prevails throughout Her Majesty's Eastern dominions."[10]

The Goomsur rebellion was no doubt put down, but the leader of the movement, Chokro Bissey, entered into other princely states to incite the people. The Government instituted enquiries to know the details about this man and Col. Campbell wrote to J.P. Grant the following: "In doing me the favour of seeking information from me it would very naturally occur to you that a person of Chokro Bissey's pretensions and importance must be well-known to one who for so many years held charge of the country which has been the scene of his exploits, and it may be of his birth, but in truth I was never even aware of the existence of such a person until the recent disturbances occurred, and know nothing of his early career and fortunes save that he is the son of Ramsingh Bukshi, who was killed while in opposition to the Government in 1837; and the nephew of Berabur Patro, the Dora Bissey of Goomsur, now a state-prisoner at Gooty, and it is supposed that when his uncle sought refuge in the Ungool territories he accompanied him thither. It has been assumed that he was the leader of the plunderers and incendiaries in the low country, but I have never yet been satisfied as to the fact."[11] Chokro Bissey was fighting against the British to place the old ruling family of Goomsur on the throne. But Campbell tried to convince the Government that Chokro Bissey had no following for the above cause. He wrote to J.P. Grant, "It will no doubt strike you as a singular fact that not a voice, except his own, has been raised for a Rajah in Goomsur since General Dyce assumed, political control. I relieved the General in May and I can assert with great confidence that no general feeling ever did, or does exist for the restoration of the Bhanj family in opposition to the wishes of a

Government whose power they have witnessed, and comprehend. It is plain that no such feeling could have obtained amongst them, as their own interests are intimately connected with the maintenance of their present rulers, and the absence of the Rajah" whose return would be as they well known, the prejudge to their punishment, in that all the Sirdars and nearly all the Peons were instrumental in his deposition. I presume Chokro Bissey is perfectly sensible of the very limited sympathy his cause excites and obtains in Goomsur, and hence his reason for fixing residence in the Baud country."[12]

Though the movement of Chokro Bissey was slighted by the British, in reality its nature was grave. The reports of the Talook authorities contain evidences of his widespread activities. In December 1846, with a gang of about 400 men he had suddenly attacked the town of Colladah, set it on fire and burnt various villages.[13] After this exploit he and his followers had installed a young man of the old Goomsur family as Rajah.[14] In February 1847, Chokro Bissey was seen at Leacotta between Goomsur, Daspalla and Angul. At the above place about 400 match lockmen of the Angul Raja had come to his help. Soon after, the rebels under him attacked the Government guards at such places as Gullery and Gaticoodah.[15] The disturbances at Goomsur had caused such anxiety in the Board of Control that the Governor-Gencral had to excuse himself with the following words to the President. "I do not interfere in the Goomsur affair. It is in charge of the President-in-Council, by legislative enactment, whilst I am separated from my colleagues. The military operations are carried on by Madras."[16]

At the beginning of 1848 the war was "going on within the Government of Bengal against the Raja of Angul."[17] Col. Campbell was directed to march against the Raja. It was unfortunate for the Raja that during his rebellion against the British, his own son went over to the enemy side. The following news appeared in 'The Englishman and Military Chronicle' on 29th January 1848: "Letters from Cuttack up to the 10th instant mention that the Madras troops had left that station some days before, the son of the Ungool Rajah, a wild looking savage, had come into Cuttack, being on bad terms with his father, it was understood that Colonel Ouseley proceeding with the Ramghur force, had granted the Raja an interview, and it was feared that the views of Government had been compromised thereby; under any circumstances the troops will probably have only to dismantle the Forts."[18] On February 8, 1848, the Governor General informed the Court of Directors, "Our little war in Ungool is at an end. Col. Campbell met with no opposition. He found preparations for resistance but encountered none: he has taken possession of the principal stronghold, and a private letter received last night informs us that the Raja himself has been captured by two of his brother chiefs who have behaved well and faithfully. It remains now to dispose of his country. It is not worth the taking: and the result will probably be that we shall propose to keep the old man in safe custody, to put the son who has fled to us some time ago in his place, making stringent conditions with him, and requiring payment of the expenses of the expedition from the territory."[19]

The Raja tried his best not to fall into the hands of his enemies. When hard pressed in flight, he "contrived to avert the attention of his pursuers by scattering rupees on the ground", but they followed him and captured him. Sirdoo, his chief counsellor, escaped and took shelter in the jungles. The influence of Angul rebellion spread to the neighbouring state of Baud, and "it was understood that Colonel Campbell would proceed now with a considerable force from Angul to Baud".[20] The Raja of Angul was sent as a prisoner to Cuttack "with his worst followers" and the Governor-General declared that "With regard to the disposal of the estate of Angul we have a perfect right to do with it what we please. It has been justly forfeited and no one could whisper a complaint if we turned out the whole lot and took it to ourselves."[21]

The defeat and capture of the Raja of Angul did not bring Chokro Bissey to submission. With his match lock men he had continued to fight and in 1847 had attacked Captain Haughton's camp. At the end of the Angul disturbance Captain Macpherson wanted to impress the Government. "It was not plain that the time had arrived for making a final movement against him (Chokro Bissey) which must have inevitably driven him from Baud a helpless fugitive."[22]

Very near to Baud was the princely state of Sonepur. When military operations began in the territory of Baud, Chokro Bissey entered into Sonepur and the Rani of Sonepur gave him shelter. There the rebel could gather his followers. The Rani's support and Chokro Bissey's exploits in Sonepur give testimony to the general discontent of the people against the British, in that territory. In March 1848, Campbell wrote to the Government, "I have information that Chokro Bissey pressed by the several parties in pursuit of him has taken refuge in the zamindary of Sonepur. I have written to the Rani and shall address the Governor General's agent in the North Western Provinces on the subject."[23] The Governor-General could feel that Chokro Bissey was "now a fugitive without followers and without power."[24] He wrote to the President of the Board of Control, "Chokro Bissey, hunted from hill to valley, has now taken refuge in the wild tracts behind Baud, marked 'unexplored' in the maps, and his followers dispersed. At present he is inaccessible, but we shall catch him some day."[25] The very determination of the Governor-General to catch Chokro Bissey, which he expressed both to the Court of Directors and the Board of Control, speaks about the dangerous influence of Chokro against the British.

Though a petty chief, up in arms against the British rule, Chokro Bissey did not think of surrender in spite of the great hardship he suffered. His followers, too, had to suffer immense hardship. Reports reached the British camp at Berhampur that Chokro Bissey was at a place near Domosinghi where several Goomsur families reached him "thus wandering about Baud in the most extreme distress." In course of time, "Eleven of the families delivered themselves up to the usual guard of sebundies at Coominghia and mentioned at the same time that others were suffering much misery and were watching with anxiety the treatment they should receive."[26] Though deserted by followers, Chokro Bissey did not give himself up. In middle of 1848 the 'Calcutta Englishman' published the following : "Letters from the south represent the state of the Northern Circars as very unsatisfactory. In Goomsur house and highway robberies are of very frequent occurrence. The ryots and traders continued in excitement and alarm from the conviction that the influence of Chokro Bissey, and the disposition of the armed population of Goomsur and Baud to rebel, so far from being killed, were barely scotched by Col. Campbell's large military operations last year. Chokro Bissey is at a place just beyond Domosinghi in Baud, where he has built houses for himself and followers. He is circulating invitations to the discontented Paiks of surrounding zamindaries to join him. . . . It had just been discovered that the Raja of Angul who is still kept at Cuttack under a guard, has been intriguing with the Sirdars and paiks of his zamindary through his women who carry his food to him."[27]

Col. Ouseley became convinced of "Chokro's importance and influence" and proposed to offer favourable terms to him. Col. Campbell wanted to punish the Raja of Baud and the Rani of Sonepur for their help to Chokro. He requested the Governor-General-in-Council to permit him to warn the Raja that "unless the Raja shall before tbe 15th of October next (1848) capture the rebel Chokro Bissey, or drive him out of his country not to return again, he shall be fined Rs. 3,000."[28] "The Rani of Sonepur should also be informed that if her officers give countenance to the rebel, or if he is permitted to enter her country, she shall be fined Rs 2,000."[29] The Governor-General sanctioned such threats to the above rulers.[30]

Failing to capture Chokro Bissey through force the British resorted to diplomatic means. The Rani of Sonepur and the Raja of Baud were played against each other as to who should be able to bring Chokro to terms. But diplomacy also failed in case of Chokro Bissey.[31]

The Raja of Baud and the Rani of Sonepur as well as other princes of Orissa seem to have been taught a lesson through the punishment to the Raja of Angul. The Government of India issued orders in reference to the ex-Raja that the old man was to be a state prisoner for life and to be confined at Hazareebag at which place the Amirs of Sind were kept. His country was to be resumed by Government and his eldest son was not to be allowed to reside nearer his old home than Cuttack. The British felt that Angul "will be a valuable acquisition to Government, for we shall thus have a district of our own, and a very productive one too, in a centrical position close to Baud and Duspollah."[32]

Notes and References

1. *Selections from Records of Govt. of India,* Madras 24 pts. I—.II.
2. *India Home Consultations,* 187-17, Report of J.P. Grant.
3. *Ibid.*

4. *IHC,* 187/14, Macpherson to Mills, 27 Dec. 1846.
5. *Home Misc.* Vol. 854, lf. 3-4.
6. *Ibid.,* Vol. 854, lf. 9-10, Governor of Madras to President, 10 Feb. 1847.
7. *Ibid.,* Vol. 853, f. 287. President to Governor of Madras, 23 March 1847.
8. *IHC,* 187/14, Extract from a letter from Lt. J.C. Haughton, 6 April, 1847.
9. *Home Misc.,* Vol. 853, f. 348, Governor-General to President, 2 May, 1847.
10. *Ibid.,* f. 362, Governor-General to President, 2 April, 1847.
11. *IHC,* 187/17, Campbell to Grant, 21 August, 1847.
12. *Ibid.*
13. *IHC,* 187/17, Report of R.A. Bannerman, 20 Sept., 1847.
14. *Ibid.*
15. *Ibid.*
16. *Home Misc.,* Vol. 854, lf. 178-79, Governor-General to President, 4 Oct., 1847.
17. *DP,* Letters to Court of Directors, 22 January, 1848.
18. *The Englishman and Military Chronicle,* 29 January, 1848.
19. *DP,* Letters to Court of Directors, 8 February, 1848.
20. *The Englishman and Military Chronicle,* 19 February, 1848,
21. *DP,* Letters to Court of Directors, 21 February, 1848.
22. *IHC,* 187/17, Macpherson to Grant, 19 February, 1848.
23. *IHC,* 187/13, Campbell's Report, 25 March, 1848.
24. *DP,* Letters to Court of Directors, 8 April, 1848.
25. *Home Misc.,* Vol. 855, f. 18, Governor-General to President, 8 April, 1848.
26. *IHC,* 187/17, Report of Campbell, 5 June, 1848.
27. *IHC,* 187/13, Extract from Calcutta Englishman, 9 June, 1848.
28. *IHC,* 187/13, Campbell's Report, 8 August, 1848.
29. *Ibid.*
30. *IHC,* 187/13, Letter to Campbell, 26 August, 1848.
31. *IHC,* 187/14, Campbell's Report, 2 Sept., 1848.
32. Allen's *Indian Mail,* 20 December, 1848.

10

Bloody Incidents in Vellore

H.S. Bhatia

T.A. Bhai Writes

In November 1805 an order was issued introducing a new type of turban, resembling hats worn by Eurasian drummers, for the native troops. Another order published in 1806 by the Company laid down that "a native soldier shall not mark his face to denote his caste or wear ear-rings when dressed in his uniform, be clean shaven on the chin and preserve a uniform quantity and shape of the hair on the upper lip." Vellore in those days was a big military station quartering several battalions. In the massive fortress, interned were the members of Tipu Sultan's family after his defeat and death at Seringapatam six years earlier. When these orders reached Vellore, the Indian guards and sepoys objected strongly.

On July 11, 1806 at about two in the morning the sepoys of the main guard stationed near the fort suddenly attacked the British troops and killed all but four who managed to escape. At about the same time an attack was made on all Europeans, present in Vellore. The British flag was pulled down and the Mysore flag was hoisted over the fort. Indians attacked with muskets, spears, swords and two six-pounders, most of which they had captured from the magazine, killing hundreds of Europeans. For about 40 hours, the Indians were again the rulers of the land from which they had been dispossessed.

Badly beaten and humiliated the Company's European forces were regrouped at Seringapatam and were reinforced by many parties of crack troopers and guns. It was planned to make a surprise assault on the Vellore fort in the early hour of morning. Colonel Gillespie led the attack. Although surprised, the Indian armed men in the fort fought valiantly and inflicted heavy losses on the Company's forces. Some one in the fort turned hostile as a rope was lowered from the ramparts of the fort which hauled up Col. Gillespie and his party over the ramparts. Col. Gillespie headed a bayonet charge to clear the way for opening a gate. The European cavalry charged into the fort and other troops also rushed in. A bloody battle ensued but the Indians were overwhelmed by a large number of guns and men and a general massacre followed. Those who escaped through the sally port were cut down outside. Hundreds of Indian men, women and children were killed.

Colonel Gillespie, chiefly responsible for all the killings at Vellore, was in 1814 shot through the heart during the Nepal War, when attacking the fort of Kalinga at Dehradun and was buried at Meerut. As if in retaliation and a spirit of revenge, the Great Uprising of 1857 started in Meerut within a mile of the grave of Colonel Gillespie who at Vellore, 51 years earlier, had mercilessly killed hundreds of Indians."

In 1825, three native regiments, stationed at Barrackpore, near Calcutta, were under orders for the Burmese war. With a caste prejudice against the sea, the sepoys demurred and refused to embark. The 47th Native Infantry became openly mutinous. The Commander-in-Chief, Sir E. Paget, marched two European regiments and some artillery to the station during the night; paraded the 47th, the next morning, and ordered them to lay down their arms. They disobeyed. The guns opened on them and they broke and fled. It did not appear that the sepoys had contemplated active resistance, for though in possession of ball cartridge, hardly any had loaded their muskets. Sri E. Paget was much blamed for resorting at once to the extrement measure; but the events of 1857, which began at the same station of Barrackpore, threw a truer light on the gravity of the crime of military mutiny.

In 1822, the 6th Madras Cavalry mutinied at Arcot; in 1844, the 34th Bengal Infantry at Ferozepore refused to march to Scinde, and the 64th Bengal Infantry mutinied at Umballa, unless their pay and allowances were increased. In 1845, the 6th Madras Native Cavalry mutinied at Jubbulpore, and the 47th Madras Native infantry mutinied when ordered to Scinde. In 1849-50 several regiments of Bengal native infantry stationed in the Punjab either broke into open rebellion or were prepared to do so.

11

Fugleman of the Great Uprising

T.A. Bhai

In 1857, Barrackpore near Calcutta was a big military cantonment having four regiments of native infantry assembled in a brigade. Since early that year great resentment was prevailing amongst the Indian troops for being forced to use cartridges for the newly introduced Enfield rifle, which were greased with a substance known to contain the fat of cows and pigs.

The cartridges and the grease supplied to the troops at Barrackpore and in other stations in the Bengal Presidency were prepared in the Arsenal at Fort William, Calcutta. When Colonel A. Abbott, Inspector General of Ordnance and Magazines, came to know the objections, he wrote on 29th January, "1 enquired the Arsenal as to the nature of the composition that had been used, and found it was precisely that which the instructions received from the Court of Directors (England) directed to be used viz., mixure of tallow and bees wax. He suggested the use of wax and oil as a substitute to the tallow till the grease of unobjectionable quality was substituted. Consequently powers were conferred on the Commander, Depot of Musketry at Dum Dum and Commanding Officers of other units to purchase *Ghee*, wax, oil and other prescribed ingredients from the *hazar* instead of obtaining grease from the Ordnance sources. But then it was found that the objection was not merely to the composition used in greasing the cartridges, but to the composition of the paper also with which the cartridges for the new rifles were made up.

The Regulation existing at that time for loading the firelock or rifle musket by the sepoys, stated :

> "1st-Bring the cartridge to the mouth, holding it between the fore-finger and thumb with the ball in the hand, and bite-off the top, elbow close to the body."

The apprehension of the Indian troops about the composition of the grease which they were required to apply to the cartridges and the wax paper which every sepoy, while loading his rifle, was to bite it off, originated by the remarks of an Ordnance *Khalasi* employed in the Calcutta Arsenal. The *Khalasi* asked a Brahmin Sepoy for some water from his *lata* but the latter refused to give the water due to reasons of caste. Thereupon the *Khalasi* said, "You will soon loose your caste, as ere long you will have to bite cartridges covered with the fat of pigs and cows." The remarks spread like a wild fire amongst the Indian troops everywhere. Describing the situation and feelings of the Native soldiers at Barrackpore, Major General J.B. Hearsey Commanding the Bengal Presidency Division in his report dated 11th Feb., 1857 to the Government of India said:

> "We have at Barrackpore been dwelling upon a mine ready for explosion. I have been watching the feelings of the sepoys here for some time; their minds have been misled by some designing scoundrels who have managed to make them believe that their religious prejudices, their caste, is to be interfered with by the Government. That they are to be forced to turn Christians."

Giving his version of the origin of the trouble, Maj. Gen. Hearsey wrote, "A sepoy from one of the regiments here (Dum Dum) was walking to his *choka* to prepare his food with his *lata* full of water. He was met by a lowcaste *Khalasi* (it is said one of the magazine or arsenal men). This *Khalasi* asked him to let him drink from the *lata*. The seyoy, a Brahmin, refused, saying—"I have scoured my *lota;* you will defile it by your touch." The *Khalasi* rejoined—"You think much of your caste but wait a little, the *Saheh-lague* will make you bite cartridges soaked in *cow* and *pork* fat, and then where will your caste be?" General Hearsey added, "The sepoy made this speech known amongst his comrades at Dum Dum; the report was not long in travelling to this (Barrackpore) and other stations."

The repercussions to the belief in the minds of the Native troops that their religion and caste were being interfered with, were serious. Several European Officers' thatched houses and the telegraph bungalow at Barrackpore were burnt by incendiaries. On the night of 5th Feb., 1857 a secret meeting was held after the eight o'clock roll call at the parade ground where about three hundred native sepoys of different regiments who had their heads tied up with clothes leaving only a small part of the face exposed, assembled. There the question of killing the Europeans and plundering the Cantonment was discussed. But the information leaked out through a native officer (Jemadar) who was present at the meeting. Emissaries were then sent out from Barrackpore to Berhampore where on 26th Feb. night, Indian sepoys of various regiments stationed there gathered in a deserted tank and took oath to protect their religion and caste even at the cost of their lives. Consequently in spite of strict orders, the native sepoys totally refused to accept cartridges having a composition of cow and pig fat.

But what happened at Barrackpore on Sunday, the 29th March, 1857 was the first violent manifestation of the deep dissatisfaction. So far it was confined to presenting applications or meeting in deputations but on that day at three o'clock afternoon a young sepoy named Mangal Panday of 34th Native Infantry Regiment suddenly appeared before the Quarter Guard armed with his musket which he took out for cleaning from bells-of-arms and a sword and ordered the bugler to sound the bugle for calling the sepoys to assemble. He declared in a loud and firm voice his intention to die for his religion and said that he would kill any European he would come across. Heexhorted his fellow sepoys to join him in this religious war against the foreigners, saying "Nikal ao, pultun; nikal ao hamara sath." Great excitement prevailed in the camp and some shouts were raised against the use of the obnoxious grease and the cartridges. Soon after the British sergeant major arrived on the scene and wanted to apprehend Mangal Panday but no native sepoy would come forward to help him. Mangal Panday dressed regimentally but with his *dhotee* took an aim and fired on the sergeant but missed. Thereupon the sergeant ran for his safety and took shelter behind the Quarter Guard. Meanwhile Lt. Baugh, adjutant, came riding up to the front. Mangal Panday presented his piece and fired, wounding the horse which fell. At this moment a sepoy Sheikh Paltoo came forward and helped Lt. Baugh to get clear of his horse. The adjutant then pulled out a pistol from his holster and saying—"That man will kill me, he is loading again" rushed towards Mangal Panday. The sergeant-major and Sheikh Paltoo followed him. He fired at Mangal Panday but missed him. On that Mangal Panday drew his sword and attacked the adjutant. A sharp hand to hand conflict ensued in which Mangal Panday faced two assailants, the adjutant and the sergeant major. He fought desperately and wounded them both severely. Both the Europeans fell on the ground and another blow from the sword of Mangal Panday might have despatched them if Sheikh Paltoo, himself injured, had not seized him round the waist with his left hand and averted further attacks. Seeing this, Jamadar Iswaree Panday, the Guard Commander and his men abused Sheikh Paltoo and said that if he did not let Mangal Panday go, they would shoot him. Both the wounded Europeans then slowly stood up and retreated quietly, several men of the quarterguard following and beating them with the buttend of their muskets.

Soon after Lt. Col. Wheler, Commanding the 34th Regiment arrived on the spot and ordered the Guard Commander to capture Mangal Pan day alive or dead. But the man would not advance. Then Brigadier Grant, Commanding at Barrackpore arrived followed by Major General Hearsey, Commanding the Bengal Presidency Division, and his two sons, both Army Captains at that time. Mangal Panday after freeing himself from the hold of Sheikh Paltoo, reloaded his musket and stood there with musket in one hand and sword in the other, determined to challenge for protection of his religion. He called upon his fellow sepoys to join him in this holy war. Reinforced by the presence of several European officers, General Hearsey ordered the guard men to load their rifles and advance towards Mangal Panday, saying that he himself would shoot with his pistol anybody disobeying the order. All the European Officers and the guard sepoys then moved towards Mangal Panday who instantly changed his mind and instead of firing on the advancing column which included his Indian colleagues also, shot himself through the chest and collapsed with his sword under him. The resultant wound although serious did not kill him.

He was immediately removed to the Quarterguard of Her Majesty 53rd Regiment where he was subjected to close questioning in order to find out his accomplices and organised plot if any to drive out the Britishers from India. On the 4th April, to a question by Major W.A. Cooke, Field Officer of the Week, Mangal Panday replied, "I acted on my own free will. I expected to die." He was asked frequently if he would give up the names of any connected with the occurrence, but he refused. Dr. T.B. Reid, Asst. Surgeon, 53rd Regiment under whose charge he was, treated him sympathetically. The Doctor admired his courage, patriotism and forbearance and tried to help him on the day of his court martial. When asked to render the fitness certificate on 6th April, Dr. Reid wrote: "Sepoy Mangal Panday has not improved his health since he came under my charge; he has been gradually becoming weaker, and is now much debilitated. The wound also presents an unhealthy appearance." But immediately after that another Doctor James Allen, Asst. Surgeon 34th Regiment, Native Infantry certified that "Mangal Panday, sepoy No. 1446, 5th Company, 34th Regiment, Native Infantry, is in a fit state to undergo his trial this day."

On the same day he was brought before a standing Native Court Martial presided over by Subedar-Major Jawahar Lal Tiwari and with fourteen native officers as members, for trial on two charges of Mutiny and Violence against his superior officers. Five witnesses including Lt. Col. Wheler who acted, as the Prosecutor also and Sheikh Paltoo the only Indian witness, gave evidence. Mangal Panday, declined to cross-examine the prosecution witnesses. When called on for his defence he was reported to have said, "I did not know who I wounded and who

I did not," and added, "I have no evidence." The trial lasted for only one day and on the same day, i.e. 6th April, 1857, the court found Mangal Panday guilty of both charges and after examining his record of service which showed him good in all respects during his military service of seven years, two months and nine days, sentenced him 'to suffer death by being hanged by the neck until he be dead.' The death sentence (eleven officers voted for it) was approved and confirmed by Maj. Gen. Hearsey on 7th April and the execution was fixed on the next morning at half-past five o'clock on the brigade parade ground in presence of all the troops off duty at the station.

In the dark cell of the 53rd European Regiment Quarter-Guard lay on the ground Mangal Panday, a young sepoy of twenty-six years, weak in bodily strength but strong in spirit.

At that time suddenly a storm started blowing. It soon grew into a tempest which uprooted trees, thatched roofs and tents and caused much damage to the buildings. It was accompanied by a violent outbreak of thunder and lightning. Confirming the outbreak of this sudden and unprecedented tempest on the evening of 7th April, 1857, Maj. Gen. Hearsey wrote in a letter, "The 84th Queen's arrived at Barrackpore from Chinsurah at 6 p.m. on 7th evening during a most violent storm. I kept them on board the steamers and when the storm had passed over at past midnight, the corps was moved up to camp."

Early morning on 8th April, 1857, all the men of the Native brigade and all other European and Native troops stationed at Barrackpore were drawn up on parade. Sepoy Mangal Panday was marched under heavy escort to the gallows. After the execution the columns of the Native infantry were advanced close to the gallows to have close look at a man whom the British rulers condemned to death for being a mutineer but who, for his countrymen, became the pioneer of the 1857 Great Uprising. The first blood had been shed.

The Cartridge Fable

Lt. Col. Gulcharan Singh (Retd.)

Although there were political, economic and administrative reasons that led to the Mutiny of 1857, but social reforms and religion were the principal causes of the dissatisfaction of the people of India, especially the soldiery. The social customs in India have religious tinge for the Indians, but to the British these appeared "inhuman" and "merciless". A few examples of these are given hereunder.

First of all take the custom of *sati,* which obliges a Hindu widow to immolate herself alongwith the corpse of her dead husband. This obnoxious and inhuman custom could not be tolerated by the British rulers, hence they legislated for its abolition. This was followed by another Act (XV of 1856), passed in the teeth of opposition, permitting Hindu widows to remarry; these, in the words of Disraeli, had disquieted the religious feelings of the Hindus. Both these customs had religious sanction as the women, unlike the Hindu males, could have only one spouse to their life time. These reforms, including the abolition of infanticide were thus taken as polluting the

Hindu religion and damaging its sacro-sanctity. However, some Indian reformers such as Raja Ram Mohan Roy co-operated with the British Government in carrying out these reforms.

In addition, the introduction of female education, the spread of English education, the introduction of railways and the telegraphs all attributed towards the danger to the native religions. The total abolition of caste and the removal of "yellow paste from the forehead" was openly preached. Also, the various publications in Indian languages issued from Serarnpore denounced the whole Hindu race for believing in their religion. The loss of caste meant the loss of everything to a Hindu. He and his family would become outcastes; his friends and relatives would look upon him with disgust and that in the next world he would be doomed.

These factors also added to the Indian soldier's disaffection towards the British. To the former service overseas, i.e. across the seas, meant loss of caste. On 1st September 1856, the Government of India issued an order that "no Native recruit shall be accepted who does not at the time of his enlistment undertake to serve beyond the seas whether within the territories of the Company or beyond them." This order, according to Field Marshal Roberts "caused the greatest dissatisfaction among the Hindustani sepoys, who looked upon it as one of the measures introduced by the *Sirkar* for the forcible, or rather fraudulent, conversion of all the Natives to Christianity."

ROLE OF CHRISTIANITY

The spread of Christianity in whatever area the British captured was the major excuse of concern. The first action on the part of the British Government in this direction was the enactment of the Inheritance Act (XXI of 1850), allowing the converts to Christianity the right to inherit their ancestral property, previously not so allowed under the Hindu as well as the Muslim laws.

On the top of it, came the Missionary education rousing the suspicions of both the Hindus and the Muslims alike. According to the Missionaries, "India needs the Gospel, needs Christianity, in order to be righted and regenerated." And according to

Metcalfe; the Missionaries asserted that "since God had laid upon Britain the solemn duty of evangelising India, the Government should not hesitate to throw its weight into the struggle." But persons like Sir Charles Edward Travely were more cautious; speaking before a House of Lords Committee, though he stressed that "nothing short of conversion of the natives to Christianity would effect any moral change," but he admitted that time for this had not then come. He did not want to lose sight of its "possible effects" upon the native army which might "excite the religious feelings of the Mahomedans and Hindoos."

Although they were, in the words of Sir Charles Wood, "very careful not to give to the Natives of India any reason to believe that we are about to attack their religious feelings and prejudices," but their grants in aid to the Missionaries for education belied all this—the Missionaries received grants for educating the backward Santhal tribes of Bihar. This considerably roused Indians' suspicions.

On the other hand, the Indians were of the opinion that "if the English continued in Hindustan, they would kill everyone in the country and utterly overthrow their religion." To the sepoy, writes T.R. Metcalfe, "the pervasive evangelical atmosphere in which his superiors live spoke louder than all the proclamations of Government neutrality." The sepoy saw not only Christian Missionaries circulating through the country but such men as Colonel Wheler. Commanding 34th Native Infantry at Barrackpore, open preaching Gospel to all classes, including sepoys and making no attempt to hide his zeal for their conversion. Talking to a member of the Oudh Artillery, Henry, Lawrence said that he "was started by the dogged persistence of the man . . . in the belief that for ten years past the Government has been engaged in measures for the forcible, or rather fraudulent, conversion of all the natives."

SCHOOL EDUCATION

Missionaries wanted the Government of India to disregard the Hindu caste system as well as their customs; not to observe Indian holidays; Bible to be introduced; as a class-book in schools; and to employ all legitimate means for the universal diffusion of Christianity throughout India. Bishop Cotton in Calcutta was convinced that "with the Bible in the school library, and voluntary instruction after school hours permitted would mean no barrier between the seeker after God and his teacher."

In 1858, Herbert B. Edwards, Commissioner of Peshawar, said: "As there can be no safe system of education without Christianity for its base, it is our plain duty to make the Bible the basis of Native education." But R.B. Champan, Education Inspector, in 1856, considered the educational system to be part of a "general scheme for the forcible conversion of the Natives to Christianity".

Many Englishmen agreed with Edwardes' idea. John Lawrence wanted to introduce Bible in the schools because it was "fraught with the highest blessings" for the people.

The grants-in-aid system was adopted in 1854 whose main beneficiaries were the mission societies. It appeared to Lord Dalhousie that "it would enable them to take the fullest advantage of missionary activity in the field of education," where there were few schools opened by private bodies.

The grants-in-aid system was adopted in 1854 whose main beneficiaries were the mission societies. It appeared to Lord Dalhousie that "it would enable them to take the fullest advantage of missionary activity in the field of education," where there were few schools opened by private bodies.

The missionaries and the British civil servants "were talking too openly about using schools as instruments of Christian conversion for these schools to be easily accepted into the culture." Thompson's rural schools, "a few foreys into educating women, and proposals to favour students of the new schools for government employment all created discontent as direct cultural challenge."

Even before 1857, there had been some pressure within the British Government to encourage government-sponsored education by making it a requirement for government employment. There had been a vague directive to this effect in the North-Western Provinces (the present U.P.) in 1856, and Sayyid Ahmad Khan had listed rumours on the subject among the causes of the revolt.

Herbert B. Edwards, Commissioner of Peshawar 1853-59, considered the Mutiny as a "national chastisement" for not disseminating Christianity. Further, in 1860, in a speech delivered in Exeter Hall, he said: "In these things we hear the voice of God. It says, 'I gave India to England for the benefit of its 180' million peoples so that you might communicate the light of the Bible and the knowledge of the true God to these my Heathen creatures. You have neglected this charge . . . and I have chastened you. But I have condoned your offences. I once raised you up, when no other hand could save you. I once more consign this people to your charge. . . and say take warning from the past. Let us take warning. A Christian policy is the only policy of hope."

The British acted as trustees to God, not to the I Indians. But Sir Bartle Frere thought it would "convince the natives generally that we meant to use our temporal power for their conversion," and provoke a full scale rebellion.

The British officials adopted another "crusadee, in that they suggested that the jails be opened to missionary teaching. In November 1858, this idea was given "hearty blessings" by the district officer Edward Prinsep. To the British Officers it was "our preference for that religion which alone we believe to be true." This meant all other religions were not true. However, this request was disallowed by the Viceroy, Lord Canning, who thought that it would mean "turning the machinery of justice and civil government to religious purposes." He further pointed out: "Let us not now, give a handle to the supposition that we sentence them to imprisonment in our jails for the same purpose under the pretence of administering justice." Thus, though the missionaries and the British Officers urged the government "to evangelize the great Indian races," but the British government refused to listen to the "Christian policy".

"The chief worry of these years (1807-14 when Lord Minto was the Governor-General in India)", writes Muir, "was the propagandist fervour of English missionaries, whose activity was due to the Evangelical Revival at that time stirring England. It sometimes took rather offensive forms which were sternly discouraged; for it was the Company's principle that the most complete neutrality and protection must be maintained towards the various religious and customs of their Empire."

The Great Uprising of 1857

FREDERICK JOHN SHORE

I

AS THE BRITISH SEE IT

Indian Mutiny, 1857-58

One of the results of reports of heavy British losses in the Crimea was to assist in bringing to a crisis the dangerous situation then existing in India. The Company's army was mainly Indian, and of these 311,000 Indians (including local levies), two-thirds belonged to the Bengal Army in which Purbiahs[1] from Oudh formed a very powerful element. Their attitude had for years been unsatisfactory and several minor mutinies had taken place, but belief in the "good fortune" of the Company had prevented a general outbreak. Now that belief was waning. Discipline was lax; regulations diminished the power of commanding-officers; and the sepoys began to consider themselves the real masters. "The chief thing that bred the rebellion", subsequently stated an Indian officer, "was the knowledge of the power the sepoys had, and the little control the Sahibs were allowed to exert over them. They naturally from this fancied the Sirkar must be afraid of them; whereas it only trusted them too well". There were of course other important contributory causes, such as discontent in certain areas over Lord Dalhousie's annexations notably Jhansi, Satara, Oudh and the wide territories of the Bhonsla of Nagpur (now the Central Provinces), which lapsed to Government on the failure of direct heirs, but these would not in all probability have led to serious trouble had the sepoys been loyal. And in all India there were but 40,000 British troops. Further, there was Brahman antagonism to the march of modern invention, such as railways, telegraphs, etc., which they considered subversive to their influence.

A Spark to the Tinder

In January 1857 a grievous mistake of the Home Government applied a spark to the tinder. The introduction of the Enfield rifle, an improved pattern of the Minie, necessitated the use of greased cartridges, and there is little doubt that the grease used at Woolwich Arsenal for the cartridges sent out to India, the ends of which had to be bitten-off, was derived from "bovine-tallow". To British troops this would not matter, but to the Hindu the cow is sacred, and to bite cartridges so greased would certainly lead to the loss of a Hindu's caste, with all that implied. Realizing the danger, the Indian Government directed that the men should use only grease of which they themselves approved, but in vain. An Indian embroidery on the original fact was that pig's fat had also been used, thus uniting Mohammedan with Hindu in a common opposition. Sepoys refused to handle even ungreased cartridges, and several cases of open defiance on parade occurred. These were dealt with, but not very decisively, and on Sunday, May 10th, 1857, the big outbreak at Meerut took place. It was timed for the hour of church parade when British troops would be unarmed. Officers were murdered, houses burnt, and prisoners released, and the revolted regiments hurried off to Delhi, where dwelt Bahadur Shah, the aged representative of the Mughal dynasty and—in title at any rate—the "Kaisar-i-Hind".

An Outworn Army

Even now the outbreak might have been confined within moderate-limits had active and energetic men occupied the senior positions; but in the Bengal Army the objection of the Government to paying pensions until the recipients were practically on their death-beds rendered this impossible. Had, for instance, the Commander at Meerut taken resolute action the Mutiny might perhaps have been nipped in the bud. But the higher ranks were filled with officers who, twenty or thirty years previously, had been efficient enough, but who had only attained responsible positions when they were far too old for decisive measures. Now, under the strain of active service they rapidly collapsed and died. The Commander-in-Chief, General the Hon. George Anson, was in the hills at Simla with his whole staff, and so was cut-off from the Governor-General, Lord Canning, at Calcutta where British reinforcements must land and plans be made.

This, fortunately, was not the whole of the picture. There were many young and able officers in India like Lawrence, but these had largely sought advancement in political posts or in the newly-raised Frontier Force stationed in the Punjab and beyond the Indus. They could not therefore prevent the outbreak of the regular sepoys down-country, but it was they and the men they commanded and raised who largely saved the situation. On May 27th General Anson died of cholera and was succeeded by General Barnard, who himself died of cholera on July 5th.

The Heroic Handful

The outstanding fact of the Mutiny is that the bulk of the hard fighting was done by the very limited number of British troops and loyal Indians available at the outset. Troops were brought back from the Persian Gulf, where a small expedition under Sir James Outram had just been brought to a satisfactory conclusion,[2] and others were intercepted on their way to China, where the second Chinese War had begun in 1856, but no considerable force was available for the best part of a year, by which time British reinforcements from home had arrived and fresh Indian units had been raised. Vast, therefore, as was the stage, the fighting was numerically against tremendous odds till right at the end, and during this critical initial period it is probable that only the fact that the rebels had no one capable, with the exception of a civilian and a woman, of any real leadership saved the situation.

Delhi, the ancient capital of India and recently refortified by British engineers, had fallen into the hands of the rebels on May 11th, when the mutineers from Meerut had arrived and been joined by the troops in the city. The Europeans who could not manage to escape were massacred. The arsenal, held by three subalterns, four warrant-officers and two sergeants only, was held against hordes of mutineers for three long hours and was finally blown up, inflicting heavy loss on the rebels. Five of the heroic defenders succeeded in escaping and were each awarded the Victoria Cross. Sir George Mac-Munn has recently brought to light the important fact that this "arsenal" only contained fifty barrels of gunpowder for practice ammunition. The main magazine in the cantonments was not blown up and fell into the mutineers' hands with 3,000 barrels of gunpowder. It was this enormous reserve which enabled Delhi to be held against the British and made it the mutineers' natural rallying-point.

The Holding of the Ridge

Delhi must at all costs be speedily recaptured and soon a small force from the Punjab, only 3,500 strong, appeared on the Ridge outside Delhi, having defeated rebel detachments on the way at Ghazi-ud-din Nagar and Badli-ki-Serai. Its commander was General Barnard, who soon found himself in the position of besieged rather than besieger. The mutineers continually issued from the city and attacked the position, and the constant tale of losses were barely made good by the reinforcements which John Lawrence, deliberately running great risks in his own province, steadily sent down from the Punjab. Throughout the summer the British barely held their ground.

In and around the recently-conquered Punjab were the fighting races who form the bulk of the Indian Army of today. The work of John and Henry Lawrence and their helpers had borne its fruit, and a martial population respected the British and despised the caste-ridden sepoys of Oudh. And—to be frank—there were the riches of Delhi, the wealth of the Chandni Chauk, the famous "Silver Street", to urge them on. Together with the British regulars they marched swiftly on Delhi, at their head the man whose name was an inspiration, Brigadier General John Nicholson. Soon there were nearly twelve thousand men before Delhi, of whom over a quarter were British. Nonetheless the odds were tremendous. Delhi had acted as a magnet to the revolted sepoys from the surrounding stations; the city was full of them; they were well-provided with artillery and ammunition and had been joined by thousands of lawless individuals who saw their chance in anarchy and the breaking-up of laws.

The Decision to Assault

At this crucial moment the strongest wills came to the front. One after another, the elderly generals died, went sick, or were overborne. The real power was in the hands of younger men, Baird-Smith, Chamberlain. Daly of the "Guides", Alexander Taylor, the brilliant engineer, and, above all, John Nicholson himself. The nominal commander, Brigadier-General Archdale Wilson, still hesitated as well he might, but he had Nicholson to deal with. Lord Roberts, then a subaltern in the Bengal Horse Artillery, was acting as Nicholson's staff-officer and knew his intention. "Delhi must be taken", he said, "and it is absolutely essential that this should be done at once, and if Wilson hesitates longer, I intend to propose at today's meeting that he should be superseded." Luckily Wilson gave way, and on September 7th orders were issued for the batteries to be laid out. Before long the breaches in the Kashmir and Water bastions were considered practicable.

"Nikkalseyn is Dead !"

The losses had been so heavy that only five thousand men could be found for the assault, after providing for the protection of the camp. They were divided into five small columns. The first, under Nicholson himself, was to assault the Kashmir bastion, the second the Water bastion, the third the Kashmir gate, the fourth the Kabul gate and the fifth remained in reserve. On the morning of September 14th the columns dashed forward to the assault. Nicholson, at the Kashmir bastion, was the first to climb the breach. The second column carried the Water bastion, and two gallant engineers, Lieutenants Home and Salkeld, blew in the Kashmir gate. Three columns were now inside the walls. Before them stretched a maze of narrow streets and lanes, desperately defended and filled with hostile snipers. Nicholson, in the narrow lane leading to the Burn bastion, sprang forward ahead of all urging on his men. A shot took him in the chest and he fell. Later, Lieutenant Roberts found an abandoned "doolie" by the roadside. In it was General Nicholson. "On my expressing a hope that he was not seriously wounded, he said: 'I am dying; there is no chance for me.' The sight of that great man lying helpless and on the point of death was almost more than I could bear. Other men had daily died around me, friends and comrades had been killed beside me, but I never felt as I felt then to lose Nicholson seemed to me at that moment to lose everything." Once again the old fire flashed forth. Hearing that Wilson contemplated withdrawing, the dying man exclaimed: "Thank God I have strength yet to shoot him, if necessary!" There was no withdrawal, and for nine days Nicholson lingered on. "His every thought", says Roberts, "was given to his country, and to the last he materially aided the military authorities by his clear-sighted, sound and reliable advice". So—in the words of the writer of "On the Face of the Waters"—"John Nicholson stands symbol of the many lives lost uselessly in the vain attempt to go forward too fast. Yet his voice echoes still to the dark faces and the light alike—'Come on, men! Come on' !"

The Capture of Delhi

The events of September 14th had placed the British in control of only a sector of the city-walls, and to avoid further heavy casualties in street-fighting such as had led to the loss of Nicholson, it was necessary on Taylor's suggestion to sap through from house to house. In this way ground was gradually gained and by September 20th Delhi was once more in the hands of the British. The mutineers and their allies fought stubbornly, but were always at a disadvantage from having no effective central command. The serious nature of the fighting is shown by the fact that in the Delhi campaign the British losses amounted to close on 4,000, of whom somewhat more than half were European, a very large percentage of the small force engaged. An episode which took place on September 21st led to much subsequent controversy. The emperor, Bahadur Shah, had taken refuge with two sons and IInd grandson at the Tomb of Humayun, the second Mughal emperor, outside the city. Hodson, the dashing leader of "Hodson's Horse", followed him there and obtained his surrender on a promise that his life should be spared. The promise was kept, but Hodson refused to make any pledge with regard to the princes who were accused of responsibility for the murder of European ladies. Having handed over the emperor, Hodson returned and seized the princes, but, being pressed on by a mob on the way back, he halted and shot the three captives with his own hand. Whether necessary or not, this act was the end of the Mughal dynasty. Bahadur Shah was sent as an exile to Rangoon where he subsequently died.

Before, however, the siege of Delhi had been brought to a successful conclusion, tragic events had been happening elsewhere.

The Tragedy of Cawnpore

Cawnpore, on the banks of the Ganges and some forty miles from Lucknow, was garrisoned by four sepoy regiments and a handful of British artillerymen, On the news of the outbreak at Meerut the divisional commander, Sir Hugh Wheeler, who had no illusions as to the loyalty of the sepoys, decided to construct a place of refuge in which the considerable European population, of whom about half were women and children, might take shelter. Not wishing, however, to precipitate an outbreak by withdrawing the sepoy guard from the magazine, which was strong and easily defensible and should at all costs have been occupied, he set about tracing out an entrenchment in the open to the south of the city. Apparently the idea was that if the sepoys did break out they would march away in the opposite direction, i.e., towards Delhi. When, on

June 4th and 5th, the sepoys rose in revolt, the Europeans took refuge within this poor enclosure, the walls of which were only about four feet high. Here, from June 6th to June 26th, less than nine hundred Europeans, of whom only three hundred were soldiers, withstood the attacks of three thousand mutineers, who had indeed marched towards Delhi and then returned, backed by the heavy guns from the magazine. Night and day the narrow space was swept by a continuous fire, the water-supply was scanty, food was short, and soon the flimsy barracks were set on fire with red-hot shot. Yet in this ghastly situation the desperate garrison beat off attack after attack, and even sallied forth and spiked some of the guns which were battering their poor defences to pieces. At last the rebels would face them no more and sought by treachery to achieve what fighting could not do.

The Infamy of the Nana

Living at Bithur near Cawnpore was Dhundu Pant, commonly called the Nana Sahib, the adopted son of Baji Rao, the last Peishwa of Poona. Though generously treated by Government, he had always cherished a bitter hatred of the British on account of the annexation of the Peishwa's domains, to which he had no real claim at all. For years he had dissembled his real feelings but on the mutiny of the sepoys, he proclaimed himself as Peishwa, and put himself at their head. It was this man who, on June 25th, sent proposals to the garrison for a safe-conduct by water to Allahabad. Though now an enemy he had previously been on very friendly terms with the European inhabitants of Cawnpore, particularly with General Wheeler, and trusting to this, the offer of a safe conduct was accepted.

On June 27th the survivors of the garrison left their entrenchments for the boats waiting by the river-bank. As they began to embark, musketry, cannon-shot and grape were suddenly poured upon them, and a horrible massacre took place. One boatload only managed to push-off into the stream. Relentlessly pursued, the boat was lost, and struggling over land or swimming for dear life in the water, only two officers and two men eventually won through to—safety. On the river-bank or in Cawnpore all the men among the survivors were put to death by the orders of the pitiless Nana, and about two hundred wretched women and children were dragged back to Cawnpore. There they were herded into a small building called the Bibigarh. But already vengeance was on its way.

The March on Cawnpore

Farther down the Ganges at Allahabad, a small force was slowly collecting as reinforcements came up from Calcutta. There were men from three battalions of the Queen's troops, the Madras Fusiliers, the famous "Blue-Caps," under their relentless Colonel Neill, Brasyer's Sikhs and some improvised European cavalry. The command was entrusted to Brigadier-General Henry Havelock, an earnest Baptist and an accomplished soldier who had grown grey waiting for the chance of command which he had never had till now. On June 20th he reached Allahabad, too late to save the victims of Cawnpore. On July 7th he marched out at the head of his little army, less than 2,000 strong, but every man filled with a consuming fire for vengeance.

This was the grimmest episode of the Mutiny. Day after day the little force marched on over the vast level plain, dotted with villages burnt and abandoned in the anarchy which had set in, along roads where the corpses of suspected rebels—often indeed suspected with very little reason—dangled from trees where the advanced-guard had hanged them. At Fatehpur on July 12th and at Aung on July 15th the rebels vainly attempted to stay their course. It was reported that the women and children in Cawnpore were still alive and the troops, though dropping in scores from cholera and heat-stroke, were not to be denied. On July 16th they were outside Cawnpore and there the rebels, led by the Nana in person, made a stand. The British charged straight at the guns and drove the enemy in headlong rout. Next day Havelock marched in, but the tragedy had already been consummated. Two days previously the Nana, fearful Jest his victims should escape, had sent five butchers into the Bibigarh armed with slaughtering-knives and these had deliberately hacked nearly two hundred women and children to death. Their remains were cast into a well close at hand. A member of the Indian Civil Service who accompanied Havelock's force wrote: "When we got to the coping of the well and looked over we saw, at no great depth, a ghastly tangle of naked limbs. . . There is no object in saying more." The well was filled up and later a garden was laid out round it with a monument, "Sacred to the perpetual memory of a great company of Christian people, chiefly women and children". The exact numbers were never known

Sir Henry Lawrence

The recovery of Cawnpore, although too late to save the beleaguered garrison, opened the way to some extent for the next task, the relief of the Residency at Lucknow. The fact that Lucknow had not already shared the fate of Cawnpore was due to the foresight of Sir Henry Lawrence who, having made a great reputation in the Punjab, was now Chief Commissioner of Oudh. He was in an immensely difficult situation, since there were four mutinous sepoy regiments in Lucknow and others might be expected to join them from the surrounding stations. He had, however, one British battalion, the Thirty-second Foot, and was able to add to them a few hundred loyal sepoys and pensioners, with whom he planned to hold an area about a mile in circumference in the centre of Lucknow, based on the hastily-fortified Residency and some adjacent buildings. On the news of the peril at Cawnpore, Lawrence sent-off fifty men of the Thirty-second who shared the fate of Wheeler's garrison, but he could do no more, and during the struggle at Cawnpore was mainly occupied in dealing with local outbreaks. Following the news of Wheeler's surrender, and the subsequent massacre, a rebel force collected near Lucknow, and Lawrence resolved to much out and disperse them. Unhappily the many years he had spent as an administrator had left him less conversant with military necessities and at the action at Chinhat on June 30th he was repulsed, and had to fall back on Lucknow with considerable loss. This was the signal for a general rising, and Lawrence found himself besieged within the ring of improvised fortifications he had previously constructed. The area was soon under shell-fire, and on July 2nd a shell burst in the room in which Sir Henry was working and mortally wounded him. Thus died one of the noblest characters in the history of British India, a man whose life-work is best described in the epitaph he had himself chosen, "Here lies Henry Lawrence, who tried to do his duty".

The Defence of the Residency

On the death of Lawrence the command passed to Brigadier-General Inglis, a determined soldier who had resolved after the tragedy of Cawnpore never to surrender. His garrison numbered some seventeen hundred, of whom slightly more than half were Europeans. There were in addition many women and children now within a hair's breadth of sharing the fate of those at Cawnpore. In spite of sickness, scanty food, assaults, constant bombardment and the ever-present risk of exploding mines under their frail defences, all alike were filled with heroic constancy, and week after week still maintained their position. But their losses were very heavy and starvation was believed to be inevitable. Actually, as Sir George MacMunn has shown, Sir Henry Lawrence had provided, in underground storehouses, immense quantities of grain. But he had not informed the military staff and so Inglis, like Townshend at Kut-al-Amara, believing himself to be nearer starvation than he really was, urged an immediate rescue. Later, as these stores were gradually discovered, they proved ample for both the original garrison and Havelock's relieving force, and when these in turn were relieved by Sir Colin Campbell, huge stores of grain had to be destroyed or abandoned. But as matters stood at the moment, the desperate appeals of the beleaguered garrison had their natural effect, and Havelock set out with little more than fifteen hundred men, determined to rescue the garrison of Lucknow or perish in the attempt.

The First Relief of Lucknow

On July 29th Havelock defeated the enemy at Unao and again at Bashiratganj, two victories in one day; but from cholera, heatstroke and sheer exhaustion, his force was fought to a standstill, and he had to fall back on Cawnpore. On August 5th he again advanced, and again defeated the rebels at Bashiratganj, but was again forced to halt. On September 15th Major-General Outram arrived, but the "Bayard of India," although his senior, generously allowed Havelock to continue in command and accompanied him in his civil capacity as Chief Commissioner of Oudh. Reinforcements had now come up, and the total force now amounted to about 3,000.

On September 19th the advance began again. At the same moment arrived another letter from Inglis with the news that the garrison were starving. On the 21st Havelock repulsed the enemy at Mangalwar and on September 23rd Lucknow was in sight. But between the relieving-force and their goal stretched a fortified position with strong loop-holed buildings, the Alam Bagh, the Charbagh bridge, the Kaisar Bagh, and the Chattar Manzil. Between these the army forced its way and plunged into the city. Fired on from every side the troops pressed on. Soon the Residency was in sight, and with one last rush the relieving force was through and on September 25th the heroic garrison was saved.

The Second Siege of the Residency

The heavy losses of both besieged and their helpers had created a difficult situation. To save the garrison Outram and Havelock had been compelled to put in every available man, and their line of communications had gone. It was impossible to withdraw the women and children through the narrow streets under fire without a much stronger force, and all that had really been done was to reinforce the garrison. At this point, however, the supplies of grain, hitherto unsuspected, which Lawrence had laid in began to be discovered. Outram therefore determined to hold on and await relief. His force was strong enough to defy effective assault, and by adopting an aggressive policy he turned the siege more into the nature of a blockade. Sickness, however, was rife, and the losses from it very heavy.

The Second Relief of Lucknow

At this stage in the campaign the new Commander-in-

Chief in India arrived, Sir Colin Campbell, almost the only senior officer who had left the Crimea with an enhanced reputation. While by no means a great general, since he was too cautious for Indian warfare and so inclined to miss opportunities, Sir Colin was as brave as a lion, always up with the vanguard and very energetic in his irascible fashion. He had few troops available, since reinforcements from England and the Cape were only just arriving, but the conclusion of the siege of Delhi made it possible to send down a column nearly three thousand strong which reached Cawnpore via Agra. With these and the reinforcements Campbell now had about five thousand men, but he was obliged to leave General Windham—known as "Redan" Windham from his share in the attack on it—with a small force to guard Cawnpore. There was a distinct risk in leaving Cawnpore, for the Gwalior Contingent—mistakenly left at a strength of over 20,000 after Maharajpur and Paniar—had now revolted, and secured as a leader Tantia Topi, a civilian hanger-on of the Nana Sahib, but a skilful and active commander. This force was now moving via Kalpi to attack Cawnpore and Outram, in one of his smuggled letters, unselfishly advised Sir Colin to deal with them first. The Commander-in-Chief was anxious to relieve Lucknow and decided otherwise. With the bulk of his force he moved on Lucknow, and occupied the Alam Bagh on November 12th and the Dilkusha on November 14, thus following a route recommended by Outram through a European clerk named Kavanagh, who with great courage has passed through the enemy's lines disguised as an Indian.[3] On November 16th progress was stopped by a fortified building called the Sikandar Bagh, garrisoned by two thousand rebel sepoys. A breach was battered in the wall and the place stormed with the beyonet. The defenders were caught in a trap and, with the exception of a handful who jumped from the wall, the whole garrison was exterminated. The troops had seen the well at Cawnpore and showed no mercy. The Shah Najif was taken in the same way, and the next day the Moti Mahal. Prominent in the capture of the latter was Captain Garnet Wolseley, who had distinguished himself both in Bunna and the Crimea and who went into every action with the determination to make a name for himself at any risk. This was the last obstacle, and that day the relieving force joined hands with Outram and Havelock. Lucknow was at last relieved.

Campbell, however, decided that it would be undesirable to lock up a force within the Residency perimeter and so, having successfully evacuated the women and children to the Dilkusha, where they would be in temporary security, at midnight on November 22nd he withdrew his whole force thither, in readiness to assist Windham at Cawnpore were it necessary. Among the sick carried out was General Havelock, worn out by dysentery. "I have for forty years so ruled my life", he said, "that when death came I might face it without fear". On the 24th he died and was buried outside the city with which his name will ever be linked.

The Advance of Tantia Topi

No news had meanwhile come from Windham at Cawnpore and Sir Colin was getting anxious. Leaving Outram with a portion of his force to watch Lucknow, be set out with the remainder for Cawnpore. As he approached the city successive messages came in with tales of disaster. The wily Tantia, as soon as Sir Colin's back was turned, had approached Cawnpore, and the impetuous Windham, disregarding to fact that his duty was to protect Cawnpore and the bridge of boats across the Ganges on which Campbell's communications depended, had on November 26th sallied out and attacked the enemy. In this engagement he was successful, but then fell back, and next day Tantia followed him up and attacked in much superior force and with a very powerful artillery. The fight went very badly and on the following day Windham was forced back within his entrenchments with a loss of three hundred men and a great quantity of transport, baggage and stores. Only the vital bridge of boats was still held, and there on the evening of November 28th Sir Colin Campbell arrived, riding far in advance of his army. A luckless officer at the bridge-head was so ill-advised as to say, "Thank God, you have come, Sir. The troops are at their last gasp". At this Sir Colin's Highland spirit blazed out: "How dare you say, Sir, of Her Majesty's troops that they are EVER at their last gasp !"

The Situation Restored

During the night the force from Lucknow came in, bringing with it the huge convoy of sick and wounded and the refugees from the Residency. Under protection of the British guns, which held off Tantia's artillery, the mass of transport was got across the bridge, taking from the afternoon of the 29th till the evening of the 30th to do so. The refugees were then sent on to Allahabad and safety, and at last, on December 6th, Campbell was free to deal with Tantia. He had at his disposal five thousand infantry, six hundred cavalry and thirty-five guns, the enemy numbering some twenty-five thousand with forty guns. In this third battle of Cawnpore the superiority of the British forces, was decisively demonstrated. Part of the rebels' position was an open plain and there Campbell delivered his main attack. It was completely successful; the enemy were routed, their camp rushed, and the flying rebels were hunted for a distance of fourteen miles. Only the failure of Campbell's chief-of-staff, General Mansfield, to arrange for the cutting-off of the enemy's retreat as Sir Colin had planned, prevented the victory from being complete. As it was, the Commander-in-Chief had captured nineteen guns and inflicted very heavy loss on the enemy with less than one hundred British casualties. This was the decisive battle. From hence forward the British were no longer struggling for existence but merely putting down a rebellion. The villainous Nana narrowly escaped at Bithur from the pursuit of a party led by Roberts and got across the Ganges into Oudh, where he twisted and turned seeking to escape the vengeance which was striving to overtake him.

The Final Occupation of Lucknow

By the beginning of 1858 Sir Colin Campbell was for the first time at the head of an adequate force. Including 9,000 Gurkhas sent by Jang Bahadur, the ruler of Nepal, he had over 30,000 men and a very powerful artillery including some 64 pounders landed from H.M.S. Shannon. With this force he determined to rejoin Outram, who was still holding on to the Alam Bagh, and finish with Lucknow once and for all. This, during the month of March he successfully accomplished, bettering down one fortified building after another but failing to cut-off or round-up the rebels in any considerable numbers. The result was that the revolted sepoys were simply driven out into the surrounding country and the final suppression of the rebellion considerably delayed. The same thing happened in May, when Sir Colin recaptured Bareilly, the centre of the revolt in Rohilkhand. The enemy were defeated but got away, thereby necessitating the employment under most exhausting conditions of many small columns for their final suppression.

The Rani of Jhansi

Nana Sahib was not the only Mahratta who cherished a grudge against the Government. Left a widow in 1854, the Rani of Jhansi had been refused by Lord Dalhousie the succession for her adopted son as Hindu custom permitted. From henceforward a bitter enemy of the British, she took advantage of the mutiny of two sepoy regiments at Jhansi—even if she did not actually instigate it—to wreak her revenge. On June 7th, 1857, the survivors of the Europeans, who had taken refuge in the Fort, found this position to be hopeless, and were tempted by the Rani's promises to lay down their arms on a promise of safe conduct. Once outside the Fort, every man, woman and child, to the number of sixty-six, was promptly massacred. Sharing the guilt of the Nana Sahib and Tantia Topi, the Rani from now on co-operated with them and showed more courage and determination than any other of the rebel leaders. With both Tantia and the Rani to deal with, the suppression of the rebellion in Central India would have been a difficult matter but for the personality of the general entrusted with the task.

Sir Hugh Rose

Major-General Sir Hugh Rose, though he had never previously served in India, displayed from the outset the very qualities of speed and activity in which Sir Colin Campbell was deficient. His force was but small, some six thousand men, of whom slightly less than half were Europeans, but he used it in a masterly fashion. It is noteworthy that his Indian troops were drawn from the Bombay Army, which with very few exceptions had remained loyal and that he was co-operating with a column of the Madras Army, of which only one regiment had given any cause for suspicion at all. The Mutiny was almost solely the affair of the Bengal Army, and the help given by the other two Presidency Armies and the Punjab Irregular Force ("Irregular" only in the sense that it was not subject to the normal organization) was of very great aid in putting it down.

On December 16th, 1857, Sir Hugh Rose arrived at Indore, and by the beginning of February, he had captured the fort of Rahatgarh; entered Saugor in triumph, and was preparing to march on Jhansi. It was in this campaign that khaki clothing was first used on a considerable scale for active service outside the Punjab, though the "Guides" and the rest of the Punjab Irregular Force had been familiar for some years with its advantages under Indian conditions.

On March 21st Sir Hugh Rose arrived before the Fort of Jhansi, which, like so many Indian strongholds, was built on a rock and rendered as impregnable as art could make it. Nevertheless at the end of ten days, the defences were being gradually battered down when suddenly an unexpected peril assailed the British.

A Double Victory

Though Tantia Topi had been defeated by Sir Colin Campbell outside Cawnpore the previous December, he had succeeded in extricating the bulk of his force. Now, at the head of 20,000 men, he was advancing to the rescue of his ally, the Rani of Jhansi, who with eleven or twelve thousand men was being besieged by Sir Hugh Rose with half that number. It was impossible for Sir Hugh Rose to raise the siege without being attacked in the rear, but somehow Tantia must be dealt with. With extraordinary resolution Sir Hugh left two-thirds of his small force to carryon the siege and with less than two thousand men sallied forth on April 1st to the R. Betwa to attack Tantia. In spite of the odds of over ten to one, the British cavalry charges on the wings and an infantry attack in the centre decided the day in brilliant fashion. Tantia was decisively routed with the loss of twenty-eight guns and almost as many killed as the total strength of Rose's attacking force. The garrison of Jhansi had remained inactive at this crisis, deceived as to the British strength, and now, on April 3rd, after only one day's rest for the British, their turn was to come. Three columns stormed and escaladed the walls of Jhansi Fort in the early morning, and for two days a desperate struggle went on. No mercy was shown, for the massacre at Jhansi had been as atrocious in its way as that at Cawnpore. As the British fought their way nearer and nearer the resolution of the murderous Rani gave way, and on March 4th she fled to join her confederate Tantia at Kalpi. By March 6th the last survivors of the rebel garrison driven out of the Fort had been surrounded and bayoneted to a man, on "Retribution Hill", just outside Jhansi.

The Counterstroke of Tantia and the Rani

As soon as possible Sir Hugh Rose advanced on Kalpi. The heat was terrible and the casualties from it very heavy. Sir Hugh Rose, himself, is said to have had sunstroke five times and yet he steadily kept on. He was now in touch with a detachment from Sir Colin Campbell's army on the other side of the River Jumna. On May 22nd he defeated Tantia and the Rani at Golaoli outside Kalpi and the following day he entered Kalpi itself. The campaign now seemed over, and indeed both commander and troops were practically worn out.

The position of Tantia and the Rani appeared desperate, but they had still one last card to play. Away to the west was the great fortress of Gwalior, still held by the Maharaja Scindia in loyalty to the British. It was the mutiny of Scindia's Gwalior Contingent which had given Tantia an army in the first place, and Scindia had other troops who might be won over in the same way. The plot succeeded, and when, on June 1st, Scindia marched out to attack the remains of Tantia's army outside Gwalior, it was only to see his whole force go over to the rebels. He fled to Agra, and Tantia Topi, who, to do him justice, seems always to have been loyal to his villainous master, proclaimed the Nana Sahib as Peishwa in the fort of Gwalior.

The Last Battles and the Final Reckoning

On the news of this reverse, Sir Hugh Rose, collecting men as he could, marched on Gwalior. On June 16th, he defeated the enemy at Morar outside Gwalior, and the next day Brigadier-General Smith won the action of Kotah-ki-Serai close to the city. In this fight the Rani of Jhansi met her end, disguised as a rebel cavalryman. A trooper of the Eighth Hussars cut her down, thus avenging the death of the women and children at Jhansi just a year previously. On June 20th Gwalior surrendered; Scindia was reinstated, and Tantia Topi set out on his amazing flight up and down Central India and Rajputana with the British for ever at his heels. For months the pursuit went on, and then at last, on April 7th, 1859, Tantia was captured. On the 15th he was tried and condemned, and on the 18th he was hanged. The fate of his master, the Nana Sahib, is uncertain to this day. By some it is said that he perished of hardship some time in 1860 in the jungles at the Terai at the foot of the Himalayas, and by others that he died in hiding many years later. Order in India was not fully restored till the end of 1859, for many small columns had continually to sweep the country, breaking up rebel bands and hunting down mutineers. By this time the British troops in India numbered 96,000 besides a large force of Indians. At last the work was done and British authority re-established throughout the length and breadth of India. But it was on a different foundation. The British troops in India were now fixed at double their previous strength; all artillery, except a few mountain batteries, was British, and the Purbiahs of Oudh had been swept almost completely out of the Indian Army. Every regular cavalry regiment of the Bengal Army had vanished and all but thirteen regular battalions out of seventy-four. Their places were taken by new units formed out of the Indian soldiers of other races who had fought by our side in the long contest.

The End of "John Company"

Even before the Mutiny was fully suppressed an "Act for the Better Government of India" passed both Houses of Parliament and received the royal assent. In accordance with it, the transfer of the government of India to the Crown, acting through the Secretary of State and the Council of India, was proclaimed on November 1st, 1858. The royal declaration was couched (considering all that had passed) in singularly noble language, the forgiving phrases of which sank deep into the Indian mind and are frequently quoted to this day. It is doubtful whether the government has ever been more finely expressed than in the words: "In their prosperity will be our strength, in their contentment our security, and in their gratitude our great reward". From that date, the European regiments in the service of the East India Company were transferred to the British Army. The infantry regiments concerned came into the British Army List as the 101st to the 109th. The 18th, 19th and 20th Hussars and the 21st Lancers were also transferred. So came to an end the distinction between "Queen's" and "Company's".

Notes and References

1. I.e., "Easterners" (from the Punjab point of view).
2. Battle honours for Reshire, Bushire, Kooshab and Persia were given.
3. Kavanagh received the V.C.

II

ORIGIN OF THE 1857 GREAT UPRISING AND ITS FIRST MARTYR

T.A. Bhai

In 1857, Barrackpore near Calcutta was a big military cantonment having four regiments of native infantry assembled in a brigade. Since early that year great resentment was prevailing amongst the Indian troops for being forced to use Cartridges for the newly introduced Enfield rifle, which were greased with a substance known to contain the fat of cows and pigs.

The cartridges and the grease supplied to the troops at Barrackpore and in other stations in the Bengal Presidency were prepared in the Arsenal at Fort William, Calcutta. When Colonel A. Abbot, Inspector General of Ordnance and Magazines, came to know the objections, he wrote on 29th January, "I enquired the Arsenal as to the nature of the composition that had been used and found it was precisely that which the instructions received from the Court of Directors (England) directed to be used—viz., mixure of tallow and bees wax. . . ." He suggested the use of wax and oil as a substitute to the tallow till the grease of unobjectionable quality was substituted. Consequently powers were conferred on the Commanding Depot of Musketry at Dum Dum and Commanding Officers of other units to purchase *Ghee,* wax, oil and other prescribed ingredients from the *hazar* instead of obtaining grease from the Ordnance sources. But then it was found that the objection was not merely to the composition used in greasing the cartridges, but to the composition of the paper also with which the cartridges for the new rifles were made up.

The Regulation existing at that time for loading the firelock or rifle musket by the sepoys, stated:

> "1st—Bring the cartridge to the mouth, holding it between the fore-finger and thumb with the ball in the hand, and bite off the top; elbow close to the body."

The apprehension of the Indian troops about the composition of the grease which they were required to apply to the cartridges and the wax paper which every sepoy, while loading his rifle, was to bite it off, originated by the remarks of an Ordance *Khalasi* employed in the Calcutta Arsenal. The *Khalasi* asked a Brahmin Sepoy for some water from his *lota* but the latter refused to give the water due to reasons of caste. Thereupon the *Khalasi* said, "You will soon loose your caste, as were long you will have to bite cartridges covered with the fat of pigs and cows". The remarks spread like a wild fire amongst the Indian troops everywhere. Describing the situation and feelings of the Native soldiers at Barrackpore, Major General J.B. Hearsey Commanding the Bengal Presidency Division in his report dated 11th Feb., 1857 to the Government of India, said:

> "We have at Barrackpore been dwelling upon a mine ready for explosion. I have been watching the feelings of the sepoys here for some time; their minds have been misled by some designing scoundrels who have managed to make them believe that their religious prejudices, their caste, is to be interfered with the Government. *"That they are to be Forced to turn Christians."*

Giving his version of the origin of the trouble, Maj. Gen. Hearsey wrote, "A sepoy from one of the regiments here (Dum Dum) was walking to his *choka* to prepare his food with his *lota* full of water. He was met by a low-caste *Khalasi* (it is said one of the magazine or arsenal men). This *Khalasi* asked him to let him drink from the *lota*. The sepoy, a Brahmin, refused, saying—"I have scoured my *lota;* you will defile it by your touch." The *Khalasi* rejoined—"You think much of your caste but wait a little, the *Suheb-logue* will make you bite cartridges soaked in *cow* and *pork* fat, and then where will your caste be". General Hearsey added, "The sepoy made this speech known amongst his comrades at Dum Dum; the report was not long in travelling to this (Barrackpore) and other stations."

The repurcussions to the belief in the kinds of the Native troops that their religion and caste were being interfered with, were serious. Several European Officers' thatched houses and the telegraph bunglow at Barrackpore were burnt by incendiaries. On the night of 5th Feb., 1857 a secret meeting was held after the eight o'clock roll call at the parade ground where about three hundred native sepoys of different regiments who had their heads tied up with cloths leaving only a small part of the face exposed, assembled. There the question of killing the Europeans and plundering the Cantonment was discussed. But the information leaked out through a native officer (Jamadar) who was present at the meeting. Emissaries were then sent out from Barrackpore to Berhampore where on 26th Feb. night, Indian sepoys of various regiments stationed there gathered in a deserted tank and took oath to protect their religion and caste even at the cost of their lives. Consequently inspite of strict orders, the native sepoys totally refused to accept cartridges having a composition of cow and pig fat.

But what happened at Barrackpore on Sunday, the 29th March, 1857 was the first violent manifestation of the deep dissatisfaction towards the ruling Britishers. So far it was confined to presenting applications or meeting in deputations but on that day at three o'clock afternoon a young Brahmin sepoy named Mangal Panday of 34th Native Infantry Regiment suddenly appeared before the Quarter Guard armed with his musket which he took out for cleaning from bells-of-arms and a sword and ordered the bugler to sound the bugle for calling the sepoys to assemble. He declared in a loud and firm voice his intention to die for his religion and said that he would kill any European he would come across. He exhorted his fellow sepoys to join him in this religious war against the foreigners, saying "Nikal ao, pultun; nikal ao hamara sath." Great excitement prevailed in the camp and some shouts were raised against the use of the obnoxious grease and the cartridges. Soon after the British sergeant-major arrived on the scene and wanted to apprehend Mangal Panday but no native sepoy would come forward to help him. Mangal Panday dressed regimentally but with his *dhotee* took an aim and fired on the sergeant but missed. Thereupon the sergeant ran for his safety and took shelter behind the Quarter Guard. Meanwhile Lt. Baugh, adjutant, came riding up to the front. Mangal Panday presented his piece and fired, wounding the horse which fell. At this moment a sepoy Sheikh Paltoo came forward and helped Lt. Baugh to get clear of his horse. The adjutant then pulled out a pistol from his holster and saying—"That man will kill me, he is loading again" rushed towards Mangal Panday. The sergeant-major and Sheikh Paltoo followed him. He fired at Mangal Panday but missed him. On that Mangal Panday drew his sword and attacked the adjutant. A sharp hand to hand conflict ensued in which Mangal Panday faced two assailants, the adjutant and the sergeant-major. He fought desperately and wounded them both severely. Both the Europeans fell on the ground and another blow from the *Tulwar* of Mangal Panday might have despatched them if Sheikh Paltoo, himself injured, had not seized him round the waist with his left hand and averted further attacks. Seeing this, Jamadar Iswaree Panday, the Guard Commander and his men abused Sheikh Paltoo and said that if he did not let Mangal Panday go, they would shoot him. Both the wounded Europeans then slowly stood up and retreated quietly, several men of the quarter guard following and beating them with the buttend of their muskets.

Soon after Lt. Col. Wheeler, Commanding the 34th Regiment arrived on the spot and ordered the Guard Commander to capture Mangal Panday alive or dead. But the men would not advance. Then Brigadier Grant, Commanding at Barrackpore arrived followed by Major General Hearsey, commanding the Bengal Presidency Division, and his two sons, both Army Captains at that time. Mangal Panday after freeing himself from the hold of Sheikh Paltoo, reloaded his musket and stood there with musket in one hand and sword in the other, determined to challenge the might of the British power and for protection of his religion. No order or appeal could disuade him to break his vow to drive out the foreigners from the sacred soil of India. He called upon his fellow sepoys to join him in this holy war against *Feringees* and for protection of their religion. Reinforced by the presence of several European officers, General Hearsey ordered the guard men to load their rifles and advance towards Mangal Panday, saying that he himself would shoot with his pistol anybody disobeying the order. All the European Officers and the guard sepoys then moved towards Mangal Panday who instantly changed his mind and instead of firing on the advancing column which included his Indian colleagues also, shot himself through the chest and collapsed with his sword under him. The resultant wound although serious did not kill him.

He was immediately removed to the Quarter Guard of Her Majesty 53rd Regiment where he was subjected to brutal treatment in order to find out his accomplices and organised plot if any to drive out the Britishers from India. On the 4th April, to a question by Major W.A. Cooke, Field officer of the week, Mangal Panday replied, "I acted on my own free will. I expected to die". He was asked frequently if he would give up the names of any connected with the occurence, but he refused. Dr. T.B. Reid, Asst. Surgeon, 53rd Regiment under whose charge he was treated him sympathetically. The Doctor admired his courage, patriotism and forbearance and tried to help him on the day of his court martial. When asked to render the fitness certificate on 6th April, Dr. Reid wrote, "Sepoy Mangal Panday has not improved his health since he came under my charge; he has been gradually becoming weaker, and is now much debilitated. The wound also presents an unhealthy appearance". But immediately after that another Doctor James Allen, Asst. Surgeon 34th Regiment, Native Infantry certified that "Mangal Panday sepoy, No. 1446, 5th Company, 34th Regiment, Native Infantry, is in a fit state to undergo his trial this day".

On the same day he was brought before a standing Native Court Martial presided over by Subedar-Major Jawahar Lal Tiwari and with fourteen native officers as members, for trial on two charges of Mutiny and Violence against his superior officers. Five witnesses including Lt. Col. Wheeler who acted as the Prosecutor also and Sheikh Paltoo the only Indian witness, gave evidence. Mangal Panday, although grown very weak due to his wound, kept up his composure throughout. He declined to cross-examine the prosecution witnesses. When called on for his defence he was reported to have said, "I did not know who I wounded and who I did not," and added "I have no evidence". The trial lasted for only one day and on the same day i.e. 6th April, 1857, the court found Mangal Panday guilty of both charges and after examining his record of service which showed him good in all respects during his military service of seven years, two months and nine days, sentenced him 'to suffer death by being hanged by the neck until he be dead'. The death sentence (eleven officers voted for it) was approved and confirmed by Maj. Gen. Hearsey on 7th April and the execution was fixed to take place on the next morning at half past five o'clock on the brigade parade ground in presence of all the troops off duty at the station.

In the dark cell of the 53rd European Regiment Quarter Guard lay on the ground Mangal Panday, a young sepoy of twenty-six years, weak in bodily strength but strong in spirit, determined to sacrifice his life for the sake of his religion and country. Unmindful of the severe pain, the ghastly wound gave him and the death sentence already pronounced, the first Indian, who took up arms and revolted against the British rulers thought over the helplessness of his country men. He remembered back the year of 1824 when in that year on the same parade ground, where he would be hanged, were slaughtered hundreds of unarmed native sepoys of 47th Regiment for their crime of petitioning the British authorities that they should not be sent by sea for service in Burma. Then his thought turned to his colleague Sepoy Hira Lal Tiwari, who had since absconded, who struck both the adjutant and sergeant-major with the butt of his musket. "What will happen to him and to Jemadar Iswaree Panday and other men of his regiment 1". He whispered to himself. Only a week back on 31st March, 1857 the 19th Regiment stationed at Behrampore was brought to Barrackpore and disbanded and all the men sent to their homes. "Would the same thing happen to his Regiment also for the second time?" "Only a few days ago we the Indian sepoys of the various units in the station were not permitted to celebrate the *Holi* festival together. Are we slaves in our own land ?" protested Mangal Panday lying alone on the ground in the small dark room on the eve of his martyrdom.

At that time suddenly a storm started blowing. It soon grew into a tempest which uprooted trees, thatched roofs and tents and caused much damage to the buildings. It was accompanied by a violent outbreak of thunder and lightning as if nature was very angry with the intended hanging of a patriot.

It also indicated the stormy days which were to follow the execution of Sepoy Mangal Panday. Waves of the Ganga flowing nearby also became most turbulent and the sky turned red as if with wrath. Confirming the outbreak of this sudden and unprecedented tempest on the evening of 7th April, 1857, Maj. Gen. Hearsey wrote in a letter, "The 84th Queen's arrived at Barrackpore from Chinsurah at 6 p.m. on 7th evening during a most violent storm. I kept them on board the steamers and when the storm had passed over at about midnight, the cops was moved upto camp".

Early morning on 8th April, 1857, Mangal Panday offered his prayers to the Almighty for the liberation of his countrymen and his thanks giving for the role allotted to him to be the pioneer in the armed struggle against the British rulers. Meanwhile all the men of the Native brigade and all other European and Native troops stationed at Barrackpore were drawn up on parade. Sepoy Mangal Panday was marched under heavy escort to the gallows. Although very weak, he walked steadily to the place of execution and even at the gallows he did not show any sign of nervousness. Rather a sign of satisfaction of some achievement was lit on his face. After the execution the columns of the Native infantry were advanced close to the gallows to have a close look at a man whom the British rulers condemned to death for being a mutineer but who, for his countrymen, became the first martyr of the 1857 Great Uprising.

III

WHEN DELHI WAS LOST AND WON BY THE ENGLISH

V. Longer

On the Midnight of May 11-12 a 21-gun salute was fired to proclaim the return of the Moghul rule to Delhi. The old, decrepit and tottering Bahadur Shah, the last scion of Babar, became the Emperor of India reluctantly. He had quailed and temporised but he was bludgeoned into ascending the throne! That was in 1857, the year of the Great Revolt, when Delhi was wrested from foreign rule and the walled city remained free for about four and a half months.

On May 12, Emperor Bahadur Shah II paraded the streets of Delhi mounted on a richly caparisoned elephant appealing to the citizens and traders to resume their normal life and advising the unruly Sepoys to exercise restraint. On the same day the English, who were in panic, had evacuated their families from the cantonment (which was where the present University campus is) and huddled them up for security in the Flag Staff Tower.

There was chaos and confusion in the city of Delhi. Arson, murder, looting and bloodshed were prevailing. Angry Sepoys and unlawful elements went out on the rampage. Englishmen who had been taken prisoners were marched to the Red Fort and sabred and sliced to death. *Two* signallers in the telegraph office, outside the city flashed a message to Ambala warning the British administration.

The Great Revolt had travelled to Delhi via Meerut. There at 5 P.M. on May 10, the fire had been ignited. The 3rd Cavalry and the 20th and the 11th Native Infantry had revolted. The next morning, most of the Sepoys who had revolted took the road to Delhi. There was a King in Delhi and a throne. Both the King and the throne were the symbol of power. The Sepoys needed *that* symbol.

The Meerut Sepoys, astride their chargers, crossed the Yamuna by the bridge of boats and were upon the Red Fort, clamouring for the King below the palace window. The Calcutta gate was closed but the Rajghat gate was thrown open and the lava of revolt poured in. The 54th Native Infantry and the 38th Native Infantry in Delhi revolted and joined the Meerut Sowars.

There was little military activity till June 8 when the English won their first *victory* at Badli-ki-Sarai and moved the Headquarters of their Delhi Field Force to the Ridge which was bare, rocky and hot. The English tents were pitched behind it. The left of the rocky chain went up to the Yamuna. The Ludlow Castle and the famous Matcalf House were situated in that direction. The right end approached the Kabul gate of Delhi. Hindu Rao's house, an Observatory, the Flag Staff Tower and an "old Pathan type" mosque, which afforded shelter and accommodation to the British troops, were located on that side.

Several attempts were made to dislodge the English from the Ridge and the biggest and most determined push came on June 23, 1857, the day which marked the hundredth anniversary of the *battle* of Plassey. It had been predicted that the English rule would disappear exactly a hundred years after Clive's victory. The Meerut and Delhi Sepoys fought valiantly and desperately. But the English won. Superior weapons, better leadership and better organisation helped.

Nevertheless, the English were facing many problems. Heat, cholera and dysentry were taking a heavy toll. The prices of foodstuff, meat and other necessities of life were shooting up; their supplies were becoming irregular and insufficient.

On the other hand, the forces within the walls of Delhi were no happier. Emperor Bahadur Shah was finding it impossible to conduct the affairs of the State with an empty treasury and an unruly mob of Sepoys. There was shortage of food and gun powder. To make matters worse there were palace intrigues, mutual suspicions and constant espionage conducted by the agents of the English who were attempting to cause disruption. There was no well thought out concerted operational plan. Discipline and leadership were lacking and treachery was not absent.

The operational situation changed when John Nicholson arrived on the Ridge on August 7. Five days later the Moghul army was driven away from the Ludlow Castle and on August 24, the British gained an important victory at Najafgarh.

The final assault on Delhi commenced on September II, when the English batteries opened up. Two days later the walls of the city were breached at two places and on the morning of September 14, the final attack, in four columns, was launched.

The Sepoys of Bahadur Shah fought with redoubtable courage and unrelenting valour. The first English column captured the Mori Bastion and the Kabul gate but a little beyond, its progress was thwarted by the Sepoys who refused to yield an inc. Nicholson himself received a fatal wound and his column had to get back to the Kabul gate. The second column too could not get beyond the point reached by Nicholson's troops. The fourth column failed and "had to beat a retreat".

However, it was the third English column, which achieved spectacular success. It blasted the Kashmir gate and as the gates fell with a remendous crash, the bugle sounded the advance. The column came up to the Church and the College, and then worked its way to the Jama Masjid. The English troops rested in Skinner's house and then fanned out in various directions. On September 20 the Red Fort and the Selimgarh fort were taken.

A terrible retribution followed. Delhi got its bloodbath. The city was ravaged and plundered by the English troops who shot and bayonetted any citizen they found. Poet Ghalib who was then alive lamented the fate of Delhi and mourned the loss of "thousands of my friends". Emperor Bahadur Shah was in hiding at Humayun's tomb. On September 21 he surrendered to Lt. Hodson and was incarcerated.

IV

THE SACK OF DELHI 1857-58 AS WITNESSED BY GHALIB

KRISHAN LAL

Greatness of Ghalib

Mirza Asad Ullah Khan, poetically surnamed Asad and Ghalib[1] was one of the greatest figures in Urdu Literature, the brightest star in the firmament of Urdu Poetry, and the most towering genius of his age, a great thinker and prose writer of eminence. Even in the contemporary world he was much honoured and respected. C.B. Saunders,[2] the Commissioner of Delhi Division, after the Mutiny wrote to the D.S. Macleod, Financial Commissioner of the Punjab on the 8th March, 1859, "Moulvie Asadullah Khan, otherwise commonly known as Mirza Nasheh, the Poet Laureate of Delhi is universally admitted to be a Persian Scholar of the greatest eminence and to be gifted with poetical talents of a high order. His only competitor in the arena of poetical fame at Delhi was the ex-king himself, but the former is considered to have been a more profound scholar and to have been a more gifted poet than the latter". Mr. M.D. Arnold,[3] Director of Public Instruction Punjab, wrote to the Financial Commissioner of the Punjab, "Assaddullah Khan is a man of great reputation and is considered, I believe a living representative in Hindustan of Persian Poetry and literature".

How could Ghalib stay in Delhi after the British Victory?

Mirza Ghalib was in Delhi when the Mutiny broke out on the 11th of May 1857. He remained there throughout the siege and also after its fall on 13th September. Fortunately he was living in Mohalla *Bili Maran*[4] in the house of Hakim Mohammad Hasan Khan. In that Mohalla there were a large number of houses of Hakims (indigenous medicine practitioners). They were in the service of Raja Narinder Singh, brother of the Ruler of Patiala State in the Punjab. The Raja had taken a promise from the Britishers that Mohalla (locality) would not be ransacked after the re-occupation of Delhi. Therefore the Raja's guard took charge of the Mohalla after the British victory and thus the Mohalla escaped wholesale destruction and its inhabitants the general massacre. The Raja was also an admirer of Ghalib.

Thus Mirza Ghalib had the good fortune of witnessing and having the first hand knowledge of the miserable plight of the citizens. He also noticed the large scale revengeful hangings of innocent citizens, the great pillage done by the British Army and the pulling down of many populous Mohallas of Delhi.

Sources of Study

We can get an excellent, detailed and reliable account of these events from his following writings:

1. *The letters written just after the Mutiny:* Mirza Ghalib wrote a large number of letters to his various friends. These letters contain good number of incidental references about the contemporary events and conditions of the people. A collection of his letters entitled "Urdu-i-Mulla" was published for the first time in 1869.

2. *Dastambu* in Persian is a narrative of incidents of the Mutiny in Delhi ranging from 11th May 1857 to 1st July 1858 and is a valuable record of contemporary events. Mirza Ghalib himself[5] wrote to Munshi Har Gopal, "I have written the account of the city and of myself from the 11th May 1857 (day of the commencement of the Mutiny) to the 1st of July, i.e. of fifteen months. The language of Dastambu is pure old Persian devoid of any Arabic words".

Mr. C.B. Saunders,[6] the Commissioner of Delhi had expressed the following unfavourable opinion about this book. "Ghalib has recently published Dastambu in which he has given a narrative of passing events during the present insurrection, principally as they had any personal effect on his own sections or in any way affected his position. With the exception of the peculiarity of the elegant but somewhat obsolete dictum in which he has written his narrative and which renders it therefore really unintelligible to all but the most abstrusive and erudite of Persian scholars, there is said to be nothing either very striking or original in the statements and opinions to which he has given expression in the work". In spite of this criticism and the fact that Ghalib has laid more emphasis on the *follies* of Indian Mutineers and has often crused them, one still gets a good account of British Revenge.

Khawaja Hasan Nizami[7] wrote, "Ghalib wrote this book after the Mutiny at a time when the life and honour of Muslims were in a very great danger. If his style and writing is hostile to the Indian Mutineers" we should not criticise him. In spite of very critical times, Ghalib wrote many things very boldly. Shaik Muhammad Ikram[8] says, "This book has got great value from historical point of view as it was written by a person who participated in these events from the beginning to the end". Gholam Rassul Mehr[9] says, "It cannot be said that Ghalib wrote this book for pleasing the English. He had started writing it at a time when hardly any body had belief in the victory of the English". Ghalib had said that he had written it during the Mutiny.

3. *An unpublished Petition* of Mirza Ghalib for the Restoration of his Pension. There is one petition of Mirza Ghalib for the restoration of his pension and robe of honour in the

Simla Record Office. A vivid account of his activities during the Mutiny which had been traced out by the British authorities, is also contained in the letters of Mr. C.B. Saunders.

4. *An elegy* (or mourning song) of Delhi.

Ghalib's activities during the Mutiny: There are two contrasting accounts of his activities. Ghalib himself wrote to Munshi Har Gopal.[10]

"I have not taken any part in the Mutiny. My innocence is well known." Again he wrote to Choudhry Abdul Ghaffar Khan,[11] "During all the period of turmoil, I have lived in this city. I have never stirred out of my house." The British authorities had in the beginning believed in this. Mr. C.B. Saunders[12] had written to the Financial Commissioner, "He certainly took no part either in our favour or against us".

But later on Mr. Saunders changed[13] his views. He wrote, "I deem it right to inform you that since writing above, I have accidently stumbled upon a passage in a news letter from Delhi during the late siege by Major Hodson, the officer-in-charge of the Intelligence Dept. which shows that the statements of the poet as to his having carefully abstained from presenting himself at the court, and from dedicating another composition to the Ex-King was not altogether veracious".

"I append a copy of the news letter for your information. It was written by one Goree Shankar of Delhi. The letter mentions that he devised and submitted for the approval of the Ex-King an Ephigrammatical superscription for the coin of the native which the later was then anxious to have struck in commemoration of his anticipated reconquest of India." This suspicion was enough to stop the payment of Ghalib's pension, Khillut and Darbar for three years.[14] But this immensely increased the hardships of Ghalib. He had already been in the habit of spending much. He used to get fifty rupees per month from the Red Fort. He was also deprived of this income after the Mutiny. He was forced to sell his clothes and live on their sale. Ghalib himself wrote to Yusuf Mirza,[15] "There are about twenty persons in this house and there is not a single pie's income. Now I don't get wine to drink".

The arrest of Ghalib : Mirza Ghalib was arrested on the 15th October 1857. We get the following account of his arrest in the book of Nawab Ghulam Hussain.[16] "Some white soldiers entered the house of Mirza Ghalib. They arrested him and brought him before Colonel Brown. As God had destined him—to live for some years more, fortunately a friend of Ghalib was sitting with the Colonel who recommended his case. Therefore, the Colonel ordered his release."

Reign of terror: The period just after the British occupation may properly be styled as the "Reign of Terror". Ghalib wrote to Munshi Har Gopal on the 5th[17] December 1857, "I am afraid of writing in more detail", he also wrote to Hakim Gholam Najf Khan on the 26th December[18] 1857. "It is quite enough to write that both of us are still alive. More than this neither you will like to write nor I shall write", he wrote again to this Hakeem on the 29th[19] January 1858. "I should thank God for safeguarding my life during these troublesome times. But I don't know what may happen the next moment. I am afraid to write a detailed letter. If God has written in our fate to meet each other again, we shall meet each other and narrate the tale of our woes and sufferings." On the 7th February[20] 1858 Ghalib wrote to Mir Mehdi Hussain "what to speak of pension, here I am afraid even of my own life."

"Here there is a vast ocean of blood before me, God alone knows what more I have still to behold".

Military regime: Delhi was handed over to the Military authorities and remained under their control up to the 24th February 1858, 'Ghalib wrote to Munshi Har Gopal on the 5th December, 1857, "There has been military rule in this City from the 11th May to the present day" (5th December 1857).

Maladministration of justice: It appears that the system of administration of Delhi was very bad for some time after the Mutiny. Mirza Ghalib wrote to Choudhry Abdul Ghaffar, "Don't take the administration of Delhi to be like that of the administration of Meerut and Agra. This Division[22] is now included in the Punjab territories. Here neither law nor constitutional conventions are followed. Whatsoever comes to the head of any administrator, is the law of this place". He wrote to Mir Mehdi Hussain,[23] "Every day a new order is issued in this city. I fail to understand what happens here". He also wrote to Yusuf Mirza,[24] "Every body is getting punishment according to his own fate. There is neither a law nor any rule here. No man's influence or his arguments can protect him. In his letter to Zulfiqar-ul-Din,[25] he pointed out, "You have not yet understood the nature of the rulers at this place, what is the use of taking a copy of order or of appeal. The orders passed by the rulers of Delhi are the recording of fate. There can be no appeal against them anywhere".

Ghalib has narrated an incident which clearly proves the truth of his remarks on Administration. In his letter to Yusuf Mirza[26] he wrote, "Now just hear an interesting story of the day before yesterday. Hafiz Memu has been released, as he was not guilty. He had made an application for the restoration of his property. His ownership to the property has already been proved. On that day he presented himself. The Judge asked 'who is Hafiz Mohammad Baksh?' He said, 'I'. 'Then again the judge asked, 'who is Hafiz Memu l' He said 'I'? He further informed the Judge, that his real name was Mohammad Baksh, but generally he was called Memo. The judge said, 'It does not matter. You are: Hafiz Mohammad Baksh, you are Hafiz Memo. You are in fact the whole world to whom the house can be restored. Therefore the case is dismissed'." Ghalib wrote to Yusuf Mirza,[27] "Fazlu lives in Arab-ki-Sarai. He came here day before yesterday. He is filing petitions for the restoration of his property, but who cares for him". About his own pension Ghalib wrote to Munshi Har Gopal,[28] "I don't know what the government : will do about my pension. In fact during the present military rule, the authorities have got no time to consider this matter." Two years later Ghalib wrote to Khwaja Gholam Abbas, "I had instituted an appeal for investigating into my conduct during the Mutiny. The reply came from the Lieut. Governor of the Punjab, 'I don't want to carryon any investigations. Therefore the case is dismissed'."

Brutal murders: The British forces shot dead many persons. Many were hanged in the Chandni Chowk. The British authorities admitted that 392 persons were hanged and quite a large number were shot dead.[29] But the Indians considered this statement to be a very meagre estimate of the deaths caused by the British authorities in their revenge. Ghalib also wrote to Mirza Hatim Ali,[30] "Thousands of my friends died. Whom should I remember and to whom should I complain? Perhaps none is left even to shed tears on my death." Ghalib wrote a mourning song of Delhi, a few lines of which are worth being translated.

. . . Nawab Ghulam Hussain—Delhi-ki-Saza, says (p. 50) Hundreds of persons were hanged. The informants were spread like a net. They were given a reward of two rupees for each arrest. Before the 24th February 1858 many innocent persons had been shot dead on the false report of the informants. Hundreds of women became widows and many thousands of children were made orphans. Mainodin: Two Native Narratives (a pro-British account, p. 71) also wrote, 'In the City no man's life was safe. All able bodied men, who were seen, were taken for rebels and shot".[31] When one comes out of the house to the bazar, one finds the blood of human beings. The crossing is a place of execution. The house is an example of Jail.

Every particle of dust of Delhi 'is thirsty for the blood of every Muslim. Ghalib also wrote in *Dastambu*,[32] "God alone knows the number of persons who were hanged. The victorious army entered the city along the main road. Whomsoever they met on the way was killed. The white men on their entry started killing helpless and innocent persons. In two or three Mohallas the English both looted the property and killed the people". In some of his letters Ghalib mentioned a few names of his friends, who were either shot dead or hanged by the British. He wrote to Yusaf Mirza,[33] "leaving aside the large number of deaths in the Red Fort, many persons have been killed in the City as well. Muzzufarul Dowla, Saiful Din Haidar Khan, Nasirul Din, nineteen years old Mustafa Khan, Artizi Khan, Murtizi Khan, Kazi Faiz Ullah, Hakim Razi ul Din Khan, Mir Ahmed Husan, Mai Kush are a few of them". He wrote to Mirza Alim Din,[34] "Count the deaths among the Muslims. Husan Ali, Mir Nasirud Din and Nazir Hussan were killed." In his letter to Nawab Anwarul Dawla,[35] he gave a pathetic description of brutal killing. "How can I write that Hakim Razi-ul Din Khan was shot dead by an English soldier in the general Massacre! His younger brother Husain Khan was also killed on the same day. Both the sons of Taleh yar Khan had come on leave from Tonk. Owing to the Mutiny they were detained in Delhi. After the capture of Delhi, both the innocent persons were hanged". Syed Ahmed Hasan[36] had inquired about the words of Sheikh Kalim Ullah. In reply Ghalib wrote to him, "A large number of persons used to live in the vicinity of Sheikh Kalim Ullah's tomb. But hardly any body escaped Death". A very large number of persons were arrested on suspicion after the Mutiny. Even the British authorities confessed that they had arrested 3306 persons. Ghalib wrote in *Dastambu,* "The Jail is outside the city and the Police lock up is in the City. The number of prisoners in them is beyond calculation". Ghalib also wrote to Shiv Narain,[37] "Out of the alive hundreds are in prison". Ghalib has fortunately given us the names of a few persons who were arrested. He wrote to Ghulam Naujib Khan, "The father of Sher Zaman is still under arrest. Mirza Bahadur Beg[38] had been arrested. Ghulam Fakhroodeen too had also been imprisoned". In his letter to Yusuf Mirza he wrote, "Hafiz Memu had been released". He wrote to Mir Ashraf Ali,[39] "Hamid Khan was arrested. He has been brought in chains".

He gave the following news about Hakim Ahsanullah Khan, to Hakim Gholam Najif Khan,[40] "The sepoys who had been posted to keep vigilance over Hakim Ahsanullah Khan has been removed. But he has been ordered to remain in the City. He has been asked to present himself once a week in the court". In *Dastambu*[41] he wrote, "Some informant falsely reported that the house of Hakim Mohammad Khan, Physician of the Raja of Patiala, had become the shelter of these rebels. Therefore, on the 2nd February 1858, the Hakim along with sixty persons was arrested. Maulvi Sadr-ud-Din Khan remained in Police custody for many days. He was presented in the court. Many witnesses were called and their evidence was recorded. In the end judgment was delivered and his life was forgiven". Nawab Mustafa Khan Arzuda[42] had been awarded seven years' rigorous imprisonment. "On appeal the order was passed confirming vigorous imprisonment on Maulana Fazl Huq Khairabadi. It was further remarked that he should be immediately exiled."

Jagirdars of Delhi province: "Even the greatest Jagirdars have been called for interrogation. There used to be seven[43] Jagirdars in the pre-Mutiny times in Delhi Division, i.e. Nawab of Jhajjar, Bahadurgarh, Ballabgarh, Farrukhnagar, Dojana, Pataudi and Loharu. Now four of them have been eliminated, only three of Dojana[44] Loharu and Pataudi remain". In *Dastambu* Ghalib has given a very vivid account of the pitiable condition of these jagirdars. *(Loharu Family).* The week in which the British occupied Delhi, Aminul Din Ahmed Khan Bahadoor and Ziaul Din Ahmed Bahadur along with their family, three elephants and forty fast running horses started towards their Jagir. But at Mehrauli they were looted and robbed of all their valuables. They were recalled to Delhi by the Commissioner and imprisoned in the Red Fort. After two or three days Abdul Rehman Khan of Jhajjar being arrested was brought to the Fort and confined in a part of Diwan-i-Am. His estate was confiscated. In this way on the 30th October 1857, Ahmed Ali Khan of Farrukhnagar was brought to the Fort and confined to it.

Raja Nahar Singh of Ballabgarh was also imprisoned in this manner. The rulers of Jhajjar, Farrukhnagar and Ballabgarh were separately hanged on the 13th June 1858. The life of Bahadur Jhang was forgiven.[45]

Bahadur Shah II: "The aged[46] emperor is under arrest and an interrogation is going on." On the death of Bahadur Shah in exile in Rangoon Ghalib wrote "Ab-ool Zuffer Sirajud Din Bahadur Shah was released from the imprisonment of the foreigners and of the body on the 7th November 1862." Most of the Royal princes were either[47] killed or imprisoned. A few of them ran away and saved their lives. Mirza Illahi Baksh,[48] one of the princes, has been asked to leave for Karachi. *The conditions of the Begums* is extremely bad. Their beautiful faces are like moon but their clothes are dirty and torn out and their shoes too worn out.

Forced eviction: Most of the citizens[49] were turned out of the city. Some of them had already left the city when they noticed the revengful attitute of the invaders. They lost all faith in the English. Most of the poor and gentlemen along with their women left the city through Ajmere Gate, Turkman Gate and Delhi Gate. They stopped in small colonies (Nizam ud Din and Mehrauli) and tombs around Delhi. In a letter to Munshi Har Gopal on the 5th December 1857 Ghalib wrote, "Don't take it as an exaggeration. The rich and the poor all have left the city. Those who remained were forcibly turned out of the city. Jagirdars, Pension holders, the rich and the citizens have all been forced to quit the city.[50] Even after a thorough search one cannot find a single Muslim here, though Hindus are still living in the city."[51]

Pass system: "No body can enter the city or go out of it without a pass. . . . On my return from Meerut I saw that great hardship is being imposed on the people. In addition to the vigilance of the English soldiers, the Thanadar (police officer) of Lahori Gate area sits on a stool—whosoever escapes the strict vigilance of the English soldiers, is caught by him and sent to the lock-up. The administrator orders him five canes or a fine of two rupees is imposed on him and is imprisoned for eight days. In addition to these measures an order has been issued to all thanadars to make an enquiry and find out those persons who are living in the City without a pass. In all than as (police stations) charts to this effect are being prepared."[52] He wrote to Choudhury Abdul Ghaffoor, "To live in the City without, the pass is very risky."[53]

Large scale loot: The prize Agents were appointed. Hundreds of labourers were employed in digging up the houses and the Fort. Ghalib wrote to Mir Mehdi Hussan,[54] "There was an indescribe loot". Ghalib's own valuables had been sent to the house of Kaleh Sahib by his wife for the sake of safety. But the house of Kaleh Saheb[55] was most thoroughly looted. All the papers, Gold, Woollen Goods and other property were taken away". Ghalib's writings had been deposited in the houses of his friends, "I have never collected the manuscripts of my own writings. Two or three friends of mine used to collect them. But their houses containing the property worth lakhs of rupees and personal libraries worth thousands of rupees have been looted, what to speak of my collections of poems. Nawab Ziaul Din Khan and Nawab Husan Mirza used to collect my books. The houses of both of them were looted along with libraries worth thousands of rupees."[56]

Destruction of Mohallas : "There was a cry that the whole city should be razed to the ground."[57] The British authorities decided in their vengeance to pull down many populous Mohallas. Mirza Ghalib noticed the destruction of some Mohallas. In his letter to Mir Mehdi Hussain, he wrote, "The area between Raj Ghat and Jumma Musjid is without exaggeration a great mound of bricks. If the debris is removed, then a vast ground shall come out. Perhaps you remember that on this side of the garden of Mirza Gohar there used to be a great lowness of ground, but now that place has been filled up. The Raj Ghat Gate has been filled up. Only the nitched battlement of the walls are apparent. The rest has been filled up with debris. . . . For the preparation of the metalled road, a wide open ground has been made between Calcutta Gate and Kabul Gate. Punjabi Katra, Dhobiwara, Ramji Ganj, Sadatkhan ka katra, Haveli of the wife of the General (General Ochterleny's native wife) godown owners houses, Haveli of the Sahib Ram and his garden, all have been destroyed beyond recognition. In short Delhi has become a vast desert."[58] In his letter to Choudhury Abdul Ghaffar, he wrote: "Here the city is being razed to the ground. Famous Bazars like Khas Bazar, Urdu Bazar and Khanam ka Bazar which were themselves small townships, have been destroyed beyond recognition. Now the owners of houses and shops cannot even locate where their property used to be."[59] In his letter to Mir Mehdi Hussain, Ghalib wrote, "If you even come here, you will see the changed condition of the roads of Jhan Nissar Khan ka Chhata and of Kucha of Khan Chand—you will also notice the pulling down of Mohalla of Balaqi Begum and the establishment of a great open space—70 yards wide around the Jumma Musjid." Syed Ahmed Hussan Khan[60] had inquired about the works of Sheikh Kulim Ullah Jehan Abadi. Ghalib wrote in reply, "The tomb of Sheikh Kulim Ullah Jehan Abadi had been completely ruined. The area in the vicinity of the tomb had the population of a good village. The descendants of the Sheikh used to live there. Now there is a vast ground and the tomb is in the middle of it." In his letter to Zulfiqar-ul Din Haider Khan,[61] Ghalib gave this news. "All the houses in the vicinity of Lal Digi have been razed to the ground." In his letter to Nawab Aminul Din,[62] Nawab of Loharu, Ghalib gave the following piece of information: "The Main gate of Dariba has been pulled down. The mosque of Kashmiri Katra has also met the same fate. The remaining portion of Kucha of Kabul Attar has been pulled down." In the letter to Yusuf[63] Mirza Ghalib gave this pathetic news, "Imam Bara of Agha Baqar is being razed to the ground. It has old holy places in it. In front of the Fort where there is Lal Digi, a vast ground shall be cleared up. The shops of Mahbub, houses of Bahlubes, Feil Khana (place for keeping elephant) from the

Kucha of Balaqi Begum to Khas Bazar shall be razed to the ground or you should take it for granted that from the gate of Ama Jehan to the ditch of Red Fort, except two or three wells and Lal Digi nothing shall remain. Today the houses of Chhata of Jehan Nisar is being razed to the ground. Many shops near the gate of Billimaran have been pulled down. Here one can see the ruins of Urdu Bazar,[64] Khas Bazar, Kucha of Bulaqi Begum and the Haveli of Khan-i-Daran. Kashmiri Katra[65] has also been pulled down . . . Dar-ul-Baqa shall be pulled down. Kucha of Khan Chand up to the Barh of Shah Bola will be razed to the ground."

Confiscation of property and pension: The property of most of the nobles and citizens on the suspicion of their taking part in the Revolt of 1857, was confiscated. Ghalib also mentions some of the cases of his friends, "Nawab Mustafa[66] Khan's Zemindaree of Jehangirabad and the property of Delhi was confiscated. . . . The property of Hakim Ahsan Ollah Khan, Mian Gholam Najub Bahadur Jung and Nobee Buksh have been sealed. . . . The Mudrassa[67] of Roshun-ul-Dawala, which is situated on the back of the Kotwali and the Haveli of Kasim were declared to be the property of Nizamul Din and were confiscated. It was auctioned and the money was deposited in the Government Treasury. All the property[68] of Hamid Ali Khan was confiscated . . . . The property of Zia-ul-Dawla,[69] which used to give a rent of 500 rupees, was also confiscated.

The pension of Mustafa Khan was confiscated.[70] Two sisters of Murtiza Khan[71] were getting a pension of 100 rupees each. The order was that "as your brother was a culprit, your pension is being forfeited. But as a matter of pity you are being granted ten rupees monthly allowance. If this is pity God alone knows what the wrath will be?" A cry[72] arose from the British for the demolition of the principal mosques on the ground that they were Muslim rallying points, that some like the Jumma Musjid had been used as strongholds in the street fighting and that it was a fitting act of revenge. The principal mosques were occupied by troops and for sometime their fate was debated. There was a proposal to sell the Jumma Musjid, and then to use it as a barrack for the main guard of European troops 'since it can never be allowed to remain in the hands of the Muslim population'. It was only after five years that it was released. Ghalib wrote on the 16th December 1862, "Jumma Musjid has been released—Maulvie Sardar-ul-Din, Fufazil Hussain Khan, Mirza Elahie Buksh and seven other persons have been appointed trustees".

Sufferings of the people: Most of the inhabitants were forcibly turned out of the city. Their condition was very pitiable. These poor persons started building places for shelter. But the British authorities could not tolerate even that. Ghalib wrote to Mir Mehdi Husain,[74] "Yesterday an order was issued saying, why are the people building houses and shops outside the City? Whatsoever has already been constructed should be pulled down immediately. No body in future will be allowed to build a house or a shop outside the city". The condition of the people after forced eviction was equally bad. Ghalib[75] made an enquiry about his friends; "I have learnt that after the brutal murder of ten persons, these persons were turned out from that place. But I don't know how they left that place, whether on foot, or riding. Whether they had any cash or were empty handed? Whether the women were provided with the Raths to ride? And what happened after their leaving that place? Where did they stay after that ?"

Even the British authorities confessed that the sufferings of the citizens of Delhi were indescribable.[76]

Notes and References

1. Ram Babu Saxena, A History of Urdu Literature, p. 158.
2. Punjab Government Record Office Simla, Delhi Division, Revenue Records, 1859, File No. 2, Letter No. 1096.
3. *Ibid.*, Letter No. 82.
4. Ghalib to Munshi Har Gopal, Letter dated 5th December 1857. Mukatib ul-Ghalib edited by Maulvi Haji Hafiz: Syed Shah Ali Husan, p. 98.
5. Makamal Urdu-i-Mula, p. 36.
6. Punjab Government Record Office, Delhi Division, Revenue 1859, File No. 2. Letters *Ibid.*, File No. 2, entitled.
7. Translation of Dastambu, p. 59, Hasan Nizam-i-Mirza Ghalib Ka Roznamcha.
8. Shaikh Muhammad Ikram-Ghalib Nama, p. 73.
9. Gholam Rasul Mehr-Galib, p. 173.
10. Mukatibul Ghalib edited by Syed Shah Ali Hasan, Letter No. 24.
11. Mukamal Urdu-i-Mulla, p. 104.
12. Simla Record Office, Delhi Revenue, File No. 2, Letter No. 1096, dated the 8th March, 1859.

13. *Ibid.* No. 1309, dated the 23rd March 1859.
14. Ghalib to Munshi Habib Ullah Khan, dated the 15th February 1858, Mukamal Urdu Mulla, p. 26.
15. *Ibid.*, p. 255.
16. Nawab Ghulam Hussain, Delhi ki Saza, Husan Nizami's edition, p. 65.
17. Syed Shah Ali Hussan, Makatib-ul-Ghalib, Letter No. 24, p. 99.
18. Mukamal Urdu-i-Mulla, p. 164.
19. Mukatib-ul-Ghalib, Letter No. 58.
20. *Ibid.*, Letter No. 39, p. 123.
21. Mukatibul Ghalib, Letter No. 24.
22. Urdu-i-Mulla, p. 98. Delhi Division was one of the five Divisions of North Western Province like Meerut and Agra in the pre-Mutiny times.
23. *Ibid.*, p. 144.
24. *Ibid.*, p. 251.
25. *Ibid.*, p. 244.
26. *Ibid.*, p. 248.
27. *Ibid.*, p. 255.
28. Mukhtib-ul-Ghalib, p. 243.
29. Delhi Gazetteer, 1883.4, p. 30.
30. Hazrat Zahir Delhvi Dastan-i-Ghadar, p. 127—"Sometimes innocent persons are killed along with the sinners. This is what happened after the Mutiny. The English soldiers began to shoot whomsoever they met on the way (p. 128). Among the men who remained in the City, there were some whose equal has never been born nor shall be born. Mian Muhammad Amin Panjakush, an excellent writer, Moulvie Imam Buksh Sabhai along with his two sons Mir Niaz Ali and the persons of Kucha Chhelan (it is said they were fourteen hundred in number) were arrested and taken to Raj Ghat Gate. They were shot dead and their dead bodies were thrown into the Jumna. As for the women, they came out of their houses along with their children and killed themselves by jumping into the wells. All the wells of the Kucha Chhelan were filled with dead bodies. My pen dare not write more."
31. A Painful Funeral rate of Delhi.
32. Dastambu Hasan Nizam's translation, p. 70.
33. *Ibid.*, p. 66.
34. Urdu-i-Mulla, p. 253.
35. *Ibid.*, p. 318.
36. *Ibid.*, pp. 181,227.
37. Urdu-i-Mulla, p. 273.
38. *Ibid.*, p. 168.
39. *Ibid.*, p. 164.
40. *Ibid.*, p. 170.
41. *Ibid.*, p. 248.

42.-45. Letter to Hakim Syed Ahmed Husan, Urdu-i-Mulla, p. 180; Mukhatibul Ghalib, Letter to Mehdi Humn, letter No. 48; letter to Yusaf Mirza, Urdu-i-Mula, p. 248; Mukhatib-ul-Ghalib, Letter No. 24; Urdu-i-Mulla, p. 136, Letter to Mehdi Hasan Dastambu, p. 68.

46.-51. *Ibid.*, p. 69; Urdu-i-Mula, Letters to Mir Mehdi Hussain, p. 119; Dastambu, p. 69, stories of shooting to death of Mirza Mughal, Mirza Khizar Sultan and Mirza Abu Bakes by Hodsu are wellknown; Letter to Munshi Har Gopal, Urdu-i-Mulla; *Ibid.*, p. 51; Dastambu, p. 66. Zahir ud Din Delhvi in his Dastan-i-Ghaddar says (p. 128); Men were turned out from the Kashmeri Gate and the women were turned out from the Kabuli Gate. One searched for the other.

52.-56. Mukhatab-ul-Ghalib, Letter No. 24, *Ibid.*, Leiter No. 48, Urdu-i-Mulla, p. 98, *Ibid.*" p. 138, Leiter to Hakeem Syed Ahmed Hasan, *Ibid.*, p. 180.

57.-59. Urdu-i-Mulla, p. 137, *Ibid.*, p. 103; *Ibid.*, p. 136.

60.-64. *Ibid.*, p. 180, *Ibid.*, p. 242, *Ibid.*, p. 286, *Ibid.*, p. 251, p. 130, Mukhatib-ul-Ghalib, Letter No. 41.

65.-72. *Ibid.*, Letter No. 40, Letter No. 48, Urdu-i-Mulla, p. 161, p. 318, p. 248, p. 250. Dr. Percival spear-Twilight of the Mughals, p. 220.

73.-75. Dr. percival Spear-Twilight of the Mughal, p. 220, Urda-i-Mulla, p. 119, Nawab Gholam Husain Khan wrote (Translation by Hasan Nizami Delhi ki Saza, p. 43 "Are the British officers not aware of the fact that many innocent and noble minded women both old and young with small children are roaming in the Forest outside Delhi. They have neither got meals to eat nor dress to wear. They have neither got the place to sleep at night nor a place to take shelter from the burning rays of the sun. The officers of Delhi have turned them out so that they may collect the moveable goods from the houses of the people. One lakh houses of Delhi have been turned into desolate ruin. This populated city has been ruined in such a bad manner that one feels like weeping over its fate." Mukhatibu-Ghalib, Letter No. 48.

76. Punjab Government Record Office-Simla General 1859, Delhi Division, File No. 2, Letter No. 42—From R. Temple, Esquire, Secretary to the Chief Commissioner for the Punjab to the Secretary to the Government of India with the Governor-General dated Lahore 21, April 1858, "After the capture of the city it was for some period utterly deserted; all the inhabitants had fled, all the moveable property had been plundered or carried away. There remained nothing but bare walls and empty houses. After that the Hindu residents were gradually and cautiously readmitted. But the Mahommedans were still excluded. Recently however the Chief Commissioner had authorised the re-admission of Mohammedans in the same manner. . . . The crime of these people has brought with it a retribution many times over. . . . After the storming though their lives, persons and honour were safe in the hands of our people, yet their property largely plundered. Lastly throughout the whole winter, which in upper India has its rigours for people of Hindustan, they have lived wretchedly from hand to mouth in the open country, without shelter. They do not now return unpunished as if nothing had happened. But after having endured hardships, they must reinhabit desolate houses."

V

FEELINGS AMONG THE NATIVES TOWARDS THE COMPANY'S GOVERNMENT

FREDERICK JOHN SHORE

. . . I now proceed to investigate the causes which have tended to produce an unfavourable disposition towards our government, and to adduce such facts in favour of my statements as bear most strongly upon the question. The principal are those so often alluded to, as having more or less influence upon all others,—the over wrought estimation in which the English are accustomed to regard themselves, and the broad line of separation from the native population, which under the mistaken idea of keeping up their dignity, they have deemed it proper to establish. An almost total ignorance of the feelings of the people has been the natural result of this most impolitic conduct; and it has had an equally mischievous effect upon our own characters; for living only among ourselves and having only our own standard of opinion wherewith to compare our conduct and ideas, self-love has been gradually gaining strength, and prejudices taking deeper and deeper root in our minds. Interested and designing men among the natives attached to us from mercenary and dishonest motives, have not been wanting to confirm these pernicious habits and ideas. No people have truer and quicker insight into character than those of India; and, like other sycophants and menials, whose sole means of livelihood is their dependence upon the great, they have found it their interest to flatter the vanity of the English functionaries, by affecting to believe *their* ideas of things in this country correct, and by representing matters so as to meet the tastes and feelings of those "in the light of whose co-intenance" (according to the original phrase), "they derive exaltation". Scorned and detested as such men are among their own countrymen, there is no species of artifice to which they will not have recourse to bring themselves into favour with the government from whom they have everything to gain.

Daily Increasing Poverty

But those who are not enveloped in the mist of official dignity, and have found their way to *the people* at large, have acquired a very different idea of their real feelings; indeed, if we consider the subject impartially for a moment, it will be difficult to arrive at any but an unfavourable conclusion. For what is there real condition under the British government? Placed by the chances of war, or negotiations in which they had no share, under our authority, they have been ruled by a system whose primary principle was self-interest and self-exaltation. They have witnessed, year by year, the gradual decay of their princes and governors, and daily-increasing poverty of the whole people, caused by the rapacity and mismanagement of their governors; they have suffered by being excluded from every office which it was possible to bestow upon an Englishman; they have seen the abolition of almost every hereditary institution by which the affairs of the country were formerly administered; and have been mocked by a harassing and vexatious system of *miscalled* justice, infinitely more expensive, and less efficient than their own, under which oppression and injustice have pervaded the land. This is, in a few words, a summary of their obligations to the British government; nor have they fared much better in the treatment they have received from the English as *individuals*. I have already spoken of the haughty tone of superiority assumed towards them in common intercourse, and of the contempt, neglect, and even insult, which they too commonly meet with in return for their politeness, patient forbearance, and attempts at civility. By the constant changes which our system induces, they have never had fair opportunities of recommending themselves to the few who were disposed to treat them well, or to entertain a favourable opinion of them; and when, by repeated instances of good conduct, they have succeeded in creating an interest in their behalf, and in some degree conquered the prejudices against them, others have been sent to take the place of those whom they were beginning to look upon as their friends. Like Sisyphus and his stone, they have been doomed to never-ending toil.

Discontentment Leads to Insurrection

It is universally acknowledged, that the constant presence of our troops alone prevents disturbances, or, in plain English, insurrection; and we have had proofs sufficient that on any opportunity a spirit of insubordination has immediately been manifested. I think it is Grotius who remarks, that if every mutiny were impartially investigated, howsoever unjustifiable it may be in the soldiers to resort to such a measure, it would be found to have had its origin in some promise broken, some right withheld, or some injustice practised towards the men: so, in civil life, I believe that inquiry would prove that almost every insurrection or disturbance has been caused by some wrong committed against the people, or some hardship suffered by them, I by no means defend the mode of redress adopted, nor do I assert that when once roused, the mob have always directed their fury against the real authors of their injuries. On the contrary, it is lamentable fact that when excited, all the evil passions of our nature are allowed full scope, little or no distinction is made and plunder and rapine are the natural results, however little intended at first. But such events are rare, without some just cause of discontent. The late Cole insurrection,[1] which cost so many lives, and occasioned such heavy losses to Government, however the unpalatable fact may be studiously concealed, and even denied by many, undoubtedly had its rise in oppressions and extortions practised on the people by the subordinate natives attached to the court, and some few individuals to whom they gave the support of their authority "for a consideration".

Down with the English

The disturbances in most of the Upper Provinces in 1824,—and there was scarcely a district which the spirit of disaffection was not more or less manifested,—arose from the same cause. I am aware that a different version was attempted to be given, and that it was asserted that the idea of our having sustained reverses in the operations against the Burmese, and of our troops being required in that quarter, was the cause of what happened; also, that many of the parties of insurgents were merely a few banditti, who were on the look-out for plunder. Certainly these were the proximate causes; but if the natives really enjoy such happiness under our government, how comes it that they are ready to unite in opposition to our authority? How is it that in the whole of the Upper Provinces not one of the leading landholders was; found to come forward in support of Government? It is also true that some of the insurgent parties originated in a gang of banditti formed merely with the hope of plunder; but what was the conduct of the people? On the first success of the robbers, numbers even of the better sort of inhabitants immediately joined them, and then insurrection, and the mere plunder, was the object. The rallying cry all over the country, repeated with the most enthusiastic exultation, was, "The English reign is over !"—"Down with the English!" It will not avail to say that it was foreign to the habits of the people to come farward, and that they stood aloof, leaving the business to our police and troops: the history of India abounds with instances in the native states, where, in the event of a disturbance those of influence called out their retainers and tenants, and boldly stood forth in defence of the Government. But it was very different at the period above mentioned: they did not merely stand aloof: even those ordinarily in frequent attendance on the different magistrates, separated immediately to their homes, under pretence of exerting their influence to preserve order in their own neighbourhood, and began raising men; but for what purpose?—to be ready, if occasion proved favourable, to turn their whole weight and power against our government; some of them did so; and it is not going too far to assert that had not the most prompt and vigorous measures been adopted and a fortunate issue not occurred at the first serious collision, or had a delay of a few days longer taken place, an insurrection would have broken out, which it would have required all the troops in the Upper Provinces to quell; and that it might have terminated in the utter subversion of our power. I have seen the official correspondence from most of the districts in that part of the country at that time. In that from Suhaurunpoor it was stated that a gang of banditti was first formed for plunder; that on their success, they were joined by others, villagers, when further plunder was perpetrated; a few days after which their numbers amounted to about twelve hundred, joined by one of the principal landholders in the district, who received them into his fort, openly defied the Government, and supported one of the party in assuming the title of Rajah; and that had the collision with the troops who were called out been delayed a day, their numbers would have swelled to at least three thousand; it having been *ascertained* that several parties of from fifty to four hundreds had been already formed, expressly to join the insurgents; and that had our forces sustained a reverse, the whole of that country would have been one scene of rebellion and outrage. So far from being controverted, the truth of these statements was acknowledged by Government, and the exertions of those engaged received their due; to them a fortunate, and, let me observe, not very common occurrence; for it has generally been the practice of Government to endeavour to show that the local functionaries have been precipitated, and have had recourse to harsher measures than were necessary; being well aware of the tendency of an insurrection to excite suspicion, that all is not as it should be on the part of the Government.

Ruin of the Upper Classes

. . . As has already been remarked, the nobles of the country have been stripped of their authority, and pensioned-off to degenerate, having no stimulus to exertion, no hope of raising themselves in the scale of existence. . . . In such a state of affairs what influence can exist, except that of fear?

Is to be supposed that those who have been deprived of their power and wealth should *like* the Government who have been the instruments of their ruin? that they should *speak well* of those by whom they have been humbled and degraded? Is it possible that their relations, friends, and former dependents, should not sympathize with them, all more or less implicated in their downfall? And, finally, will not the people at large, who are taxed with much greater severity than they ever were before, be ready to concur in their complaints? The ruin of the upper classes has been (like the exclusion of the people from a share in the Government) apologized for by saying that it was the necessary consequence of the establishment of the British power. That it was so of the system we have acted on,—that of immediate and temporary profit, without looking to future results,—is lamentably true. But the mere occupation of the country by the English required no such proceedings; indeed, had we acted on a more liberal plan, we should have fixed our authority on a much more solid foundation than that on which it now rests; and probably have ultimately realized as much *net profit* as we are likely to obtain under the present system. Had we allowed the upper classes, particularly the landholders, to retain their authority, modified, perhaps, in a certain degree, under proper check and control, and employed them to assist us in the government of the country, instead of being the objects of their hatred, we should have had the incalculable benefit of their assistance and influence, and that of their numerous relations and dependents in supporting our power in any agency. But the dislike to see any *native* in possession of authority has been carried to an extraordinary degree. No sooner have we become masters of a province, than the blight begins to fall indiscriminately on all; those who lent us their assistance, and those who opposed us, receiving generally the same treatment,—a remark I have often heard made by the people. Strange as it may sound, I believe that it would have been, in reality, far better for the country, had we even pursued the usual plan of barbarous conquerors, in parcelling out the lands among our own followers, and giving them to English gentlemen. But had English settlers been permitted to obtain possession of estates by fair means, it would have been far better; for then there would have been a connecting chain of links between the highest and the lowest, all of whom would have had an interest in preserving order and supporting lawful authority; but under the system hitherto adopted, there is no middle class between the foreign rulers and the native working classes; and their respective situations in society have been rendered almost as distinct as that of masters and slaves.

Company's Indian Empire like an Island of Sand

. . . Our empire is, indeed, like an island of sand thrown up by an inundation; it possesses no stability in itself, and nothing has been done to give it any. No embankments have been raised, no trees planted, whose roots might extend beneath and bind it together. The whole attention of those who have taken possession of it has been absorbed in *digging for gold;* while a few individuals have been employed from time to time in repairing, with fresh heaps of sand, whatever damage it has sustained. This may succeed for a time, but the whole fabric is liable to sink by its own weight, or to be carried away by another flood. A rathole has been carried away a dyke in Holland which is composed of a much firmer material than sand. I do not imagine that this will ever be effected by a combination among the native princes, or by a premeditated insurrection; it is more likely to happen when totally unexpected and to have its origin in some petty disturbance where the insurgents may be fortunate enough to defeat the first small body of troops sent to subdue them; and then the feeling would spread like a burning forest, till the whole country was in a blaze beyond the power of extinguishment.[2]

Notes and References

1. This occurred in 1832, in the provinces between Calcutta and Nagpoor.
2. This nearly came true in 1857. A detailed account of the Great Uprising and earlier mutinies has been given in volume eight of this book.

14

Bahadur Shah and the Administration Court of the Mutineers

S.K. Banerji

Muhammad Bahadur Shah II was the last Mughal otentate. He was very old and infirm when the Indian Mutiny ook place at Delhi in 1857 and he was dragged by the nutineers from his palace to be seated on the throne of his orefathers. He took up his task seriously and made earnest fforts to conduct the administration, e.g., in order to conciliate is Hindu subjects he had issued orders that no sacrifice of a ow, bullock or calf would be permitted on the Baqar-i-id Day.[1] Vhile he had to look after the civil administration, he had also defend the city against the British besiegers. He had also to eep a careful watch on his insolvent and lawless soldiery, but ere his efforts were mostly futile and infructuous.

Amongst the Mutiny papers is a unique document, 57-539 f the Press list published by the Government of India in 1921, hich testifies to Bahadur Shah's anxiety to control his unruly soldiery. A court of ten members was appointed and among its aims and objects was included getting riddance of the terrible mess to be noticed in the several military and civil departments.

The following regulations were made to establish the court and direct its deliberations:

1. A body named the Administration Court be established for the proper administration of the civil and military affairs of the country.
2. The Court shall consist of ten members of whom six were to be chosen from the military and four from the civil, and of the six military members, two will represent the infantry, two the cavalry and the remaining two the artillery.
3. The President and the Vice-President shall be elected by the members from among themselves and the Court shall resolve itself *into* five committees to look after the administration of the different departments.
4. At the time of appointments, every member shall declare on oath that he would discharge his duties with integrity and not be subject to greed, malice or deception, his sole consideration to be to improve the administration and add to the peace and happiness of the ryots. Before the publication of the minutes of the proceedings, no member shall divulge them without permission from the President and the Court.
5. Only those members are to be chosen from the army who have put in approved service and are known to be prudent and likely to be of use to the State. In exceptional cases, one possessing the requisite qualifications but not the length of service may be selected; the other members shall not raise any objection to his choice.

The same shall apply to the selection of the civil members.

6. A member guilty of partiality or dishonesty shall be forthwith removed by the Court and recourse will be taken to regulation 5 for the selection of his successor.

7. All matters of the government shall be placed before the members and decided by the majority of votes. The decision shall next be placed before the Saheb-i-Alam Bahadur for his consent and then finally for Huzur-i-Wala's approval.[2] If there be a conflict of opinion between the Court and the Saheb-i-Alam Bahadur, the matter will be placed at the Court meeting for reconsideration. If disagreement still persists the proceedings in full shall be placed before the king whose decision shall be final.
8. No one but the members is to have access to the meetings of the Court. The Saheb-i-Alam Bahadur and the king shall have the right to be present whenever they choose.
9. A resolution or amendment proposed by a member shall have the consent of at least one other member.
10. The proposer of a resolution shall speak first on it and without any interruption from the other members; after him an opposer will speak and then the supporter of the resolution and lastly the other members by turn.

10A. After the passing of a resolution by the Court and its approval by the king, it shall be circulated among the secretaries of the different departments for information and necessary action.

11. The persons chosen from the military sections are also to act as their supervisors. To the two supervisors in each section shall be attached four other members to form a committee, one of whom will act as its Secretary. The resolutions of the committee will be placed by a supervisor before the Court.
12. The Court shall, with the consent of the majority of its members, make alterations in these regulations.

Let us make some observations on these regulations:

1. A crude attempt was made by Bahadur Shah to introduce a popular element in the administration. But the details of the procedure of selection of the members of the Court are not forthcoming and we surmise that

in the midst of stress and storm of war, he was content to nominate them. Since the military members were to control important sections, they must be senior officers.

2. Occasionally additional members of experience were invited if their presence was helpful to the deliberations.
3. No regulation is put down for the selection of the civil members. The civil departments were numerous and the choice of a member must have been restricted to the few important ones.
4. It is not clear how the two members from one military section correlated with each other especially when each acted as the convener of an important committee. Probably the two mutually agreed on the division of their work
5. The decisions of the Court were not final but subject to the approval of the Saheb-i-Alam Bahadur and the king.
6. The Court dealt with all affairs under the sun. In the then disturbed state its exact military and civil duties are not clear. More than once it helped the authorities by encouraging the mutineers against the English.

The document though undated is valid but bears no official confirmation and is not written on special paper.

In the Mutiny papers there were several references to the Administration Court:

(a) In some of the papers, it is seen acting as an advisory body, e.g., on a few occasions it informs the officers of the army that the king had promised to reward them if they carried the enemy trenches by assault and if they fell, their surviving heirs would be supported.[3] Similarly, it advised the king to agree to grant rewards to the soldiers in case of victory.[4] It also supplemented the orders of the military headquarters by issuing instructions to the officers to oppose the approaching English[5] and informing a colonel of the shortage of ammunition in camp.[6] It approved of a Brigade

Major's proposal to construct a bridge and strengthen the guard at a particular post.[7] It tried to maintain discipline in the army by forbidding plunder while fighting was going on.[8] We have serious doubts whether all the instructions of the Court were attended to at all.

How disturbed the conditions were at Delhi may be granted from another document[9] where the king direct the Court to stop the soldiers and elephant drivers from destroying the royal and private gardens. If the king felt helpless in the matter how could an advisory body like the Court be expected to be more effective? We presume that the complaint was made merely for the information of the Court and no prompt measures were expected of it.

There is another document[10] which bears witness to the king's distress. It is addressed to his military officers and (a) expresses his weak state of health, aggravated by their lawlessness; (b) a request is made to them to remove the military guards placed on his *hakims* and to desist from laying hands on the people's property; (c) a warning is given that the plunderers will be severely dealt with by the Court and they are told that if punishment be not palatable to the soldiery, he would either retire to the shrine of the Khawaja Sahib[11] or commit suicide by swallowing a diamond and even be ready to be killed by his own lawless men.

The document written in Urdu for the benefit of his common soldiers, gives a vivid picture of the king's plight and his unfitness to act as leader at such a stormy period. He weeps over Hakim Ahsanullah Khan's death piteously bewails that now there was none else but God to look after him and pleads for the release of another of his *hakims* so that he might get a regular treatment and be cured of his malady. He goes on to complain of his misdoings of the soldiery and asserts that the spoliation of his subjects' property was nothing less than the spoliation of his own. The last, no doubt shows his concern for his subjects—but to no purpose; for when he threatens to set the Administration Court to punish them, he knew perfectly well how little he could rely on it. Probably, for this reason, he threatens at the close of the *hukmnama,* as it has been termed, of his resignation or putting an end to his life.

We are further enlightened of the king's distress by the document, 60-71, of the Press list, where a protest is lodged against the king's policy of obtaining money by raising loans from the local money-lenders. The petitioners point out that two such loans had already been raised in past on promise of their repayment in full, together with an addition of twenty-five per cent of the loan but the sum thus raised mostly remained with the corrupt middlemen, allowing only a meagre sum to reach the king. They also complained against the Administration Court, darkly hinting at some member being in secret league with the English and suggesting the substitution of a Council of only four men in its place.

We do not know whether the king approved of the last suggestion, but think it would not have improved matters at all.

In conclusion it may be stated that the whole atmosphere was steeped in suspicion, corruption, intrigue and lawlessness and no one was really interested in the affairs of the state and least of all, the Administration Court, and the king who alone seemed to think of the people, was infirm and powerless to do any lasting good to his suffering subjects.

Such is the gloomy picture of the conditions prevailing at the headquarters of the mutineers at Delhi.

Notes and References

1. See, Press list of the Mutiny papers, 1857, pp. 61-245.
2. Saheb-i-Alam Bahadur, it appears from another document (Persian O.R. 135-67) addressed by the king to the chief of Jaisalmiar to refer to Muhammad Bakht Khan; Bahadur Shah's deputy and entitled Lord Governor-General Bahadur. The Huz:ur-i-Wala refers to Bahadur Shah.
3. See papers 426-27, 429, 431-33, 437, 447 all belong to section 57.
4. 57-445.
5. 57-470.
6. 57-449.
7. 57-488-89.
8. 57-56-60.
9. 57-573.
10. 135-167-70.
11. *Ibid.*

    Qutbuddin Kaki, Muinuddin Chishti's successor. The Khwaja Saheb's tomb lies in the neighbourhood of the Qutb Minar.

15

Military Trial of Delhi Emperor

Given below are important extracts from the proceedings of the trial of Bahadur Shah Zafar, the last Mughal King of Delhi by a Military Commission in January 1858 *held in Diwan-i-Khas upon charges of murder and treason. The trial was a sequence to the unsuccessful Great Uprising of Indian soldiers which started in Meerut on* 10 *May* 1857 *against the British rule and* for reviving the Mughal Empire in India. Ironically the English on arrival in India in 1607 and thereafter were granted trading, Diwanee and revenue rights by the Mughal rulers, but in course of time they became so powerful as to try and sentence a Mughal Emperor. The trial lasted about forty-one days, had nineteen hearings, twenty-one witnesses and over a hundred documents in Persian and Urdu, each one with English translation, were *produced in the court. The King tendered his defence in Urdu on the twentieth day of trial. The prosecution evidence was in many parts contradictory and heresy but the accused King evinced* little interest in the proceedings and did not cross-examine even the clearly weak and worthless witnesses. After the findings of guilty by the Military Tribunal, the King was awarded a term of—life imprisonment in exile[1] and transported to Rangoon where he *died in early November 1862 at the age of* 87. *(Ed.)*

Proceedings on the Trial of *Muhammad Bahadur Shah*, Titular King of Delhi before a Military Commission, held at Delhi on the 27th day of January 1858, and following days by order of Major-General Penny, C.B., Commanding the Division, pursuant to instructions from Sir John Lawrence, Chief Commissioner of the Punjab, for the trial of such prisoners as may be duly brought before it.

President — Lieutenant Colonel Dawes, Artillery.
Members — Major Palmer, Her Majesty's 6th Regiment
Major Redmond, Her Majesty's 61st Regiment.
Major Swyers, Her Majesty's 6th Carabineers.
Captain Rothney, 4th Sikh Infantry.
Interpreter— Mr. James Murphy.
Prosecutor for Government—Major F.J. Harriot, Deputy Judge Advocate General.

Charges

1st. For that he, being a pensioner of the British Government in India did at Delhi, at various times between the 10th of May and 1st of October 1857, encourage, aid and abet Muhammad Bakht Khan, Subadar of the regiment of Artillery and diverse others, native commissioned officers and soldiers unknown, of the East India Company's army in the crimes of mutiny and rebellion against the State.

2nd. For having at Delhi, at various times between the 10th of May and 1st of October 1857, encouraged, aided and abetted Mirza Moghal, his own son a subject of the British Government in India, and others unknown, inhabitants of Delhi, and of the north-west province of India also subjects of the British Government, to rebel and wage war against the State.

3rd. For that he, being a subject of the British Government in India and not regarding the duty of his allegiance, did, at

Delhi, on the 11th May 1857, or there abouts, as a false traitor against the State, proclaim and declare himself the reigning King and Sovereign of India, and did then and there traitorously seize and take unlawful possession of the city of Delhi; and did moreover, at various times between the 10th of May and 1st of October 1857, as such false traitor aforesaid, treasonably conspire, consult and agree with Mirza Moghal, his own son, and with Muhammad Bakht Khan, Subadar of the regiment of artillery, and diverse others false traitors unknown, to raise levy, and make insurrection, rebellion, and war against the State, and further to fulfil and perfect his treasonable design of overthrowing and destroying the British Government in India did assemble armed forces at Delhi, and send them forth to fight and wage war against the said British Government.

4th. For that he, at Delhi, on the 16th of May 1857, or thereabout did, within the precincts of the palace at Delhi, feloniously cause, and become accessory to the murder of 49 persons, chiefly women and children of European and mixed European descent; and did, moreover, between the 10th of May and 1st of October 1857, encourage and abet diverse soldiers and others in murdering European officers, and other English subjects, including women and children, both by giving and promising such murderers service advancement, and distinctions; and further, that he issued orders to different native rulers having local authority in India, to slay and murder Christian and English people, whenever and wherever found on their territories; the whole or any part of such conduct being an heinous offence under Act XVI of 1857 of the Legislative Council in India.

The prisoner pleaded *Not Guilty.*

Translation of the Written Defence put in by Bahadur Shah, ex-King of Delhi

The real facts are as follows : I had no intelligence on the subject previously to the day of the outbreak. About eight o'clock a.m., the mutinous troopers suddenly arrived and set-up a noisy clamour under the palace windows, saying they had come from Meerut after killing all the English there; and stating, as their reason for having done so, that they had been required to bite with their teeth, cartridges greased with the fat of oxen and swine, in open violation of the caste of both Hindus and Mussulmans. When I heard this, I immediately had the gates under the palace windows closed, and sent intelligence to the commandant of the palace guards. On receiving the message, he came personally, and wishing to go out where the troopers were collected, requested that the gate might be opened. I kept him from this purpose, however, and when I would not allow the gate to be opened, he walked up to the balustrade, and said something to the troopers, who then went away. After this, the commandant of the palace guards left me, saying he would make arrangements immediately to put down the disturbance. Very shortly after, Mr. Fraser sent a message for two guns, and the commandant another for two palanquins, saying that two ladies were staying with him, and requesting that I would have them taken to and concealed in my private female apartments. I sent the palanquins immediately, and gave orders at the same time that the guns should also be taken. Very soon after this, I heard that before the palanquins could reach them, Mr. Fraser, the commandant of the palace guards and the ladies, had all been killed. Not long after this the mutinous soldiery rushed into the hall of special audience itself, and the hall of devotion, surrounding me completely, and placing sentries on all sides. I asked them what their object was, and begged of them to go away. In reply, they told me to remain a spectator, saying, that they had staked their lives, and would now do all that might be in their power. Fearing that I should be killed, I kept quiet and went to my own private apartments. Near evening, these traitors brought, as prisoners, some European men and women whom they had found in the magazine, and resolved on killing them. I had recourse to persuasion, and succeeded in getting their lives spread for the time. The mutinous soldiers, however, kept them prisoners in their own custody. Subsequently, on two 'occasions, they again determined on killing these Europeans, when I again restrained them from their purpose by entreaty and persuasion, and saved the lives of the prisoners. However, on the last occasion, though I again did all in my power to reason with the rebellious soldiery, they would not heed me, and carried out their purpose of slaying these poor people. I gave no orders for this slaughter. Mirza Moghal, Mirza Khair

Sultan, Mirza Abul-bakr, and Basant one of my own personal attendants, who had leagued with the soldiery, may have made use of my name: but I have no knowledge that they did; nor do I know that my own armed retainers, acting independently of my orders, joined in the slaughter. If they did so, they may have been urged on to it by Mirza Moghal. Even after the massacre, no one gave me any information regarding it. In reference to what some of the witnesses have said in evidence regarding my servants having joined in killing Mr. Fraser and the commandant of the palace guards, I make the same answer, viz., that I gave them no orders. That if they did so, they did it of their own free will. I had no knowledge of it, and this matter also was not communicated to me. I swear by God, who is my witness, that I did not give orders for the death of Mr. Fraser or any other European; Mukund Lal and other witnesses in saying that I did, have spoken falsely. That Mirza Moghal and Mirza Khair Sultan may have given orders would not be strange, for they had leagued with the revolted soldiery. After these occurrences, the rebellious troops brought Mirza Moghal, Mirza Khair Sultan, and Abul-bakr, and said they wished to have them as their officers. In the first instance, I rejected their request; but when the soldiery persisted, and Mirza Moghal in anger went off to his mother's house, from dread of the soldiers, I kept quiet in matter, and then by mutual consent on both sides, Mirza Moghal was appointed to be Commander-in-Chief of the army. As regards the orders under my seal, and under my signature, the real state of the case is, that from the day the soldiery came and killed the European officers, and made me a prisoner, I remained in their power as such. All papers they thought fit, they caused to be prepared, and bringing them to me compelled me to affix my seal. Sometimes they brought the rough drafts of others and had fair copies of them made by my secretary. At other times, they brought the original letters intended for despatch, and left copies of them in the office. Hence several rough drafts in a diversity of hands have been filed in the proceedings. Frequently they had the seal impressed on the outside of empty unaddressed envelopes. There is a no knowing what papers they sent in these or to whom they sent them. There is a petition in the proceedings without an address from Mukund Lal to some unknown party, in which a list is given of the number of orders issued on that date. In this catalogue it is distinctly specified that so many orders were written under the direction of so and so; so many others under that of such a one; and so on, but not one is ascribed to me. Accordingly, this also proves, that whoever wished, had orders written as he chose, without my authority, not even acquainting me with their purport, while I and my secretary being in jeopardy of our lives, could not dare to say anything in the matter. It was just the same case as regards the petitions bearing orders in my own writing. Whenever the soldiers or Mirza Moghal, or Mirza Khair Sultan, or Abul-bakr, brought a petition, they invariably came accompanied by the officers of the army, and brought the order they desired, written on a separate piece of paper, and compelled me to transcribe it with my own hand on the petition. Matters went on so far in this way that they used to say, so that I might hear them, that those who would not attend to their wishes would be made to repent their conduct, and for fear of them I could say nothing. Moreover, they used to accuse my servants of sending letters to and of keeping in league with the English, more particularly the physician Ahsan Ullah Khan, Mahbub Ali Khan, and the queen Zinat Mahal, whom they said they would kill for doing so. Thus one day, they did actually plunder the physician's house, and made him a prisoner intending to kill him but refrained from their purpose only after much entreaty and supplication, keeping him a prisoner, however, still. After this, they placed others of my servants in arrest, for instance Shamshir-ud-dowlut, the father of the queen Zinat Mahal. They even declared they would depose me, and make Mirza Moghal king. It is matter for patient and just consideration then, what power in any way did I possess, or what reason had I to be satisfied with them? The officers of the army went even so far as to require that I should make over the queen Zinat Mahal to them that they might keep her a prisoner, saying she maintained friendly relations with the English. Now, if I was in the full exercise of power and authority, should I have permitted the physician Ahsan Ulla Khan's and Mahbub Ali Khan's imprisonment; and should I have allowed the physician's house to be plundered? The mutinous soldiery had established a court in which all matters were deliberated on, and such measures as after deliberation, were sanctioned by this council they adopted; but I never took any part in their conferences. Thus, without my knowledge or orders, they plundered, not only many individuals, but several entire streets, plundering, robbing, killing and imprisoning all they chose; and forcibly extorting whatever sums of money they thought fit from the merchants and other respectable residents of the city, and appropriating such exactions to their own private purposes. All that has been done, was done by that rebellious army. I was in their power, what could I do? They came suddenly, and made me a prisoner. I was helpless, and constrained by fears, I did whatever they required otherwise they would immediately have killed me. This is universally known. I found myself in such a predicament that I was weary of my life, while my officials had no hopes of their being spared. In this state of things, I resolved to accept poverty, and adopted the garb, coloured with red earth, of a religious mendicant, intending to go first to the shrine to the Kutb Sahib, hence to Ajmir, and from Ajmir eventually to Mecca; but the army would not allow me; it was the soldiery who plundered the Government magazine and treasury, and did what they pleased, I took nothing from them, nor did they bring any of the plunder to me. They, one day, went to the house of the queen Zinat Mahal, intending to plunder it, but did not succeed in breaking open the door. In addition to all this, it is worthy of consideration that no person demands the wife of the poorest man, saying, "Give her to me, I will make her a prisoner." As regards the Abyssinian, Kambar, he obtained leave from me to go on a pilgrimage to Mecca. I did not send him to Persia, nor did I send any letters by him to the Persian king. As regards the behaviour of that rebellious army, it may be stated that they never saluted me even, nor showed me any other mark of respect. They used to walk into the hall of special audience and the hall of devotion with their shoes on. What confidence could I place in troops who had murdered their own masters? In the same way that they murdered them, they made me a prisoner, and tyrannised over me, keeping me on in order to make use of my name as a sanction for their acts. Seeing that these troops killed their own officers, men of high authority and power, how was I, without any army, without treasure, without stores of ammunition, without artillery, to have resisted them, or make arrangements against them? But I never gave them aid in any shape. When the mutinous troopers first arrived, the gateway under the palace windows being in my power, I had it closed. I sent for the commandant of the palace guards and acquainted him with what had happened, and prevented his going amongst the mutineers. I also immediately sent two palanquins for the ladies, and two guns for the protection of the palace gate, on the several requisitions of the commandant of the palace guards and the agent to the Lieutenant-Governor. Moreover, I despatched a letter the same night by camel express to His Honour the Lieutenant-Governor of Agra, acquainting him with the calamitous occurrences which had happened here. So long as I had power, I did all that I was able. I did not go out in procession of my own free will. I was in the power of the soldiery, and they forcibly did what they pleased. The few servants I engaged, I engaged for the protection of my own life, in consequence of my fears of the revolted and rebellious troops. When these troops prepared to abscond, finding an opportunity, I got away secretly under the palace windows, and went and stayed in Humayun's Mausoleum. From this place I was summoned, with a guarantee that my life would be spared, and I at once placed myself under the protection of the Government. The mutinous troops wished to take me with them, but I would not go. In all the above, which I have caused to be written from my own dictation, there is not the smallest falsehood nor deviation from truth. God knows, and is my witness, that I have written only what is strictly true, and the whole of what I can remember. I told you with an oath, at the commencement, that I would write only the truth, without addition or deficiency, and so I have now done.

Notes and References

1. "Who pulls about mercy? The agonised wail
   Of babies hewn piecemeal yet sickens the air,
   And echoes still shudder that caught on the gale
   The mother's, the maiden's, wild Scream of despair."

   "Our swords come for slaughter, they come in the name
   Of Justice: and sternly their work shall be done;
   And a world now indignant beholds with acclaim,
   That hecatomb, slain in the face of the sun."

"And, England, now avenge their wrongs by vengeance deep and dire, Cut out this canker with the sword, and burn it out with fire;
Destroy those traitor legions, hang every Pariah-hound,
And hunt them down to death, in all the hills and cities round."

Miss E. Leslie in *Sorrows, Aspirations and Legends from India* (1858)

2. Of the heroic nine, three died at their post, Willoughby and five others escaped with their lives. Forrest, Raynor, Shaw, Buckley and Stewart lived to receive the Victoria Cross (they were the first winners of Victoria Cross in India) but Willoughby, their leader, survived the explosion to die at the hands of a village mob on his way to Meerut. Surendra Nath Sen: *Eighteen Fifty-Seven*.

16

From Company to the Crown

SIR GEORGE DUNBAR

The shock felt in England due to the events of the Mutiny gave the East India Company its death-blow. It was realized that the system of "double government" with its division of powers and responsibilities could not be allowed to go on, and Lord Derby's Conservative ministry brought in a Bill "for the better government of India." By the Act of 1858[1] the East India Company—a mercantile corporation which had built up an empire was dissolved, and the British government stood openly responsible in its place. Instead of the old board of control and court of directors there was a parliamentary secretary of state with an India Office Council. The secretary of state was answerable to Parliament, and as in a genuinely democratic constitution Parliament is responsible to the people the ultimate power lay with the electors of the United Kingdom. But Indian affairs tacitly held to be outside the range of party politics, aroused little practical interest until Indian nationalism became a disturbing force.

The transfer of the government to the Crown and the appointment of Lord Canning, last of the Company's governors-general, as first viceroy and governor-general under the new regime, was announced in India on November 1, 1858. The royal proclamation was drafted in accordance with the expressed wishes of Queen Victoria, to be proclaimed Empress of India in 1877, and two of the clauses ran as follows:

> "We hereby announce to the Native Princes of India that all treaties and engagements made with them by or under the authority of the Honourable East India Company are by us accepted."
> "It is Our will that, so far as may be, Our subjects, of whatever race or creed, be freely and impartially admitted to offices in Our service, the duties of which they may be qualified, by their education, ability and integrity, duly to perform."

From 1858 onwards British India was to be ruled by a civil autocracy in which authority was concentrated at the centre, and exercised by the viceroy's executive council. This was in fact a cabinet whose members were the ministers in charge of the departments of state. "In this oligarchy", to quote Sir William Hunter, "all matters of imperial policy (were) debated with closed doors." Nor did the oligarchy include an Indian until 1909 when Satyendra Sinha,[2] an eminent Bengal lawyer, was appointed legal member of council.

On Hunter's remark the comment made by Romesh Dutt in 1903 is fair and to the point: "In this brief but pithy sentence we detect all the strength and all the weakness of Indian administration. The 'oligarchy' comprised the ablest British officials in India, but has never, within a half century of the Crown administration, admitted an Indian within its body. . . . The people of India have no place within the cabinet; no consultative body of representatives has been organized to advise the cabinet; no constitutional method has been devised to bring the cabinet in touch with the people. The best of governments must fail of success when the people are so rigidly excluded from the administration of their own concerns."

In one respect the Councils Act of 1861 took a short step forward. The governor-general in council could legislate for all the territories under the Crown and for this purpose his council was reinforced up to 12 "additional" members, amongst whom some of the non-officials appointed were Indians. It was not a substantial concession as their number made them no more than advisory, and private bills could not be introduced. Nor were they truly representative, because the early members came from the cautiously conservative aristocracy, religious leaders and government pensioners. The Indian universities had only been four years in existence and the modern progressive type of leaders and representatives had not yet appeared.

Crown and Company Courts Amalgamated

The Indian High Courts Act, passed the same year, amalgamated the Crown and Company courts. Indians could be appointed as judges, and Ram Prasad Roy of the Calcutta High Court was the first of a line of distinguished Indian judges whose numbers were to increase considerably after 1919.

But to the great mass of the people living in the villages scattered over the countryside government at its higher level meant nothing until the days of a powerful and energetic National Congress and the reforms which brought with them a limited right to vote. The one authority visible and known to them was the civil servant in charge of the district who was, until after 1919, British with the rarest exceptions.

There is all the difference in the world between a civil servant in the British Isles and a civil servant in India. In Britain, government officials are collected in a number of large offices, where they remain segregated from the general public, absorbed in their files, forms and correspondence. Their work is specialized and concerns only their own department; it is seldom technical. But, although there are big secretariats in India where red tape can hardly be said to be unknown, the total number of officials employed in them is relatively small. The civil servants are mainly distributed all over the country to do their work as individuals with variety of their duties: "Lecturing in universities or bridging rivers, fighting epidemic disease or dealing with widespread riots, excavating a prehistoric city or installing a water supply for a new one."

District Officer Evolved

From the servants of the East India Company, whose earliest official duties amounted to little more than those of a revenue collecting agency, the British district officer was evolved. On him the whole system of administration in practice depended. In the eyes of the people in his charge he was the Government of India "at once autocrat, counsellor and friend", an incorruptible authority unbiased by any religious influences. Lord Curzon, speaking of the British officials who died at their posts during the famine of 1896, touched upon an aspect of British rule in India which is too often forgotten: "These men did not die on the battlefield. No decoration shone upon their breasts, no fanfare proclaimed their departure. They simply and silently laid down their lives, broken to pieces in the service of the poor and the suffering among the Indian people; and not in this world, but in another, will they have their reward."

This reference of Curzon's brings us to a matter that vitally affects the vast population of the country whatever the government of the sub-continent may be. Agriculture is the greatest of its industries, and famine the recurring calamity which threatens the great areas that are dependent on the monsoon rains. As Lord Curzon remarked, "to ask any government to prevent the occurrence of famine in a country the meteorological conditions of which are what they are here, is to ask us to wrest the keys of the universe from the hands of the Almighty." What can be done is to insure against its worst effects, stark starvation and the epidemics of disease which come; with it, by efficient, organized relief during the emergency, and by a long-term policy to improve the general position of the peasantry.

Famine and Flood

Famine cannot possibly be fought successfully in the absence of good communications and rapid, adequate transport.

This had been the insuperable difficulty of the Mogul government when taking their relief measures. By the 1860's communications were easier with the extension of the railway system and the improvement of the roads, but these advantages had not then reached the eastern coast, and when a catastrophic famine fell upon that part of India in 1865 "the people of Orissa, shut up in a narrow province between pathless jungles and an impracticable sea, werein the condition of passengers in a ship without provisions". No government schemes were then in existence and "on every measure relief there seemed to be written the fatal words 'too late'." Between the famine and the added calamity of floods more than a million people were estimated to have died in Orissa alone.

Lord Lawrence,[3] who was then viceroy, persuaded the secretary of state that irrigation works were of more urgent importance as regards famine than the completion of the railway system, and an irrigation department was established. Twelve years later the total area irrigated by government works in India was 10½ million acres; in 1931 it stood at 31 million; and by 1935 the Lloyd barrage, the largest work of its kind then in existence, had increased this total under government schemes by another million acres.

The Orissa famine was the starting point of the government campaign to grapple with these calamities. But it was not until Curzon took the matter in hand after the great famine of 1900 not merely a crop famine, but a fodder famine on an enormous scale"—that the government of India finally evolved machinery for famine relief that could, humanly speaking, be considered complete. Weekly reports kept the supreme government informed as to rainfall and the state of the crops; provincial schemes for every detail of famine camps, public assistance, and medical services stood ready for immediate action; the cooperation of provinces unaffected by the famine was carefully worked out. The scheme remained the sure remedy and bulwark against the catastrophic effects of famine until provinces became autonomous, and the central administration no longer had direct executive powers over them.

Cooperative Societies Started

But more than this emergency scheme was necessary in the agricultural interest. Curzon, who said that "the peasant has been in the background of every policy for which I have been responsible, of every surplus of which I have assisted in the disposition", gave the whole sub-continent a benefit second only in the everyday lives of the farming population to irrigation canals and artesian wells. Other viceroys had passed Acts to give security of tenure to the cultivator, but it was Curzon who started the cooperative societies of India. He had already appointed an inspector-general of agriculture and founded, with the generous donation of Mr. Henry Phipps of Chicago, the Institute of Agricultural research. The cooperative societies opened savings banks, encouraged cattle and mule breeding, began to reassure a suspicious peasantry with the object of merging fragmented holdings into "pool" farms, sank numerous wells, and converted previously waste land into productive fields. These societies were quickly appreciated not only in what was British India until 1947, but also in the larger states whose revenues enabled the princes to establish them.

British Administration Entirely Western

Before attempting to describe twentieth century India, its constitutional changes and the turbulent scenes that accompanied them, something must be said of the situation from which they sprang. The earlier conquerors of India were Asiatic in race and methods of government and had identified themselves with the people, but British administration was entirely Western in its standards and operation; the ruling race kept aloof and no Indian had a voice in the government. It was a guardianship unparalleled in its magnitude and efficient control of Asiatics; and whatever else British dominion may or may not have done it set-up a standard of scrupulous integrity, and of even-handed justice between Indian and Indian, it brought with it the maintenance of internal peace and security, and it imposed political unity in the sub-continent. This administration, with the smooth working of a machine, reached the height of its efficiency under Lord Curzon; but at the same time the inevitable effects of completely alien rule and the reactions to it became more and more pronounced.

Curzon's Reforms

Imperious in character, imperial in his outlook, it was said of Curzon by a secretary of state for India that he "had his way more than any viceroy of modern times". Some of his measures of reform, notably for famine relief and the encouragement of elementary education, could not be gain-said by anyone, but his Universities Act to tighten government control met with vehement Indian opposition. That great Indian statesman, Gopal Krishna Gokhale, while welcoming reform, looked upon the Bill as a retrograde movement which cast an unmerited aspersion on the educated classes of the country and was destined to perpetuate "the narrow, bigoted and in expansive rule of experts".

In the event the Act had little or no effect on the universities. But this must be said of their condition in 1904. The Indian universities had been modelled on the University of London, and the corporate life of Oxford and Cambridge was lacking, though it had not been absent in an older India. This could be remedied by hostels, but the colleges were little more than collections of lecture rooms and laboratories. University life was entirely dominated by examinations, and cramming was the art most enthusiastically pursued as matriculation qualified the successful candidates for one of the 11,000 subordinate posts in the government of India. There came into existence a *bloc* of educated men, chiefly Bengalis, who thankfully accepted things as they were until saturation point was passed when, with no hope of employment, serious discontent among these graduates began. On the other hand, in the viceroy's mind, technical education on businesslike lines would "open a real field to the youth of India", and in this he took a lively interest. For elementary education he secured a large and permanent annual grant which made it possible to open thousands of new schools.

But Curzon was frigidly uninterested in the political opinions that were due to English education and, far-seeing and sincere as was, for instance, Gokhale's opposition to some government measures in the legislative council, the viceroy could see nothing in the national leaders but the ambitions of a few men to gain place and power. Curzon in his whirlwind drive to improve the administration by greater centralization genuinely felt that the efficiency he ruthlessly demanded was only possible with British occupants of the higher posts. It was the negation of the policy which had been first officially proclaimed for British India, however unhonoured in the observance, by the East India Company 70 years earlier. And yet the paradoxical fact stands on record that Curzon believed that as viceroy he had "done much (whether wisely or unwisely) to accelerate the lifting of India from the level of a dependency to the position which is one day to be hers, if it is not so already, namely, that of the greatest partner in the Empire".

Curzon's attitude to the states was founded on the axiom that "the native chief has become, by our policy, an integral factor in the imperial organization of India. He is concerned, not less than the viceroy and the lieutenant-governor, in the administration of the country. I claim him as my colleague and partner". To make this more effectual he revived the idea of a former viceroy, Lord Lytton, to form a council of princes, but the home government did not then approve. Curzon had to rely upon his own not unfruitful but distinctly disturbing intervention, when he thought this necessary, and the financial straits which famine brought upon some of the states gave him special opportunities.

A ruler of Curzon's forceful character is bound to arouse strong disagreement and opposition, and the viceroy was to find it both in London and India. His final differences with the home government reacted upon himself, but one decision which he made started a conflagration that swept across the sub-continent with devastating results.

Curzon's surveying India from his personal standpoint of what would benefit the country, cast his eye upon Bengal, the great presidency in which until 1911 stood the capital of British India. On the highest provincial level it was far too unwieldy for the lieutenant-governor, alternating between Calcutta and Darjeeling, effectively to control. To descend to the districts, where the police force was inadequate to keep law and order, an example of the difficulty of satisfactory local administration could be seen in Mymensingh, a huge waterlogged district with a population of 4,000,000 and only one British executive officer.

Partition of Punjab and Bengal Provinces

On the grounds of imperial responsibility and military requirements Curzon had, in 1901, abruptly announced to the Punjab government the division of that province and the formation of the North-West Frontier Province under a chief commissioner. In the interests of internal administration he now decided to divide Bengal by creating a new province of Eastern Bengal and Assam. With the support of the officials the viceroy consulted, and the approval of Parliament, this was carried out in 1905.

Resentment throughout India

The partition raised a storm of passionate resentment, not only in Bengal but throughout India, in every educated and politically-minded Hindu, a feeling which swept aside all argument of administrative benefit. The agitation was fundamentally communal and sprang from the instinctive fear of Moslem preponderance in the new province, but there was added to this the belief that the partition was a political move to weaken the national movement by dividing the province which had begun to take its leadership. Curzon, who seems to have failed to realize the change which had for some time been taking place in the outlook of the educated classes, gave no weight to the hostility which greeted the announcement of the partition; it was for the good of the masses, and that was enough for him. But the storm clouds were gathering fast, and were to break over India two years after Curzon left the country.

Dual Military Control

The controversy between the viceroy and his commander-in-chief Lord Kitchener over the question of "dual military control" in the council of the Government of India hardly comes within the scope of this book. It need only be said that Kitchener's proposals would have led to a military autocracy, and that the additional functions laid upon the commander-in-chief by the abolition of the military administrative member created "an impossible burden for one man to assume"—as they were to prove in Mesopotamia in 1915. The decision of every other member of council was against the commander-in-chief when the question came up in March 1905. The home government, standing between the masterful personalities and great public services of Curzon and Kitchener, offered a wavering compromise which the viceroy could not accept, and he resigned in August 1905.

The dramatic departure of the last of the great pro-consuls whose personal authority impressed itself over all-India closed the era which had opened under Canning. For a time the efficient machinery of British bureaucratic administration continued to work as before. But the claim for immediate independence was to rise uncompromisingly beyond the policy of a succession of secretaries of state whose declared aim came to be the establishment step by step of that release from control in a dominion government of the Indians themselves.

The new viceroy, the Earl of Minto, whose ancestor had been governor-general 100 years earlier,[4] had the cool judgment, the sense of justice and the courage needed in a situation of growing discontent and violence.

His predecessor's university policy and the partition of Bengal were the most obvious causes, but there were others. It was most galling to men whose outlook had been widened by education and travel to be under the restrictions of an Arms Act which applied to pure-bred Indians only, and the system of indentured emigration to South Africa, which the Government of India did its best to improve, gave the impression that Indians held an inferior status among the subject of the King-Emperor.

Indians Excluded from High Positions in Civil and Military Services

But there was something more. For a succession of

generations, whatever, might be the policy proclaimed, Indians had in practice been excluded from high responsible positions in the civil and military services of British India. In 1904 there was no idea of granting King's commissions to Indian military officers; and, in that magnificent cadre holding viceroy's commissions, the senior Indian officer, the colonel's right-hand man, was junior to the newest British subaltern still struggling with his language examination. In the Indian Army, with the close understanding between all ranks and the relationship between the regiment and the villages where one generation after another supplied its recruits, the situation was a happy one in what may be called a traditional and conservative atmosphere. But in civilian life the fact that no Indian had any authority in the government of his own country was bound to have a deteriorating effect upon the manhood and self-respect of the British-educated and political minded classes. There was, too, the insistent influence of Western materialist ideas and the stream of new inventions coming-in from Europe, all of which gave the Indian people the impression that this foreign civilization was higher than their own.

Lapses in British Behaviour

That was the Indian point of view at the turn of the century and it was accentuated far too often, outside the body of civil servants and officers of the Indian Army, by a British attitude that can be summed up as the eminently Victorian idea and application of the word "native". Acute racial superiority and colour prejudice were not an earlier English characteristic, but they had become increasingly evident during the nineteenth century. This had possibly originated when steam brought England to India and British residents began to abandon their Eastern way of living and lost their earlier contacts; it could not exist with any knowledge of India's art, culture and history. Indians of good family, with an English public school and university education, who were received everywhere in London society, came back to India to be barred from clubs under British management in their own cities; and in everyday life they were liable to meet with deplorable lapses in British behaviour. It was an example of that insularity which breeds contempt; and, in Mahatma Gandhi's restrained comment, "the average Indian was content to accept his inferiority".

Nationalist Movement

But the years 1904-05 brought a change in the outlook of Indians which was most impressive to any observer. The course of the Russo-Japanese war was giving Oriental Japan a succession of spectacular victories over the vast Western power that had been the bugbear of British foreign policy for 70 years. The East had awakened from her long sleep and the educated classes in the Indian cities began to recall the past greatness of Asiatic peoples which had for generations been forgotten. British mechanical inventions did not seem so marvellous after all and Indian culture, viewed with a new sense of proportion, came to be judged as certainly not inferior to the civilization of Europe. The Indian inferiority complex, though it might be difficult to get rid of it altogether, was now less persistent, and the Nationalist movement was given its first organized impetus, through the Indian National Congress. It embodied the claim of the East for due recognition of status.

English Radical Ideas

India had been accustomed to autocratic hereditary rule for more than 2,000 years. It was the educational system brought in by Bentinck and Wood that enabled upper-class Indians to read and appreciate English radical ideas, to study the revolutionary storm that swept over Europe in 1848, and in the twentieth century to become strongly impressed and influenced by the course of events in Ireland.

But until female education began to make headway English ways of life and thought meant nothing to the masses of the Indian people. The controlling influence of Hindu mothers was against any changes in family life, and that girls should work in factories, and women have votes and enter into politics, would have indescribably horrified the old matriarch whose word was law in the joint family. The agricultural classes had no use, nor had they much opportunity, for education. Their horizon was bounded by their fields, their interests lay in a world made up of their homes, their crops, and what they owed the local money-lender.

Pioneers in Education

Moslems as a body held aloof from the new learning and what came with it; they had been chilled and affronted by the substitution of English for Persian as the official language. The renaissance of Muhammadan education did not begin until the 1870's, when it was inspired by Sir Syed Ahmad Khan who did for his co-religionists what Raja Ram Mohan Roy had done earlier for the moral and intellectual advantage of the Hindus. Syed Ahmed Khan founded the Muhammadan Anglo-Oriental College at Aligarh, and a Hindu writer said of him in 1919 : "There would be no educated Muhammadan community existing and flourishing today but for the heroic pioneer efforts and far-sighted vision of this great man, who did not see in the utter collapse of the Mogul Empire an argument for racial estrangement and enmity."

Interest in politics two generations ago was consequently confined to a small group of educated townsmen. Whatever their mother tongue might be they could all speak English together. Another form of Westernization helped to unite the politicians of India, for railways and telegraphs had brought the cities within easy access and close contact with each other.

Indian National Congress Founded

All this gave birth to new aspirations and hopes for the future; a retired member of the Bengal Civil Service, Alan Hume, took a practical interest in giving these political opinions a voice; and with the unofficial blessing of the viceroy, Lord Dufferin, the Indian National Congress was founded. Indian political life had begun with an influence on public affairs hardly greater than that of the Oxford Union. But Congress "as it attained man's estate became more and more conscious of its strength and capacity, and its outlook was soon widened. From an attitude of prayerfulness and importunity, it developed self-consciousness and self-assertion".

In December 1885, 72 delegates from different parts of British India, including Hindus, Moslems, Parsees and Indian Christians, assembled at the Sanskrit College in Bombay to hold the first session of Congress. The attitude of this representative body was reflected by one of the opening speakers, who declared that "by a merciful dispensation of providence" Britain had rescued India from centuries of external aggression and internal strife, and summed up the benefits of British rule "in one remarkable fact, that for the first time in the history of the Indian populations there is to be beheld the phenomenon of national unity among them, of a sense of national existence". The initial aim of Congress was to remodel the administration on Western lines which its first president, W.C. Bannerji, emphasized to be in no way incompatible with a through loyalty to the British government. For many years the sessions ended with cheers for the British imperial sovereign.

Twenty years later the atmosphere had changed, and while the British connexion still appeared a blessing British rule was now held to be the reverse, and self-government "similar to what exists in the self-governing colonies of the British Empire" was proclaimed to be the essential remedy. For the Indian Liberals, voicing the general political opinion, were convinced that the educated classes could only be conciliated by association in an increasing extent with the government of their own country—a policy to which England had pledged herself in the past.

Demand for Home Rule

Gokhale's demand for home rule came at the moment when self-government within the Empire was in the air. In South Africa, the British government took the road which led to the creation of a prosperous Dominion loyal to the person of the Sovereign, but in Ireland and in India no such policy was pursued. It is within the bounds of possibility that there was then in India a favourable though short-lived opportunity to take definite measures which could have brought an agreed political settlement of India's future constitution. For in 1905 Moslem sympathies with the Congress movement had not been alienated by the course of the anti-partition campaign, and in

Minto there was a viceroy in sympathy with Indian Liberal views.

All-India Muslim League

But when the King's Speech at the opening of Parliament in 1907 gave the first hint of Indian constitutional reform, unity between Hindu and Moslem had withered. The All-India Moslem League was founded in 1906 to safeguard their own political interests, and communal differences which up to then, under the British Raj, had been entirely religious, now entered the field of politics.

Nor was this the only split in Congress. The formula "Swaraj" had been adopted in 1906 to keep the two Hindu wings united. To the Liberals led by Gokhale it meant home rule by constitutional means, while the left wing led by Bal Gangadhar Tilak saw Swaraj as the slogan in a fight for independence. The policies clashed at the presidential election of 1907 when the moderates were victorious, and they kept control of the organization until after Gokhale died in 1915, while Tilak and the extremists went out into the wilderness.

But feeling over Bengal had risen by 1907 to fever-pitch and represented an opposition to British rule which had been unknown for 50 years. While prominent Liberal elder statesmen, such as Surendranath Bannerjee, headed an intensive agitation which they declared to be not anti-British but intended to awaken public opinion in England to the seriousness of the situation by constitutional means, left-wing nationalists appealed to force.

Tilak, a man of deep learning, remarkable ability and immense popularity defeated though he had been in Congress, launched a formidable campaign. A Chitpavan Brahman, as were the Peshwas, he used the cult of the Maratha Sivaji against two civilizations alien to India by recalling past Moslem defeats and by inflamming public opinion against British rule. His weapons were his newspaper and the youth movement, and his tours through the Deccan attracted hosts of followers until his trial and imprisonment for an article he published on political murder.

The Terrorist Movement

The Hindu protest had involved throughout India a boycott of British goods which was enthusiastically supported by the student community, the younger and more hot-headed generation of the politically interested classes. This brought into the nationalist movement the unbalanced and explosive element which was directly responsible for the terrorism that broke out in 1907: a criminal form of protest which it is the plain duty of any government to stamp out.

The terrorist movement had its origin in the gymnastic societies started in Bombay at the beginning of the century and taken up in Bengal. Insofar as these societies were a reaction against excessive Westernization and had for their object a revival of the soul and culture of ancient Hindu India, they represented the ideals of Rabindranath Tagore and the future gospel of Mahatma Gandhi. The tragedy lay in the methods they employed, Hindu middle-class lads, in a movement which included neither peasant nor Moslem, were enrolled to become compromised, after an initial training in the highest standards of moral purity, in revolutionary conspiracy and sheer gangsterism. In taking this course, the extremist wing of young political India sought to justify cold-blooded murder as the warfare of a legitimate government and robbery with violence as tax-collecting. Calcutta, where an attempt was made to assassinate the lieutenant-governor, the prelude to attempts on Minto and Hardinge, and Madras were scenes of inflammatory meetings and dangerous noting. In the Punjab, where the local government had handled a canal colony with less than its usual wisdom and something distinctly like a breach of faith, there were serious riots at Lahore and Rawalpindi that April and May.

At the same time Eastern Bengal was the scene of grave disorder, but here it was not a revolutionary demonstration against the British Raj. Communal feeling was running high in the new province where the Moslems viewed the partition from a very different angle than the Hindus. The Moslem population was against the violent agitation and the boycott of British goods, and they vigorously resisted the intimidation and terrorism that swept the country. In May 1907, there was a general rising of the Moslem peasantry of Mymensingh, a district as difficult to police as any in India, against their Hindu landlords and creditors.

First Step in Constitutional Progress

In this atmosphere of unrest and widespread defiance of authority, which the government were obliged to supports by stern measures, the first step in constitutional progress was taken by the Indian Councils Act of 1909, known as the Morley-Minto reforms. The Act was an enlargement of the 1861 legislation. It extinguished the official majority in the provincial legislative councils, and it increased the membership of the central legislative council mainly by non-official election from the provincial councils. But the "additional" Indian members, mostly selected representatives of local authorities, large landowners, trade associations and special Moslem members, were not numerous enough to be more than advisory; they could only give their views, and thus hope to improve legislation. In the governor-general's council the official majority held absolute control. Lord Morley, the Liberal secretary of state, would have no part in launching democratic government in India, and in this he had Conservative support, Lord Curzon, however, adding the comment that the new councils would inevitably become "parliamentary bodies in miniature."

Notes and References

1. *Government of India Act*, 1858 (21 *and* 22 *Viet*., c. *106)*

   I. The Government of the territories now in the possession or under the Government of the East India Company, and all powers in relation to Government vested in or exercised by the said Company in trust for Her Majesty, shall cease to be vested in and exercised by the said Company; and all territories in the possession or under the government of the said Company, and all rights vested in or which if this Act had not been passed might have been exercised by the said Company in relation to any territories, shall become vested in Her Majesty, and be exercised in her name, and for the purposes of this Act India shall mean the territories vested in Her Majesty as foresaid, and all territories which may become vested in Her Majesty by virtue of any such rights as aforesaid.

II. India shall be governed by and in the name of Her Majesty, and all rights in relation to any territories which might have been exercised by the said Company if this Act had not been passed shall and may be exercised by and in the name of Her Majesty as rights incidental to the Government of India; and all the territorial and other revenues of or arising in India, and all tributes and other payments in respect of any territories which would have been receivable by or in the name of the said Company if this Act had not been passed, shall be received for and in the name of Her Majesty, and shall be applied and disposed of for the purposes of the Government of India alone, subject to the provisions of this Act. . . .

2. Afterwards the first Lord Sinha, who became governor of Bihar and Orissa in 1920.
3. Sir John Lawrence, previously the first lieutenant-governor of the Punjab.
4. The first Lord Minto had also held vice-regal rank, in the remarkable appointment of viceroy of Corsica.

Muslim Politics in the Punjab, Pro-1857

N. GERALD BARRIER

MUSLIM MILLET-ADHERENTS, HINDU UNITED CONGRESS, EDUCATION, SIKH, GURUDWARAS, NATION

Serious gaps exist in the historiography of the Muslim community in the Indo-Pakistan subcontinent. Scholars have tended to focus on the pre-British period and the growth of the demand for a separate Muslim state following the Curzon era, but with a few notable exceptions, little detailed attention has been paid to political developments among Muslims during the nineteenth century. This is unfortunate because communal tensions, pressures, and separatism emerged during the nineteenth century which later found expression in formal political channels. It seems likely, for example, that future investigation will demonstrate that Hindu-Muslim antagonism in the 1920's, the resurgence of Muslim political associations in the 1930's, and even the movement for the creation of Pakistan had their roots in the turbulent history of Bengal and the Punjab prior to 1900.

Within the last decade, however, that reconstruction has begun. The Research Society of Pakistan and the Historical Research Institute (Punjab University, Lahore), for example, have preserved old newspapers and published several studies dealing with pre-1900 Muslim society and politics in the Punjab.[1]

Origins of Muslims Political Activities

This essay with appended documents attempts to make a small contribution to the ongoing study into the origins of Muslim political activity. The first purpose of the paper is to examine some of the events culminating in the 1888 anti-Congress demonstrations among Punjabi Muslims. Although the discussion is based on government records and hitherto unused primary sources, it should in no sense be considered a final assessment of the period. Rather, the essay aims at suggesting basic processes and problems which require further analysis. The second goal is to make available translations of two significant Urdu political tracts written during the anti-Congress movement. The tracts illuminate Hindu-Muslim relations and the shifting ideologies within the Muslim community. Their translation and publication also will underline the existence of such contemporary material and encourage fresh use of tracts and collections in scattered depositories.

Three Types of Political Activities

Muslim politicians were primarily engaged in three types of political activity prior to 1881. First, both educated and illiterate urban Muslims worked within cultural organizations, or *anjumans*, to strengthen their own community. Muslim leaders also carried out extensive agitation to force the British to give their co-religionists more representation in the bureaucracy and educational system. These two activities did not prevent a third, Muslim alliance with Hindu in opposing acts of British *zulm* (oppression) or defending issues affecting the western-educated class as a whole. Muslims occasionally joined Hindus in organizations or specific demonstrations. The alliance dissolved as soon as common issues were removed, but the potential remained for future co-operation.

Hindu Rise—A Threat to Muslims

Muslims responded to a number of diverse pressures following annexation in 1849 by organizing and joining associations which tried to protect and strengthen the Muslim community. Missionary proselytization, often backed formally or informally by British civil servants, spurred the creation of a network of Muslim anjumans. These societies, such as the Delhi and Lahore Anjuman-i-Islamia, were initially concerned with guarding Muslim endowments and stemming apostasy.[2] By the 1870's additional crises had emerged which propelled Muslims further toward reform and self-strengthening. First, the Brahmo and Arya Samajees contributed to Hindu militancy.[3] At the same time that Hindus seemed to become more anti-Muslim, it was becoming evident that Muslims had fallen far behind Hindus in the race for western education and employment. Besides the loss of potential income, Hindu ascendancy in the public services posed a serious threat to Muslims because official posts were sources of power which could be manipulated to support communal claims and to attack religious opponents.[4] Muslims consequently began to convert existing anjumans into organs of reform and revival, a process exemplified by the Lahore Anjuman-i-Islamia. The Anjuman had originally been supported by conservative aristocrats and chiefly supervised endowments, but when a retired government servant, Barkat Ali, became secretary in 1877, the Anjuman was transformed into a reform society supporting the leading social and religious 'modernizer' of Indian Muslims, Syed Ahmed Khan.[5] Under Barkat Ali's leadership, the Anjuman built schools, established a newspaper, and tried to revive the spirits of Muslims by organizing branches in twenty Punjab and adjoint districts. A few Muslim lawyers and college students initially joined in the new effort, but they soon became dissatisfied with the aristocratic inclinations and limited program of the Anjuman-i-Islamia.

"Middle class Mohamedans" revived another Muslim association, the Anjuman-i-Himayat-i-Islam (Society for the Defence of Islam) and Reforms carried out their *own reforms*.[6] The heads of the new Anjuman included government officials and two barristers influenced by Syed Ahmed, Muhammad Shafi and Shah Din. The two Anjumans co-operated, but the new one was more bold in its attempt to westernize Muslims. It made English compulsory in Anjuman high schools so that Muslims would acquire more government posts, stressed female education, and defended the more advanced ideas of Syed Ahmed.[7] In addition to reform and education, Anjumans became platforms for countering Hindu propaganda. Taking a lead from the Arya Samajists, who quickly deployed new techniques of agitation and propaganda, Muslims organized a system of street-preaching, published papers defending Islam, and founded a tract society.[8]

The Second Era—Urdu *vs.* Hindi

The second era of Muslim activity was an organized campaign to influence official policy affecting Muslims. These campaigns revolved around, but were not limited to, the bread-and-butter issues of education and employment.[9] In 1877, for example, the Delhi Anjuman-i-Islamia held meetings on the problem of Muslim backwardness in new professions and petitioned the British to reserve special places for Muslims until all offices contained "half Hindus and half Muhammadans."[10] Although the government denied the request, sporadic demonstrations over the issue continued. In 1881, Muslim leaders decided to make a more systematic representation on the occasion of the calling of the Hunter Education Commission. Punjabi Muslims hoped that the commission would recommend that their community be given special advantages such as reserved scholarships. Hindus opposed this, but they wanted the commission to recommend a change in language policy. Hindus wished to replace Urdu, the official language in courts and secondary education, with Hindi, a language they considered the *lingua franca* of Hindus throughout India. Muslims opposed the change on the grounds that Urdu closely resembled Persian, a vernacular some Muslims thought to be their "national language." Muslims also feared a shift toward Hindi would give Hindus further employment advantages.[11] Each community thus tried to influence the commission on the issues of language and Muslim favouritism. Hindus and Muslims excitedly prepared petitions and held public meetings. Local anjumans sponsored Muslim rallies, while Hindu reform societies were behind the effort to rally Hindu "public opinion".[12] When the British did not listen to the remonstrances, controversy subsides but each subsequent inquiry reopened the issue.

Lahore Indian Association—A United and Divided House

Despite the intensity of communal competition, Hindus and Muslims could co-operate in a political organization transferred to the Punjab from Bengal in 1877, the Lahore India Association. Defence of community did not necessarily preclude other types of political activity, particularly, on occasions when urban Punjabis felt under common attack. Until 1883 the Indian Association had been a predominantly Hindu organization which criticized the British through the Lahore *Tribune* and tried unsuccessfully to interest educated Punjabis in agitation over broad, secular issues.[13] In 1883, however, a change in the political climate widened the scope and membership of the Association. That year the government tried to enact the Ilbert Bill permitting Indian Judges jurisdiction over Europeans. The Bill met with unexpected opposition from Europeans, who demonstrated loudly and formed "defence associations". Civil servants and English businessmen in Lahore held meetings and wrote stinging letters to local newspapers. Criticism often degenerated into racist charges concerning Punjabi morality. Mounting European hostility evoked a counter-agitation by the Lahore Indian Association. Punjabis rallied to the support of the Association and denounced the overt bigotry of local Europeans. Hindus and Muslims spoke from the same platform, for the issue was no longer Hindu *versus* Muslim, but Punjabi *versus* European.[14]

Hindu-Muslim Unity Societies Formed

The Ilbert Bill and similar racial incidents paved the way for temporary co-operation among urban Punjabis. Hindus and Muslims formed "unity societies" to improve communal relations and mixed socially.[15] Growing co-operation also was reflected in the transformation of the Indian Association into a broad-based organisation representing all urban Punjabis. In 1883, a Brahmo Samajist, Dyal Singh, became president, two Bengalis were secretaries, and the executive council included several Muslims and Arya Samajists.[16]

The highpoint in Hindu-Muslim collaboration was Syed Ahmed Khan's visit to the Punjab in January of 1884. Syed Ahmed made the tour to collect funds for his Aligarh projects but he also spent considerable time attending political meetings and urging communal accord. At each town on his itinerary Syed Ahmed was met by joint Hindu-Muslim delegations. In Amritsar and Lahore he stated that Hindus and Muslims were members of the same "Indian nation", and he called on them to work together in "patriotic" organizations such as the Indian Association to improve the political condition of India.[17]

Despite Syed Ahmed's pleas the fragile entente fell to pieces. Mutual threats had temporarily driven the diverse Punjab communities together, and between, 1884 and 1887, new sources of tension drove them apart. As Muslims responded to these new elements by organizing once again to protect their own interests, opportunity for political co-operation across religious lines declined.

Urban Punjabis and Communal Politics on (1884-87) Kine Slaughter

Systematic Arya campaigns against Islam and the spread of communal rioting contributed to widening cleavages among urban Punjabis. Following the death of Dayananda in 1883, one section of the Arya Samaj increasingly assailed Muslims. The resulting controversy in public meetings and the press hardened existing divisions and tended to institutionalize old patterns of conflict and distrust.[18]

The cow protection movement and sporadic violence accompanied religious controversy. Ranjit Singh had formerly prohibited kine slaughter in the Punjab because Hindus and some Sikhs considered the cow a sacred animal. The British removed the ban, but in order to protect the religious feelings of the volatile Sikhs and Hindus, the government ordered Muslim butchers to slaughter cattle in isolated areas and to cover the meat in public. Few incidents occurred over the explosive issue during the first decades of British rule.[19] Nevertheless, between 1883 and 1891 more than fifteen major riots took place over kine slaughter or related issues such as playing instruments in front of religious institutions. The outburst was due primarily to three factors. First, Aryas established cow protection societies in many towns and fanned Hindu resentment over slaughter. These societies and Arya efforts to force officials to alter traditional locations of butcher shops often generated rioting.[20] Spread of cow societies coincided with three years (1885-87) in which Ramlila, a Hindu festival of merry-making, fell in the same period as Muharram. When Muslim funeral "processions and Hindu parades collided, or when kine sacrifice came to the attention of Hindus, riots followed.[21] The spread of communications which made possible the rapid transmission of news and rumour also added to unrest. The *Akhbar-i-Am*, for example, printed a rumour of rioting in Lahore and almost precipitated a real disturbance.[22] Although the government had regained control of the situation by 1893 and prevented further rioting, the decade of violence left a lingering scar of bitterness.

Municipal Elections aroused Hindu-Muslim Tension

Elections and control of municipal institutions also divided Hindus and Muslims. Before the granting of "local self-government" in 1884 under Lord Ripon, opportunity for continual competition by religious communities had been limited. The Punjab had no legislative council and municipal posts were almost universally filled by appointment.[23] This changed in 1884 when the government gave Punjabis the opportunity to elect municipal committees. The initial elections were savagely contested because control of the institutions meant the power to distribute public funds and appoint, salaried officials.[24] Hindus had a majority of voters and won most of the elections. The election campaigns especially aroused Hindu-Muslim tension in Delhi, Lahore, Multan, Amritsar, Hoshiarpur and Ludhiana. The elections occasioned such unrest that eventually the British intervened and set-up separate electorates so that members of a constituency could only vote for co-religionists.[25] The committees nevertheless remained a source of tension, with Hindu or Muslim factions manipulating patronage to support their religious community.[26]

These fresh or renewed sources of tension had an almost immediate effect on Hindu-Muslim co-operation. As the *Tribune* warned, elections and riots threatened the "new-found friendship."[27] Muslims nominally remained in the Indian Association until 1885 but when the Hindu members of the Association defended a Hindu interpretation of riots during the summer of 1885, most prominent Muslims cut-off support to the Association with Hindu members who joined the Congress.[28]

Association and Congress almost Hindu Bodies

Withdrawal from the Indian Association, which left Muslims without formal channels for voicing their opinion and needs to the government, came at the very time when Punjabi Muslims felt under increasing pressure to improve their position in the public services, Communal favouritism had spread in the lower branches of Punjab administration, with Hindus and Muslims often giving appointments and jobs only to co-religionists. An official investigation in 1895, for example, revealed that for a decade Hindu Khatris controlled several district offices and prevented qualified Muslims from rising above clerkships.[29] Not only was nepotism rampant, it was also receiving more publicity. By the late 1880's Punjab editors were publishing frequent exposes of ugly incidents in which officials mistreated individuals because of their religion.[30] These reports, whether rumour or fact, exasperated the aggrieved community, and accentuated the tendency to defend communal interests. As one newspaper noted, "bigotry in the public services" meant that "unless our community makes every effort to help and defend our co-religionists, we are lost."[31]

Frustration over Muslim backwardness set the stage for the Aitchison Public Service Commission agitation in 1886 and 1887. Three questions connected with the inquiry stimulated rivalry: simultaneous examinations for the civil service in India and England, the nature and method of recruitment of administrative cadres subordinate to the civil service, and reservation of appointments for Muslims. It was commonly acknowledged that if simultaneous exams were held in India, the increased number of Indians in the ICS would primarily be Hindu; similarly, Hindus would probably dominate open competition for the lower services because of their education.[32] Muslim concern over their plight and the exertions of an outside Muslim organization, the Central National Mahomedan Association of Bengal, made the resulting demonstrations more bitter and hotly contested than the earlier ones over the Hunter Commission. The Mahomedan Association, begun by Amir Ali in 1879, had promoted the "well-being of Mussulmans of India" with a series of petitions calling for Muslim advantages in education and employment.[33] The Association had little influence in the Punjab for several years, but in 1885 a young Muslim editor, Muharram. Ali Chisti, began to champion Amir Ali in his paper, the *Rofiq-i-Hind.* At the age of 23 Muharram Ali already had a reputation for instability and impetuous action.

Communal Hate Circulars given to Attickson Commission

He was a strong opponent of Syed Ahmed Khan whom he felt was a heretic undermining Muslim civilization. In politics, he supported the Indian Association fight against Urdu in 1882, spent a month in Jail in 1885 for libelling a Hindu officer, and the same year denounced the Indian Association as an "arrogant" Hindu organ.[34] Through his efforts, six branches of the Mahomedan Association action were formed in the Punjab by 1886. Most of the members were petty officials or aristocrats without knowledge of English, and several, like Muharram Ali, were known for their opposition to Syed Ahmed Khan.[35] The

Punjab branches led the assault-on Hindu domination of official posts. Meetings were held, and petitions prepared for the Aitchison Commission. Circulars bordering on hate literature counselled witnessies to emphasis Hindu-Muslim antagonism and to demand an end to "clerical clerk" monopoly of "places of power."[36] Hindus conducted counter-meetings and called on Muslims to "quit acting like children" and "fight their battles like men."[37] The Commission arrived in Lahore in December and for a month heard Muslim witnesses' plea as per their leader for special privileges and Hindu witnesses as told by their Association—Congress Frontman defend competition. Muslim agitation continued after the Commission hearings. Delegates from the Anjuman-i-Islamia and the Mahomedan Association met the new Lieutenant Governor, James Lyall, with requests that Muslims be given a share of posts equal to their proportion of the population Lyall refused, but that refusal did not prevent further demonstrations.[38]

The issue of militant agitation tended to divide Punjabi Muslims. The patron and chief advisor of many anjumans, Syed Ahmed Khan, "preached the doctrine that the economic and political future of Indian Muslims depended largely upon British patronage. If Muslims abstained from agitation, avoided offending the rulers and convinced them of Muslim loyalty, he argued the British would protect Muslim interests. Syed Ahmed consequently frowned upon prolonged demonstrations against the government.[39] Syed Ahmed's opponents attacked this philosophy, arguing instead that Muslims could progress only by continued agitation under the leadership of Amir Ali and an all-India Muslim organization. In early 1887 Syed Ahmed's Punjab followers defended his strategy and called on "respectable" Muslims to give up anti-British agitation. The Mahomedan Association branches soon collapsed. Muslims ceased bombarding the government with demands and tended instead to concentrate upon education and "expressing loyalty" to the British.[40]

Moreover, they expelled from their anjumans "trouble-makers" who questioned the religious or political views of Syed Ahmed. The first to go was Muharram Ali Chisti, an advocate of Muslim militancy.[41]

The problem of how to improve the Muslim position had thus brought to the surface in the Punjab two conflicting strategies, pressure upon the British and a campaign to win official patronage through self-help and expressions of loyalty. The latter temporarily won out among Punjabi Muslim politicians. Although, as will be subsequently shown, this strategy did not mean that Muslims gave up politics, it did result in Muslim hesitancy to associate with agitation directed against the British. This commitment and the continued influence of Syed Ahmed Khan in the Punjab became crucial determinants of Muslim relations with the Punjab Congress.

Muslims Oppose Congress, (1885-90)

Although only one Punjabi Muslim attended a Congress session prior to 1888 the initial response of the Punjab Muslim community toward the Congress, as reflected in the Punjab press, was neutrality and "watchful waiting."[42] In 1888, however, the anti-Congress movement headed by Syed Ahmed and the virulent reaction of Punjab Congressmen helped transform Muslim neutrality into opposition.

Syed Ahmed had originally considered the Calcutta Indian Association "patriotic" and lauded Bengali politicians as models for young Indians.[43] By 1888 his views had changed. The Muslim leader distrusted the Congress because it championed programs such as open competition and elective legislative councils which seemed to threaten the Muslim community. Hindus would have an advantage in competition. While as a majority group they would control the legislatures too. The government appeared to be anti-Congress, and Syed Ahmed believed that Muslims could advance only by repairing on good terms with the British. Patronage and self-improvement would lead to the betterment of Indian Muslims; association with the Congress, whose program hurt Muslims and whose opposition to the government might alienate British support for Muslims, would be disastrous.[44]

Opposition to Congress Spreads

The first indication of concerted Muslim opposition to the Congress came in December of 1886. The *Aligarh Institute Gazette* and the National Mahomedan Association denounced the organization and warned Muslims to remain clear of "Bengali babus" and sedition.[45] Gaining momentum in 1887, the anti-Congress movement culminated in the Lucknow and Meerut speeches of Syed Ahmed in which he publicly attacked the Congress and called for a reaffirmation of Muslim loyalty to the British. The speeches were followed with the formation of a "United Indian Patriotic Association" whose platform was Congress opposition and emphasis on improving relations between Indians and Englishmen.[46] Syed Ahmed's call evoked a positive response from many of his Punjabi followers. At least 15 of the 54 Muslim organizations affiliating with the new Association were Punjabi, mostly branches of the Anjuman-i-Islamia and the Anjuman-i-Himayat-i-Islam.[47] The Amritsar Anjuman-i-Islamia also prepared resolutions publicizing Syed Ahmed's arguments and in February of 1888 distributed 600 copies of his Lucknow speech.[48]

The Congress Meet the Challenge in Bombay

The Congress tried to meet the challenge by cultivating Muslim support in Bombay, for example, a prominent Muslim Congressman, Badruddin Tyabji, attempted to undercut the influence of Syed Ahmed and prevent Muslims from attending an anti-Congress conference.[49] Following the lead of its parent organization the Punjab Congress Committee (the executive council of the Lahore Indian Association) adopted a three-prong strategy for halting the anti-Congress moves. First, the *Tribune* personally attacked Syed Ahmed. Claiming that the "Pope of Allighur" had no right to speak for Indian Muslims, the *Tribune* published editorials and letters harshly criticizing Syed Ahmed.[50] Too, Hindu leaders of the Congress attempted to integrate Muslims into public meetings in order to validate the claim that "only a few followers of Sir Syed who were much deceived" actually opposed the nationalist organization.[51] Finally, the Congress imported outside speakers, particularly Muslims, who whipped up enthusiasm among Punjabis of each community. In the fall of 1888, for example, Badruddin Tyabji,

Mohammed Ali Bhimji, and other Muslim politicians toured Punjab district towns in an effort to increase Muslims attendance at the coming session.[52]

Energetic Congress Campaign

The energetic Congress campaign accelerated the anti-Congress efforts of Punjabi Muslims. In addition to the goal of divorcing themselves from the Congress Muslims also concentrated on labelling the Congress as a seditious Hindu organization. The underlying assumption was that if it could be shown that the Hindu commercial class, which dominated public services, formed the Punjab Congress, the government would then take jobs a way from these "disloyal" Hindus and give a larger share to "loyal" Muslims. Muslim leaders adopted a variety of tactics to achieve these dual goals. First, they tried to neutralize Congress claims of Muslim support, by holding anti-Congress meetings attended by prominent Muslims. Wherever the Congress held demonstrations for visiting "Muslim politicians, anti-Congress Muslims countered with "oppositionallies."[53] Secondly, an attempt was made to isolate and question the motives of Muslims openly siding with the Congress. Social and religious pressure was brought to bear in cases of obstinancy, with several Muslim merchants and lawyers coming under economic boycott.[54] A final move was dissemination of anti-Congress propaganda.The charges of the *Tribune* and the vernacular Congress papers to the effect that Muslims were being taught "to lick the feet of the powers that be" aroused.

Notes and References

1. For example, articles and commentary on publication plans in the *Journal of the Research Society of Pakistan*, I, Pt. II (Oct. 1964) and the issue of the *Journal of the Panjab University Historical Society* (XV, Jan. 1963) which reproduces valuable archival documents on the Central Muhammadan Association of Calcutta and Muslim agitation in the Punjab. The *Journal of the Asiatic Society of Pakistan* and the *Panjab: Past and Present*, Patiala also are publishing an increasing number of informative articles on this period.

2. Mian Shah Din, "Mohamedan Societies in the Punjab," *The Indian Magazine*, 1888, pp. 188-90, Muharram Ali Chisti, *Jawab Mazmun ka Risala Masamma ka Muraqqa-i-Tohsib* (Lahore, nd), pp. 11-12.
3. The following on the Arya and Brahmo Samaj: Jamiat Rai, *Hamare Nau Jawan* (Lahore, 1889), pp. 1-7; B.C. Pal, *Memories of My Life and Times* (Calcutta, 1932-51), II, 25, 68-82; Lajpat Rai (ed. V.C. Joshi), *Lajpat Rai Autobiographical Writings* (Delhi, 1965), pp. 23-29. A detailed discussion of this militancy is in K.W. Jones, "The Arya Samaj in the Punjab," unpub. diss., U. of Calif., 1966, Ch. II.
4. "Thagi Report on Communal Unrest, 1880-89", sec. I, Punjab Government, General File (PGG), Jan. 1887, 12-12a. Unless otherwise noted, citations to PG files are to printed records in the India Office Library. Citations including "KW'. (Keep-with) are in the West Pakistan Record Office.
5. Mian Shah Din, "Mohamedan Societies", 188-90, For a succinct discussion of his program and ideology, W.C. Smith, *Modern Islam in India* (London, 1946), pp. 15-23; Bashir Ahmad, *Justice Shah Din* (Lahore, 1962), pp. 278-319.
6. Mian Shah Din, "Mohamedan Societies", p. 190.
7. Mian Shah Din, "Mohamedan Societies", pp. 191-92; Bashir Ahmad, *Shah Din*, pp. 251-57.
8. Ghulam Sadiq, *Ek Musalman ki Iltimas Qaum Ki Khidmat Men* (Amritsar, 1893), pp. 9-11; "Thagi Report", sec. 3. The Mohamedan Literary and Tract Society of Lahore was founded in 1882, and by 1892 had published at least twenty items either attacking Hinduism or defending Islam.
9. Other issues included compulsory Vaccination and official interference in pilgrimages.
10. Memorial, official reply, and notes, .Government of India Home File (GIH), May 1817, 11A. GI records from NAI, New Delhi.
11. Commission discussed in Zafar-ul-Islam and Raymond L. Jensen, "Indian Muslims and the Public Services, 1875-1915," *Journal of the Asiatic Society of Pakistan*, IV (1964), 85-193. Also see relevant documents in *Journal of the Punjab University Historical Society* (XV, Jan. 1963).
12. Lajpat Rai commentary, *Autobiography*, pp. 22, 26, 79; Hindu and Muslim testimony, *Punjab Committee of the Education Commission* (Calcutta, 1884), pp. 104-5, 194-95; 246-47, 471. Also, resolution 306A, Oct. 2, 1883, PGG Feb. 1889 (KW), 14-22A.
13. Ruchi Ram Sahni, "Self-Revelations of an Octogenarian" (mss in possession of V.C. Joshi, Indian Institute of Public Administration, New Delhi), pp. 201-03; B.C. Pal, *Memories*, II, 20-21. Also, *Tribune*, March 24, 1883.
14. *Tribune*, March 17, Sept. 15, 1883. Also following letters in *Civil and Military Gazette* (CMG): "An Old Anglo-Indian" (March 1, 1883); "An Older Settler" and "One of the Garrison" (March 7, 1883). Apparently a few Muslim and Hindu aristocrats were afraid to support the Bill. A general view of Muslim reaction is in Zafar-ul-Islam and J.M. Woldman, "Indián Muslims and the Ilbert Bill: 1883-84", *Journal of the Asiatic Society of Pakistan*, VIII, No. 2 (Dec. 1963), 131-56.
15. *Tribune*, June 9, 1883. Also, Ruchi Ram Sahni, "Self-Revelation," pp. 204-08. A second issue bringing Hindus and Muslims together was the arrest

of Surendranath Banerjee for criticizing the demand of a High Court judge that an idol be brought into court (the "Norris Case").

16. *Tribune,* March 10, 1883, Also, "Thagi Report", sec. 1.
17. The tour and Punjab response admirably discussed in Syed Hameed Ahmed, "Sayyad Ahmad Khan's Visit to the Punjab," *Journal of the Panjab University Historical Society,* XV (April 1963), 49-69. A contemporary assessment in *Tribune,* Feb. 2, 9, 1884.
18. K.W. Jones, "The Arya Samaj and Communal Tensions in the Punjab, 1877-97," *Journal of Asian Studies* (Dec. 1968), 4-15.
19. PG Proclamation, March 29, 1849, appendix to "Thagi Report", sec. 1.
20. Thagi and Dakaiti Department Special Branch Note on the Agitation against Cow-Killing, Aug. 9, 1893 (pp. 1-7), GI Public (P), Jan. 1894, 309-414B. An example of how Aryas heated the issue was their effort in Ferozepur to force the closure of butcher shops. Correspondence and notes, PGG, Nov. 1888, 2-6A.
21. Delhi Com. to PG, 8C, Oct. 30, 1886, and enclosures, PGG, Jan. 1887, 12-12A; Note on Cow-Killing Agitation, p. 8.
22. Lahore Com. to PG, 530, Oct. 27, 1885; PG to GI, 598, March 26, 1886, PGG, March 1886, 11-26A.
23. PG resolution 34-619, May 3, 1872, PG Revenue (R), May 1872, 4A.
24. New committees discussed in PG to GI, Sept. 1, 1883, and subsequent correspondence, GI Legislative (L), Oct. 1884, 16-104A.
25. Based on an examination of two years of Punjab committee proceedings, 1883-84, For separate electorates, "Review of Punjab Municipal Administration", sec. 1, GI Municipal, Jan. 1892, 7-9A.
26. For example, incidents discussed in PG Committee (C), Jan. 1886, 15-16A; PGG, May 1887, 3-8A.
27. *Tribune.* May 17, 1884.
28. Ghulam Sadiq, *Musalman,* p. 2; also, "Thagi Report", sec. 3.
29. Undated memo on "relationships of district officials", PGG (KW), Dec. 1896, 49-141A.
30. For example, *Singh Sahai,* Aug. 13, 1890, *Selections from the Punjab Vernacular Press, (SPVP), 1890,* p. 309; *Tribune,* February 2, 1884, Dec. 1886.
31. *Rafiq-i-Hind,* Jan. 26, 1886, attached to "Thagi Report", Also, comments of author, Muharram Ali Chisti in *Jawab Mazmun,* p. 16.
32. *Proceedings of the Public Service Commission; Punjab Commission and Evidence* (Calcutta, 1887), 1, 17-19. Analysis of the agitation and findings of the committee are in Zafar-ul-Islam and Jensen, "Indian Muslims", pp. 95-112.
33. *Central National Mohammedan Association, Rules and Objects* (Calcutta, 1885), pp. ii, 1-24. Also, "Memoirs of the Late Right Hon'ble Syed Amer Ali," *Islamic Culture,* VI (1932), 9-18, 163-71; documents in *Journal of the Panjab University Historical Society,* XV (Jan. 1963).
34. *Tribune,* March 28, 1885; comments on Muharram Ali in "Report on the Panjab Vernacular Press, 1885-86," GIP, June 1887, 22-24A. For religious views, review of his book on Syed Ahmed, *Catalogue of Books Registered in the Punjab* (Quarterly Report, June 30, 1893), pp. 38-39.

35. *Triennial Report of the Central National Mohammedan Association of India* (Calcutta, 1898), pp. 4-6. List of Punjab members given in the report and in *CMG,* April 7, Nov. 17, 1888.
36. Circular printed in *Tribune,* Jan. 19, 1887.
37. *Tribune,* Dec. 15, 18, 1886.
38. *Tribune,* April 27, 1887; *CMG,* April 25, 1887.
39. For discussion of Syed Ahmed's political views, the following: "Rafiq Ahmed Zakaria, Muslims in India: A Political Analysis (1885-1906)," unpub. Ph.D. diss., SOAS, London U., 1948, pp. 93-97, Bashir Ahmad, *Shah Din,* pp. 320-47, Ram Gopal, *Indian Muslims* (New York, 1959), pp. 65-67.
40. *A Briel Report of the Third Muhammadan Education Conference* (Lahore, 1888), pp. 4-6, 23-21, Muharram Ali, *Jawab Mazmun,* pp. 31-32. The process is not altogether clear and requires further study.
41. Drawn from the following press accounts: *Tribune,* Nov. 16, Dec. 17, 1887, Jan. 2, 1889; *CMG,* Nov. 17, 1887.
42. *Tribune,* April 7, 27, 1887.
43. *Tribune,* Feb. 9, 1884. Also, speeches in Syed Hameed Ahmed, "Syed Ahmed Visit", pp. 56-61.
44. Speech in *Pioneer Mail,* Jan. 18, 1888; United Patriotic Association, *Showing the Seditious Character of the Indian National Congress* np, nd).
45. *Triennial Report of Mahommedan Association,* pp. 21-22; *Tribune,* Dec. II, 1886, Jan. 18, 1888.
46. *Pioneer Mail,* Jan. 18, 1888, For a discussion of the Association's constitution, Zafar-ul-Islam, "Documents on Indo-Muslim Politics", *Journal of the Pakistan Historical Society* (Jan. 1964), pp. 14-18.
47. List in "Documents", pp. 17-18; Zakaria, "Indian Muslims", appendix B.
48. *Tribune,* Feb. 4; 1888.
49. Discussed in Husain B. Tyabji, *Badruddin Tyabji* (Bombay, 1952), pp. 194-205; Ram Gopal, *Indian Muslims,* pp. 65-67.
50. *Tribune,* Sept. 29, 1888, A series of Lajpat Rai-letters were printed separately as a volume and are reproduced in V.C. Joshi (ed.) *Lala Lajpat Rai : Writings and Speeches* (Delhi, 1966), I, 1-25.
51. *Tribune,* May 23, 1888.
52. Reports in *Tribune,* Sept. 29, Oct. 3, 1888.
53. *Tribune,* Oct. 3, 1888. Also, discussion of counter-agitation in the documents following this section.
54. Letters and reports in following *Tribune* issues: Sept. 12, 29, Oct. 3, 6, 10, Nov. 21, 1888. Kay Robinson, editor of the *CMG,* was intimately involved in the controversy because he sided with the Muslims in order to wean them away from the Congress. Robinson to PG, Nov. 6, 1888, PGG, Feb. 1889 (KW), 14-22A. For an example, *CMG,* Sept. 20, 1888.

Sikhs : Gurudwaras/Nation

PROF. KHUSHDEVA SINGH

Shri Atal Bihari Vajpayee, a former Hon'ble Prime Minister of India once remarked: "Send a Sikh into the space (Moon). His first act there will be to make a Gurudwara", the Sikhs have immence love and affection for a Gurudwara which is their sacred place for siparchuism and religious, social and political centre. (Ed.)

The Britishers were great exploiters and shrewed administrators. They came to India as traders, and soldiers and established their headquarters at Calcutta after completely defeating Mir Qasim, the Nawab of Bengal, Bihar and Oudh, Nawab Shah Alam, King at the battle of Buxur (1761), with the name of East India Company. They soon realised that for boosting their trade they needed the patronage of sovereignty and to achieve this end, raised armed force and started annexing one territory after another[1] through military campaigns wars and all means, both fair and foul. Wealth looted by the British forces was mostly sent to England. They made treaties with the ruling princes, which were of mutual benefit. If some ruler put in resistance, they succeeded in overthrowing him, using all political tactics.

Ultimately after Ferozshah war they established their foothold in Punjab, after the first Anglo-Sikh war 1845-46 and took over Punjab in second Anglo-Sikh Gujarat war fought in 1848-49 after the death of Maharaja Ranjit Singh.[2] The British government fully well knew that the Sikhs were very sore at the loss of their sovereignty and it would be impossible for them to run the government on the strength of their army alone. They realised that the government should find ways and means to get co-operation and support from their loyal people.

Knowing that Gurudwaras are the main source of Sikhs' revival of power the British officers and the police encouraged and supported occupation of Gurudwaras and Dharamshala by Non-sikh Mahants and their men. The Sikh could not tolerate this. The British also evolved a formula of saints, soldiers and helpers, under which their missionaries reached the farthest corners of the state and sought those poor, ignorant and low caste people who were living a life of misery. They started dispensaries and schools for them and served them in many other ways. After gaining their confidence and good will, they preached them the gospel of Christianity, i.e. Fatherhood of God and Brotherhood of man, and freedom to all to pray to God and enter their churches. This appealed to the suppressed section of the society and they became Christians. The British army guaranteed them protection of life and property, and the rulers provided them with ample chances for their economic, social and educational development.

A Gurudwara is a social, spiritual and prayer centre for Sikhs. During the Anglo-Sikh Wars, the government had been a witness to the extraordinary bravery of the Sikh Jawans. They sought their cooperation by recruiting them in their army, named the regiments as Sikh Regiment and provided every regiment with a Granthi, and a copy of Guru Granth Sahib. Who teaches a disciplined life, secular society and honest labours was ceremoniously kept in a room. The British officers encouraged the Sikh Jawans to live according to the Sikh traditions.

All this was done to get support and cooperation from the local public but all their efforts failed to suppress the feeling of the Sikhs for long.

Akali Dal Agitation

After Kuka (Namdhari), Akali movement commenced to liberate Gurudwaras under control of Mahants who took the wine and opium and abused the holy place by gambling drinking and smoking.

On November 15, 1920, a proclamation was made from Akal Takhat to the effect that a committee of 175, to be known as the Central Gurudwara Managing Committee, was set-up for the management of Sikh gurudwaras. This Committee was later given a Punjabi name, i.e. Shiromani Gurudwara Parbandhak Committee.

A great historical event occurred on December 14, 1920 when an organisation under the name of Akali Dal was founded. The aim of this body was to raise and train volunteers for "action" to take over the gurudwaras from recalcitrant mahants and to provide a democratic management for them. The Akali Dal achieved the highest glory during the Gurudwara Reform Movement, as it was the first mass demonstration of the efficacy of passive resistance in which thousands of men and women voluntarily submitted themselves to brutal violence at the hands of the police supported by British officers.

Glowing tributers to Akalis for their Non-Violence practical example of non-violence brought glowing tribute to the Akali Dal from national leaders like Mahatma Gandhi, who wrote to Baba Kharak Singh : "First battle to India's freedom won", learning that one thousand non-violent Akali Sikhs have been murdered by the Mahant and his men; Jawaharlal Nehru, Rev. C.F. Andrews, the Ali brothers, Sarojini Naidu and many others. Dr. Rajendra Prasad observed in his autobiography that the saga of heroic determination enacted on a mass scale during the Gurudwara Reform Movement demonstrated that non-violence was not a mere slogan but a practical mode of struggle.

The Mahants who were backed by the government also used force against non-violent Sikhs who visited the gurudwaras to protest against the Mahants for misusing the place of worship. One hundred Sikhs were killed at Nankana

Sahib and the Government supported the Mahants. Police were posted near the disputed Gurudwara. The Sikhs grouped together as jathas to court arrest and persecution at Darbar Sahib, Amritsar and Guru-ka-Bagh at Amritsar, Bhai Pheru gurudwara at Lahore and at Jaito in Nabha state.

The Sikhs taking part in jathas at Guru-ka-Bagh and Jaito were brutally kicked and put under horses feet and also killed by bullets. Many died and sacrificed their lives. Many were burnt alive at Nankana Sahib but took the path of non-violence. Over 30,000 went to jail, 500 were killed and Rs. 15,00,000 fine was levied on Sikhs and hundreds of families were humiliated by government personnel.

The Martial Sikhs and Non-Violence

Wg. Cdr. Mohan Singh wrote : "On 13th September, Rev. C.F. Andrews, narrated all that he witnessed at Guru-Ka-Bagh to the Governor at Lahore and every other officer that he met.

After the seriousness of barbarous atrocities of the Englishmen had been driven home by an English brethren, that Governor decided to pay a visit to Amritsar the same day i.e., 13th September. He put a stop to the merciless beating of the Akalis by the Police that had been going on for days. Then onwards the government resorted to arrest of Akalis. This carried on un-abated till mid-November, 1922 and by then over 5,500 Akalis had been lodged in different jails. But nothing deterred the brave Sikhs from their righteous path, since for them, no sacrifice was too much, to free their holy shrines from the clutches of the Mahants.

Then to put a stop to this unending woeful drama of British creation, emerged on stage, Sir Ganga Ram C.I.E., a retired Engineer. He purchased the land in question at Guru-Ka-Bagh, from the Mahant and gifted it to the Akalis. Immediately thereafter on 17th September, 1922, he wrote to the British Government that he did not require police protection there. Unless this too was government's own manipulation, it served as a face saving device for the prestigeous British Government to wriggle out of the ugly situation.

With immediate effect on 17th September, 1922, the government stopped arrests of Akalis and heaved a sigh of relief. But, still it took another three long years for the British Raj to reconcile itself to the reality of the situation—par-excellence unity and sincerity of purpose of the Sikhs. It was not till 7th July, 1925, that the mighty Empire condescended to pass the Gurudwara Reform Bill into an Act, giving the Sikhs absolute control over their holy shrines and freedom of *Kirpān*. The Act came into force from 1st November, 1925.

That is how the Akalis emerged victorious in their long drawn adherence to non-violence under utmost provocation, beating and brutalities. The Akalis triumphantly carried the day, in this one sided saga of reprisals, recrimination and repression.

The Akali Dal agitation proved to be a powerful and significant movement of civil disobedience which brought about great awakening in the country. It was in this context that the Indian National Congress meeting at its annual session at Gaya in January 1921, passed a resolution recording with pride and admiration its appreciation of the "unexampled bravery of the Akali martyrs and the great and noble example of non-violence set by them for the whole nation". As a result, the Gurudwara Reform Movement brought about orientation of the Sikh mind which, by and large, turned against the British.

Akali Jatha marching to Guru-ka-Bagh

Babar Akali Movement

Another revolutionary movement arose in the Punjab which is known as Babar Akali Movement. The Babar Akalis evaded arrests. They attacked policemen and their lackeys. Their chief aim was to punish the agents of the foreign rulers who spied upon the Indian patriots or helped the police against them. Leaders like Master Mota Singh, Jathedar Kishan Singh, Amar Singh of Delhi and Jagat Singh alias Bijla Singh were the moving spirits of this movement. The organisation was a secret one, but it issued public proclamations from time-to-time warning the internal enemies of the country's freedom and issuing their death warrants which were to be carried into effect by its members.

Participation of Masses

S. Hukam Singh, a former honourable speaker of Parliament (Lok Sabha) wrote in his article on Sikh Affairs : The Sikhs though in minority have always made contribution of all proportion to their population. It is a pity that very few Sikhs have taken the trouble to record facts as they happened it Satluj into Guru-ka-Bagh. Regarding Anglo-Sikh wars, it is said that during the struggle for independence from British rule the role of the minority Sikhs have been glorious as the sacrifice chart given below tells us.

	Sikhs	*Non-Sikhs*	*Total*
Hung by the neck on gallows	93	28	121
Life Sentence to Kale Pani (Andamans)	2,147	499	2,646
Killed at Jallianwala Bagh Amritsar	799	501	1,300
Killed at Budge Budge Ghat (Calcutta)	67	46	113
Killed in Kuka Movement	91	—	91
Total	3,197	1,074	4,271
Courted voluntary arrest during 19 months of Emergency during 1975-77	45,000	—	45,000

The chart is prepared meticulously by Lt. Col. Gulcharan Singh, is a noted writer of Sikh historical events.

"It will be seen that during the struggle for the independence of India the Sikh sacrifices population-wise have been far greater than the other communities. In nationalist anti-British activities the contribution of Sikhs has been very great".

The people made a wonderful response to the clarion calls of the national leaders. Instead of scattered incidents of courage and heroism, the whole mass of people joined the national and Akali movements. Punjab's contribution to the mass struggles of 1930-32, 1933-34 and the Quit India Movement of 1942-45 was worthy of its past traditions. In every town and village of the Punjab, Congress Committee, Bal Bharat Sabhas, War Councils and Workers' Councils were enthusiastically organised, and people in thousands rallied round the national flag. In the Quit India struggle of 1942 workers and leaders in hundreds were rounded up then thrown behind the bars.

Thus, Punjab's and Sikh's role in the movement for the nation's liberation is as colourful and romantic as the Punjabi character itself. Historic incident that shook the entire nation, like Jallianwala Bagh tragedy, took place on this sacred soil of ancient heroes, warriors, saints, soldiers and gurus. The Punjabis were in the front ranks in the Khilafat Movement, Praja Mandal Movement and in the Indian National Army organized during World War II.

Even at the time of attainment of independence by the country, Punjab had to write its history with blood and tears of lakhs of Punjabi people who had to leave their hearths and homes in the area now known as West Punjab and sacrificed their kith and kin and all that they possessed at the altar of freedom.

—Inputs by T.A. Bhai

Notes and References

1. **Territories Captured and Looted** : Isle of France (1810), Java (1811), Deccan (1817, 1818), Burma (1824, 1825, 1826), Bhurtpore (1826), Coorg (1834), Ghazni (1839), Kalat (1839), Sind (1843), Pegu (1852, 1853), Persia (1856, 1857), Delhi (1857), Lucknow (1858).
2. Lord Macauley wrote : We now come to the most desperate series of battle that the British war fight in India.

19

Anglo-Sikh Wars : Some Prominent Features

A. PROCLAMATION OF WAR

The plan of operation of the Sikh leaders on crossing the Sutlej seems to have been far from badly laid. Part of the force was to cut-off Sir John Littler at Ferozepore, while, if possible, the Ludhiana force was to be met and crushed by the main body before the Umballa troops should have effected a junction; the theory being that the danger of Ferozepore would compel the Ludhiana force to advance at once in the hope of effecting a relief. The design, however, was frustrated, as will be seen, by the great marching achievement of the Umballa regiments.

On the 8th December he heard from Major Broadfoot, his political Agent, that there was no longer any doubt whatever that the Sikh were making preparations on large scale to cross the Sutlej and the following day he sent the too-long-deferred orders to the Commander-in-Chief for the immediate advance of troops from Umballa, Meerut and elsewhere towards the frontier. On the 12th he heard of the actual crossing by the Sikhs, and on the 13th he issued his proclamation declaring war, dated from his camp about 25 miles from Ludhiana.

B. SIKH SOLDIERS BRING HUMANITY TO BATTLE FIELD

British Officer Mistakenly in Sikh Army Escorted Back

Mercy in the field of battle is not a thing understood by Orientals. One instance, however, deserves to be recorded to the credit of the Sikhs. About the time that the Sutlej was crossed, an officer, Lieutenant Biddulph, on his way to join his regiment at Ferozepore, fell into their hands, and although his life was in peril, it was spared, and he was made over to the charge of an officer of Sikh Artillery; the gunners became his friends; and, strange to say, after the Battle of Moodkee, he was allowed to return to the British camp, wither he was escorted by the artillery officer's brother. Sir Henry Hardinge very rightly would not allow Lieutenant Biddulph to take part in the subsequent battle at Ferozeshah; remarking that he owed that at least to the generous enemy who had released him. It is pleasant to be able to record occasional traits of civilisation and generosity on the part of our brave enemy, for, as a rule, their conduct on the field of battle was merciless in the extreme. Another striking act of generosity will, however, fall to be related in connection with the Battle of Ferozeshah.

Sikh Soldier Carries on his back War Wounded British Officer Miles away to Camp Hospital

The wounded during Mudki War many of whom had been lying for twenty-four hours on the ground unattended, were now looked after. Their sufferings had been terrible, and many had fallen victims to the merciless cruelty of the Sikhs; but it is again gratifying to be able to give one instance of humanity on the part of the enemy. Lieutenant Sievwright, an officer of H.M.'s 9th Foot, had been desperately wounded in front of the Sikh battery, and lay all that night in dreadful anguish on the field with a shattered leg, helpless and unable to move. At daylight, finding that the Sikhs were cutting up the unprotected wounded, he managed with incredible difficulty to drag himself some short way further off. Seeing a Sikh soldier approaching. Sievwright grasped his pistol and challenged him; to his relief, the Sikh replied, "Salaam sahib." Seeing that he was clearly kindly disposed, Sievwright called him up; the man sat down beside him, and after some conversation it was arranged that the Sikh soldier should carry him to the nearest succour. This good Samaritan took his wounded foe on his back, and carried him, at the peril of his own life, some two miles to the rear, where he met a dooli, in which Sievwright was placed, and conveyed into Firozepore. Acts of kindness between enemies have often been heard of on a battle-field, but never one that could surpass this. The Sikh remained with Lieutenant Sievwright, and tended him in hospital; but it is melancholy to relate that the gallant young officer himself died only a week after from the effects of his wound, which necessitated the amputation of his leg above the knee. Records do not show what became of the brave and kindhearted Sikh but it may be certain that his generous humanity did not pass unrewarded.

C. SIKH EMPIRE LOST BY TREACHERY

Jammoo Rajah Betrays Sikh Cause

During this war of the Sikhs against the English, the Rajah Gholab Singh remained away at Jummoo, in the mountains. It is true he promised his support to the Sikhs, but he hesitated in fulfilling them as long as possible. A short time previous to the last battle, at Sobran, some hundreds of the Sikh delegated punches (deputies) succeeded in drawing out the "bear", as they used to call him, from Jummoo, his den. This agreed with his views, the Sikhs having already stood up in two battles; the third being fright and it was more than probable that the fourth, which must decide the destiny of the country, could be their last.

Residue Sikh Power Weakened

To enfeeble the country, it was divided into three parts; one was left to the Sikhs, the second was annexed to the English possessions, and the third, Cashmere, comprising a part of the mountains, was appointed to Gholab Singh, as a reward for the services he had rendered, and also in consideration of a large sum of money he had delivered over to the conquerors. He was promoted to the title of Maharajah of Cashmere, which was made independent of Lahore, but under English protection. Dulleep Singh, after having paid the expenses of the war, remained the ruler of Lahore, and Lall Singh was appointed his wuzeer. Sir H. Lawrence was appointed by the English as Resident, into whose hands the reins of government were entrusted. One of his first measures was the reduction of the army, and the suspension of several establishments for the manufacture of military stores, including my powder-mill, etc.

Treachery Rewarded

Whereas Gholab Singh was made Maharajah of Cashmere, Rajah Lall Singh, who had risen from the rank of mulcteer to be minister of state, did not long enjoy the title of wuzeer; being, a crafty Brahmin, of great influence among his partisans, and in possession of immense riches, which he acquired at the time when he was Runjeet Singh's treasurer (he never having rendered any account of the funds under his charge), such a man appeared to the English to be dangerous, and his removal was considered necessary.

Another Treachery

On the 10th of February, 1846, the battle of Sobroan took place, which decoded the fate of the country. Teja Singh, the traitor, took to his heels, and, on passing the Sutlej, he ordered the bridge to be broken down, leaving the greater part of his troops behind in a helpless state. The betrayed soldiers cried, with their hands folded and grass in their mouths, making themselves emblems of their holy animals, the cattle.

The Sikh army having passed the Sutlej, the soldiers became aware that their leaders were playing the part of traitors, not doing anything they ought to have done. In the history of Major G.C. Smyth, we find the following passage :

> "They gave vent to their alarm and indignation in fierce reproaches on the treachery of their leaders; but that was

all they could do. 'We knew', they said to their leaders, 'that you had leagued with the court to send us against the British, and to pen us up here like sheep, for them to come and slaughter us at their convenience; but remember, that in thus acting, you play the part, not only of traitors to your country, but of ruthless butchers and murderers. You destroy a whole army, which, whatever its faults and crimes may have been, has always been ready to obey the orders of the state and its officers. We might even now punish you as you deserve; but we will leave you to answer to your gooroo and your God; while we, deserted and betrayed as we are, will do what we can to preserve the independence of our country'," etc. etc.

Lord Dalhousie, Governor-General of India wanted Sikh Government Defeated and their Dynasty Abolished

In adopting the second course, e.g. smaller, Lord Dalhousie acted directly on the principle—precisely the reverse of Lord Hardinge's—which avowedly guided his policy throughout his administration. In his own words, used on a subsequent occasion, it was his "strong and deliberate opinion that in the execution of a wise and sound policy, the British Government is bound not to put aside or neglect such rightful opportunities of acquiring territory or revenue as may from time to time present themselves." While the war was in progress, he wrote (February 1st, 1849) to Henry Lawrence, "I do not seek for a moment to conceal from you that I have seen no reason whatever to depart from the opinion that the peace and vital interests of the British Empire now require that the power of the Sikh Government should not only be defeated, but subverted, and their dynasty abolished."

Index